305. 896073

M363

The
White
African
American
Body

D0160975

CHARLES D. MARTIN

The White African American Body

A CULTURAL AND LITERARY EXPLORATION

RUTGERS UNIVERSITY PRESS
NEW BRUNSWICK, NEW JERSEY, AND LONDON

Library of Congress Cataloging-in-Publication Data

Martin, Charles D., 1962–

   The white African American body : a cultural and literary exploration / Charles D. Martin.
       p.   cm.
   Includes bibliographical references (p.   ) and index.
   ISBN 0-8135-3031-8 (alk. paper)—ISBN 0-8135-3032-6 (pbk. : alk. paper)
       1. African Americans—Race identity.   2. Albinos and albinism—Race identity.   3. Albinos and albinism—United States—History.   4. African Americans in popular culture.   5. African Americans in literature.   6. Human skin color—Social aspects—United States.   7. Human skin color—United States—Psychological aspects.   8. Racism—United States—History. 9. United States—Race relations.   I. Title.

E185.625.M33   2002
305.896073—dc21

                                                                                    2001031780

British Cataloging-in-Publication information is available from the British Library.

Manufactured in the United States of America

For Celia

CONTENTS

ILLUSTRATIONS

ACKNOWLEDGMENTS

I extend my heartfelt gratitude to those institutions and people who made my way a little easier. Research librarians are saints, and I want to single out the following people who took time to help me work through their collections: Phil Lapsansky of the Library Company of Philadelphia; Annette Fern of the Harvard Theater Collection; Gigi Barnhill of the American Antiquarian Society; as well as the kind folks at the Hertzberg Circus Collection and Museum and the Special Collections Department of the Syracuse University Library. Florida State University also deserves much credit. The money and time I received through a graduate student travel grant from the English department and a university dissertation fellowship from the graduate school was invaluable.

In this long journey, I have gathered a small community of readers, friends, and guides, all of whom, through their encouragement and scholarly insight, have made this project worthwhile. Many thanks to Bruce Bickley, Darryl Dickson-Carr, Leonard Cassuto, Donald Gibson, Jerrilyn McGregory, Neil Jumonville, Leslie Mitchner, Dennis Moore, Anne Rowe, and Gabrielle Stauf. A special thanks to Rip Lhamon, who has been for me a mentor, a colleague, a friend, and a cheerleader.

I devote my last words of appreciation for Celia Kingsbury, a talented scholar and my best friend. For her sharp eye and her compassionate ear, I will always be indebted.

The
White
African
American
Body

A Ballyhoo for the Exhibition

ere I present to you the body of the white Negro.
   White skin on an African body. Spotted Child. Leopard Boy Pie-bald Girl. Albino Family. Negro Turning White. Hybrid. Enigma. Transgressor of boundaries.

For more than two hundred years, natural philosophers, scientists, and showmen have exhibited the bodies of African Americans with white or gradually whitening skin in taverns, dime museums, and circus sideshows. The term *white Negro* has served to describe individuals born with albinism as well as those who have vitiligo, a disorder that robs the skin of its pigment in ever-growing patches.[1] Founding Fathers, laborers, and Irish immigrants, among many others, gathered to witness the spectacle of whiteness on skin that the audience expected to be black. To a great extent, it seems inconceivable from our jaded, early-twenty-first-century perspective that, for so long, the white Negro body presented a fantasy of racial transformation, a belief that, under the right conditions, black skin could turn white and the African American could become indistinguishable from the European. But the white Negro spectacle did induce dreams of change, and those yearnings died hard, lasting well into the twentieth century, infiltrating the culture and the literature.

Witness the exhibition. Staged before millions, for the pleasure of philosophers and princes, literati, and statesmen.

I find it hard to clear my voice of the inflection of a barker who narrates the unveiling of another sport of nature. We encounter the white Negro, and we react viscerally to the complete and universal whiteness of the Albino Family, the growing white patches of the Leopard Boy. At first, even for a moment, if we are willing to admit it, we marvel as we do at others with radical bodily difference—the legless and armless wonders, the two-headed women, the hermaphrodites. Leslie Fiedler has observed, "Nobody can write about freaks without somehow exploiting them for his own ends."[2] He admitted that he could not. And I have discovered, in spite of my best efforts during the course of this book's creation, that neither can I exonerate myself completely. In these chapters, I have become exhibitor. As I present these images and arguments at conferences and in consultation with colleagues, I have noticed in the faces of my audience a mixture of fascination and embarrassment. In spite of ourselves, even as we try to avert our gaze from the racial spectacle, the patches of white skin still draw.

Scholars have tried to explain the appeal of those with anomalous bodies: dwarfs and giants, human skeletons and Siamese twins, bearded women and wild men of Borneo. Fiedler finds the source in our own intense "psychic need," an impulse developed in childhood to discover the limits of the self in the extreme conditions of others. The freak's body "challenges the conventional boundaries between male and female, sexed and sexless, animal and human, large and small, self and other, and consequently between reality and illusion, experience and fantasy, fact and myth."[3] The challenge presented by the display of the anomalous body helps constitute the normality of the audience. For my argument, I will add to Fiedler's list the boundary between black and white, which I believe the figure of the "white Negro" both embodies and frustrates. The blurring of racial categories presented by the white Negro compels the audience to define racial difference further and map its boundaries. The preternatural whiteness calls attention to the pigmentation of the audience and creates a self-conscious need to delineate the difference between the shade of the exhibit and that of the viewer.

Susan Stewart identifies the freak show as "an inverse display of perfection" which consequently establishes an ideal. "To know an age's typical freaks," she argues, "is, in fact, to know its points of standardization." In this statement, she implies the artifice of what she calls "a freak of culture": as our standards for the average shift, so do our standards that make up the margins.[4] Although we must acknowledge the reality of the physical body on exhibit—the bearded lady does have facial hair, the Siamese twins are conjoined, the Leopard Boy has vitiligo—the status of the disabled body is a social construction.[5] Robert Bogdan contends that the presentation on the stage is what marks a freak. "Showmen," he writes, "fabricated freaks' backgrounds, the nature of their conditions, the circumstances of their current lives, and other personal characteristics."[6] The presenters concocted "true life histories" and dressed them to exoticize or aggrandize their physical condition. In a way, the white Negro is a sham, a P. T. Barnum humbug. Like other so-called freaks, the figure exists in our imaginations, the lack of pigment calling for a designation, its own nomenclature. But the audience's fascination, our inability to turn away, is not fabricated. We react to the black-white body because it fathoms a need.

Bogdan also argues for the volition of the exhibit, that these people with possibly unusual physical traits chose to exhibit themselves and in the process found community with others on the margins of show business, yet his prose betrays the central problem of agency in the presentation. Even though he sees a kind of liberation in the carnival display, he does admit that those on exhibit did not author their histories, choose their costumes or backdrop, or even speak for themselves on most occasions. The carnival talker served as the mediating voice, offering ballyhoo and blather. The nineteenth-century white Negro suffered the same silence. The Leopard Child did not speak. Diaries, if they existed, do not survive. Only the voice of Henry Moss, the most famous of the eighteenth-century white Negroes, echoes through the accounts of his self-promoted displays in Philadelphia.

In her landmark study *Extraordinary Bodies: Figuring Disability in American Culture and Literature*, Rosemarie Garland Thomson repositions the discussion of anomalous bodies on display from a focus upon the effect on the audience to that on the exhibit, those that she terms "extraordinary bodies" in order to reclaim for people with disabilities an exalted position lost during the decades of silent display and clinical observation. In spite of her intention to reclaim the freak, the body that deviates, the extraordinary, she does not neglect the exhibition's benefit to the audience. According to Thomson, the extraordinary body helps constitute what she terms the "normate," the so-called average body of the citizen she identifies as white, male, and able-bodied. In the process of this constitution, though, the disabled body is estranged, stigmatized as a freak by virtue of its physical difference from the normate, which in turn "legitimates the status quo, naturalizes attributions of inherent inferiority and superiority, and obscures the socially constructed quality of both categories." Thomson creates a simple binary: freak and normate. The disabled body plays a distinct role in the creation of the American self by violating the principles of "self-government, self-determination, autonomy, and progress." In other words, such a body is not self-reliant. The freak show exhibit instead "mocks the notion of the body as compliant instrument of the limitless will and appears in the cultural imagination as ungovernable, recalcitrant, flaunting its difference as if to refute the fantasy of sameness implicit in the notion of equality."[7] It is important to note that at this point in time the bodies of African American men and women, as well as the bodies of women defined as "white," qualified as disabled under this rubric since they were deemed incompetent to perform the rites of citizenship. Mikhail Bakhtin as well includes among "traditional representations of the grotesque body" in these satiric processions the extraordinary bodies of "negroes and moors (a grotesque deviation from the bodily norm)."[8] Like giants and dwarfs and bearded women, the blind and the halt and the lame, people with dark skin defy and define the average, their bodies marked simultaneously as excessive and insufficient.

For her argument, Thomson proposes a narrative of regression. The extraordinary bodies of the people with congenital disabilities began, in a distant era, as revered and feared figures pregnant with portent, living examples of God's grace and wrath, yet always functioning "as icons upon which people discharged their anxieties, convictions, and fantasies." In the era of festivals and fairs, the disabled body became a wonder, an esteem that did not last under the eventual imposition of scientific scrutiny. "The once marvelous body that was taken as a map of human fate," she writes, "now began to be seen as an aberrant body that marked the borders between the normal and the pathological."[9] To support this narrative, she embraces Bakhtin's concept of the carnivalesque—the disorderly body as a challenge to religious and secular authority and hierarchy—as a means essentially to resacralize the extraordinary body and imbue it again with the ability to provoke awe and turn the world upside down.

A historical narrative of social change, though, is not that simple. Ideological and philosophical shifts are never immediate or complete. Beliefs linger and practices continue in spite of official efforts to contain and dampen them. New commercial needs to commodify difference and medical curiosity to divine its source may have authorized the demise of the disabled body as a prodigy, but the seemingly sudden arrival of the Enlightenment and its embrace of reason never fully stifle the carnivalesque: the marvelous continues to surface in popular culture; the sideshow attraction still troubles its audience and defies definitions.[10] In their study of English carnival and coffeehouse culture, Peter Stallybrass and Allon White have identified two strains in Bakhtin's thought on the carnivalesque body. The first strain enunciates the challenge the grotesque body poses in that halcyon, pre-Enlightenment time to authority through the inversion of hierarchy: the low is made high, the high low, the fool crowned, the clergy parodied, the extraordinary body exalted. The effect on the extraordinary body is literally revolutionary and liberatory.[11] But this inversion is momentary and conditional: it is specific to the ritual and limited still by the toleration of authority. The extraordinary body itself does not change its constitution. The lame do not walk, the blind do not see. The inversion of this status still relies upon the uncomplicated oppositions of popular/official, high/low, extraordinary/normate. The extraordinary body—the low still "the low"—discovers its place in the procession, anointed in the face of official disapproval, an emblem of "the right to be 'other' in this world."[12]

The second strain of thought Stallybrass and White read in Bakhtin eschews the easy oppositions and opts for a more complicated model of the marketplace. "Against the populist element in Bakhtin," they write, "we must emphasize the fair as a point of economic and cultural intersection, of hybridization, to use his own term, not just as the potential space of popular and local subversion." The fair does not solely exist for the frivolity of a populace seeking license to tweak the nose of authority; it was also, if not primarily, a commercial event, a crossroads for goods from all points on the compass. The pageants and processions of bodily difference existed side-by-side with "the marketable wonders of the colonized world." As empire spread, so did the display of goods, an ever-increasing spectacle of colonial wealth. As the goods grew more exotic, so did the exhibits of extraordinary bodies. The one-time manifestation of God's great bounty became the splendor of the king's coffers. Crowds filled the marketplace to view the juxtaposition of the exotic and the mundane, "the commingling of categories usually kept separate and opposed: centre and periphery, inside and outside, stranger and local, commerce and festivity, high and low." In this spirit of hybridization, "the heterodox merging of elements usually perceived as incompatible . . . unsettles any fixed binaryism" and, as a result, influences the exhibition of extraordinary bodies.[13] Out of this celebration of hybridity, the mixed bag of booty from the colonies, arises the contradictory figure of the white Negro.

The idea of the white Negro first originates in colonial contact. Balthazar Tellez, a seventeenth-century historian of Jesuit exploration and missionary work, coined the term *albino* to describe white-skinned tribe members encountered on the first European incursions along the coast of West Africa.[14] Not coincidentally, the white African body arrives with the first inventions of racial difference. According to the prevailing critical narrative of racial construction, the economic exploitation of a continent requires the perception of its people as significantly and irredeemably different. Abdul JanMohamed contends that nascent colonialism and imperialism necessarily establish a "manichean allegory" as a means of rationalizing the open theft of resources. Dark skin becomes black, light skin grows white. Moral qualities begin to attend these simple oppositions: black receives the attributes of evil, inferiority, laziness, uncontrollable emotion, licentiousness; white acquires their virtuous opposites.[15] This development of polarized racial difference, the blackening of the African, as it were, coincides with the equally fabricated whitening of the European. As the thesis for his own treatise on the foundation of whiteness, Theodore W. Allen argues that as the early colonizers confronted irreconcilable customs, laws, and institutions that precluded easy acquisition and exploitation of resources, the national differences between European peoples dissolved into what he has identified as "a political act: the invention of 'the white race.'"[16] With whiteness invented and beatified, the albino body of the white African emerges as a possible challenge, an obstacle to this new binary of black and white.

The appetite for economic exploitation fosters the urge to colonize, to strip away the traditions, laws, and culture of a conquered people and replace them with a likeness of European polity, to create in the now-black body a duplicate citizen, what Homi Bhabha has called "the figure of mimicry." This desire to reform the behavior of the "black" body creates as well a threat to whiteness. "From such a colonial encounter between the white presence and the black semblance," Bhabha writes, "there emerges the question of the ambivalence of mimicry as a problematic of colonial subjection."[17] As a colonial mimic, the "black" body simultaneously reflects the difference required for dominance and a sameness, a virtual whiteness, that troubles the binary of black and white by rendering the fabrication of European whiteness visible and reproducible. Like the appearance of the colonial mimic, this first sighting of white skin on a black body sets in motion a scene of narcissistic colonialist desire for whiteness that will repeat and reproduce: the hybrid figure of the "white Negro," the translated body as colonial insignia, colonized by whiteness, transforming yet never quite transformed. The "white Negro" reenacts the whiteness of the colonizer and serves as its interrogator.[18] The transparency of whiteness, its pretensions to naturalness, ends in the body of this white mimic.

Even with these efforts to reform and civilize the "black" body, the unadulterated native—the South Seas islander or Native American tribe member or Zulu warrior in full costume—arrives in Europe as an ethnological specimen and entertainment for the heads of state who funded the exploration and the paying public, the armchair colonizer. In 1550, whole Brazilian villages appeared on the outskirts of Rouen for the pleasure of Henri II; Martin Frobisher, having failed yet again to discover the Northwest Passage in 1577, lured a group of Nova Scotian Eskimos aboard his ship for future profit in their exhibition in the Old World.[19] These exhibitions, these rehearsals of culture, if you will, allow for the homebound European citizen to participate in adventurous exploits, to see and temporarily partake in the possession of the world. Steven Mullaney writes, "Difference draws us to it; it promises pleasure and serves as an invitation to first hand experience, otherwise known as colonization."[20] The spectacle of these strange dark bodies, the radical difference of their new blackness and the curiosity of their proclaimed savage customs, further rationalizes the economic domination of foreign peoples.

Later collected in cabinets of curiosity, early natural history museums, and public fairs, these representatives of a world elsewhere, imported and exported for popular consumption, established the tradition of the racial freak, a figure of bodily difference to be displayed alongside fat women and dog-faced boys. To discuss the bodies of colonized peoples alongside those of more traditional freaks will potentially offend some sensibilities, yet I do not casually graft the figure of the prodigious body of the freak to the figure of the black-skinned African. The conjoined twin that this operation creates is neither monstrous nor disjunctive. Both figures are culturally constructed tropes, equally unnatural by themselves. The same mechanism of colonialism that radicalizes the body into blackness affords that body to be commodified as a freak and, in this exhibition, exposes it to slavery. In fact, as Maja-Lisa von Sneidern argues, the exhibition of the extraordinary body, the uneven relationship between showman and display it inevitably creates, establishes an atmosphere in which slavery can take place: "The human anomaly who materializes physical deviation from a norm is a body capable of locating a place where a person slides into property."[21] From the exhibition of the freak at the fairgrounds, so the tale goes, comes the rationale for enslavement.

The racial freak and the slave have a shared origin in the colonial formation of the manichean allegory. In its staging, the exhibition inevitably allows for the easy slippage between person and property, citizen and thing. The exaggeration of bodily difference between peoples results in the creation of what Leonard Cassuto prefers to call the "racial grotesque." Instead of emphatically erecting rigid and unchanging racial categories, he argues, the objectification of the racial grotesque "never fully succeeds."[22] Humanity still flickers before the audience of the spectacle of blackness. Although I am not convinced that the audience of racial exhibitions necessarily experiences the humanity of the display, Cassuto's argument provides a foundation for understanding the effect of these spectacles upon their audiences. Rather than secure identity for the audience of the freak show—as previously stipulated in freak show criticism—the grotesque offers "the anomalous embodiment of cultural anxiety."[23] In the exhibitions, categories are violated and left unresolved. As a result, the audience feels more unease than reaffirmation.

As the displayed black body of the African wavered between man and beast, civilized and savage, the transformed body of the white Negro produced an additional problem by reversing the apparent stigma of blackness. Since dark skin itself marked the African body for display, whiteness should have logically restored humanity and endowed citizenship. It did not. As the melanin melted away from the skin, the audience's expectation of blackness remained and altered the arriving whiteness, rendering it likewise visible as an anomaly. Rather than furnish a foil for the whiteness of its audience, the white Negro defied the opposition, presenting instead the haunting figure of the doppelgänger, the mimic that masters its master.

To be seen. The Wonderful White Negro Woman, (From the Island of Jamaica) A Phœnomenon so extraordinary that it is believed her equal cannot be found.

—London broadside, ca. 1790.

As we witness the bodies now, we marvel as did the first audiences. In spite of ourselves, the awe returns. The photographs, etchings, lithographs I display before you still maintain a kind of currency, a moment of puzzlement and curiosity. Part of this fascination, we may confess, resides in the lingering expectation of a world divided into an ineluctable blackness and whiteness, discrete racial essences that begin to collapse and confuse in the body of the white Negro. The simple biological phenomenon of dark skin drained of its melanin conjures in the imagination social and political possibilities, synecdoches of blurred identities and hopeful aspirations for full citizenship, an object lesson of utopian racial harmony, the fantasy of bodily difference evaporating into a naturalized whiteness. It is for these tropes that we should reserve our wonder. We must turn our gaze upon our spectatorship and those mechanisms we employ and have employed to transform the body of the white or whitening African American into a central cultural figure, one produced out of our continuing struggles to contend with the failures of representative democracy.

At first, explorers, plantation owners, and medical doctors shipped the transforming bodies of white Negroes back to Europe as a New World wonder; sometimes they commissioned paintings or engravings to circulate as artifacts of the endless variety found in colonial possessions. White Negroes were showcased in the exhibition spaces of seventeenth-century London, before the Royal Philosophical Society, in the salons of eighteenth-century Paris, and later at English fairs. By studying the illustrations of these exhibited bodies, we get a better understanding of the white Negro's place in the European imagination. The 1740 *Portrait of Maria Sabina* shows the young girl from a Jesuit plantation near Cartagena standing in a tropical landscape dotted with rustic churches adorned with prominent crosses. Her skin starkly mottled from vitiligo, she is nearly naked, with a beatific smile and stark black and white coloring. A parrot perches on her left forefinger as if she has called it from the trees. The anonymous artist presents Maria Sabina as a child of nature, a marvel of God's creation, a sign of God's benevolence and ceaseless invention. Likewise depicted as a sport of nature in a 1789 lithograph, John "Primrose" Boby, "the Celebrated Piebald Boy, a native of the West Indies," suffers a reduction to tropical exotica, palm trees swaying in the background, naked save for a cloth strategically draped across his loins. The illustration suggests the allure of the New World, the mystery of nature's effects on the body in equatorial climes.

Fig. 1. *Portrait of Maria Sabina*. By permission of the Colonial Williamsburg Foundation.

Fig. 2. "Primrose, the Celebrated Piebald Boy," lithograph. By permission of The Library Company of Philadelphia.

The paintings and prints, the etchings and woodcuts have demonstrated a remarkable reproductive capability, a confirmation of the persistence and popularity of white Negro display. The *Portrait of Maria Sabina*, in particular, offers a history of prolific exhibition. Initially displayed by her mother before the priests from the local college and paying customers, Maria Sabina grew in regional fame until a painting of the child's marvelous body was commissioned for export to Europe.[24] Portraits of Maria Sabina began to circulate and multiply after her initial exhibition. According to legend, an American ship captured the Spanish vessel carrying the picture. Entranced by the spotted girl, the new owners of the portrait commission more copies for distribution.[25] Consequently, no more than a year or two later, the French capture an English ship bearing a portrait of Maria. This painting, copy or original, eventually comes to the attention of Georges LeClerc, the Comte de Buffon, who produces an engraving from it as an illustration for his *L'histoire de l'homme*, translating the extraordinary body of Maria Sabina into an object of natural history. The image of the transforming white Negro, reproduced and disseminated, becomes a kind of capital, an object valued enough to be copied and spread through the Atlantic region in a process Stephen Greenblatt has identified as the "mimetic circulation" of spectacle.[26]

Nowhere was the traffic in white Negro exhibitions and images more prolific than at the great fairs of England. Advertisements and illustrations from these exhibitions depict the mottled bodies as colonial marvels from the New World. To augment their box-office receipts, exhibitors of white Negroes sold illustrations at the performances. At Bartholomew Fair in the 1790s, coins bearing the likeness of Mrs. Newsham, the "Albino Negress," served as souvenirs. A Mr. Richardson, a Bartholomew Fair theater owner, offered for sale copper plate engravings of George Alexander, "the Spotted Boy," to supplement the exhibition of the young child's body. The engravings of George Alexander, like those of Maria Sabina, emphasize the marvel of his extraordinary, transforming body. In the picture, the young boy sits on the back of a turtle in the midst of a tropical landscape as he reaches out to a small, equally spotted dog at his side. He smiles joyfully. Imported from the Virgin Islands, the small boy was exhibited from the age of fifteen months and was only four years old at the time of his death from cancer of the jaw. Between acts of the gothic melodrama "Monk and Murderer," Richardson paraded him on the stage of his theater to the delight of the crowd. Like other British white Negroes, George Alexander was simply a marvel from the New World, a professed object of mystery and beauty. The playbill describes him as "the offspring of Negroes, beautifully covered by a diversity of Spots, transparent brown and white; his hair interwoven brown and white; this fanciful Child of Nature, formed in her most playful mood." According to his obituary in

F I G . 3 . Piebald girl from
Buffon's *L'histoire de l'homme*.
By permission of The Library
Company of Philadelphia.

1813, he "was the theme of universal admiration, not only for the very singular marks which it pleased the Almighty to distinguish the works of his creation from the rest of the human race, but the playful and endearing manner with which this late wonderful infant prepossessed all ranks of persons in his favour that visited him."[27] Although one nineteenth-century publication called him "the last of the great natural curiosities exhibited" at Bartholomew Fair, even his death did not end the circulation of his image for display.[28] Shortly after his death, a Bartholomew Fair museum advertised the exhibition of his likeness in wax.

As the British displays of white Negro bodies faded, exhibitions in the United States flourished, their appeal reaching beyond the merely marvelous into public concern over the nature and potential mutability of racial difference, worries over slavery and miscegenation, and yearnings for a national identity. In the American exhibitions, the disappearance of blackness from the African American body entertained fantasies of transformation and philosophical speculations upon the origin of skin color. Displays in the American exhibition spaces of the tavern, the natural history museum, and

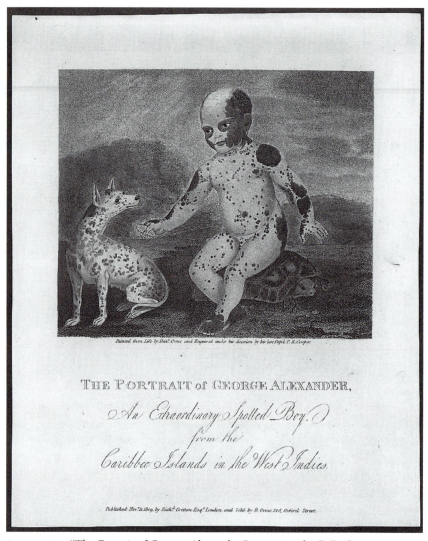

FIG. 4. "The Portrait of George Alexander," engraving by P. R. Cooper after Daniel Orme. By permission of The Harvard Theatre Collection, The Houghton Library.

the philosophical society took on the tone of objective scientific inquiry that obscured an obsession with the African American body. The traffic in white Negro wonderment continued. Like the reproduction of images, documents of white Negro displays—newspaper reports and scientific papers—transmitted from point to point on the Atlantic compass: Barbados, Jamaica, London, Paris, Philadelphia. In 1697, William Byrd II published in the *Transactions of the Royal Philosophical Society* "An Account of a Negro-Boy That Is Dappel'd in Several Places of His Body with White Spots," which announces the exhibition in England of an unnamed eleven-year-old African American boy, a slave from the colonies.[29] Tales abounded from the plantations. James Bate, a surgeon from Maryland, gave an account to the Royal Society in 1759 of "colonel Barnes's negro woman," who possessed "four parts in five" of a skin as "white, smooth, and transparent as . . . a fair European."[30] Another member of the society announced the appearance in London of an albino Virginian slave and suggested the color derived from the African mother's shock of seeing Europeans for the first time. For the remaining decades of the eighteenth century, these scientific reports continued to circulate in American newspapers as the interest in white or whitening African American bodies intensified.

The scientific attention accorded the body of the white Negro betrays the figure's importance in the development of an American national identity based upon a clear and defined idea of whiteness. Reflecting upon the influence of white Negro exhibition, Dana Nelson argues that "scientific discourse offered helpful equipment to U.S. national formation coextensive with its hierarchizing mobilization of the concept of 'race.'"[31] Haunted by the black body and the presence of slavery in a new democracy, an anxious white American public saw in the body of the white or whitening African American the manifestation of their anxieties, not only about race but of the attendant unease about their status as white citizens. The exhibition of white Negroes also spurred in scientific discourse concerns over the troubling presence of poor, immigrant, and laboring peoples, a population that the more elite, philosophical observers saw as not quite white.[32] In their increasing struggles to define themselves as white, the emerging American working class constructed as its opposite the "blackness" of both the free and enslaved African American populations. Historian of the working class David Roediger contends that "by considering a range of comparisons with Blacks in weighing his status as a white worker, the white laboring man could articulate a self-image that, depending on his wont, emphasized either his pride in independence or his fears of growing dependency."[33] Although I am unwilling to accept a reading of racial formation based exclusively upon, in Alexander Saxton's words, "sustained important interests of ruling classes or class coalitions," the tension between pride and fear proposed by these theories of whiteness illustrates the uncertainty and distress experienced before the body of the white Negro by audiences who presumed their whiteness.[34]

In contrast to the theorists of the freak show, we must be careful not to homogenize the audience of white Negro exhibition as middle class and identifiably white nor the effect of the exhibit on the audience as universally normalizing.[35] Philosopher and burgher, amateur scientist and working stiff, the audience before the displays in Peale's natural history museum or later in the cacophony of Barnum's American Museum could feel simultaneously superiority and anxiety in the midst of the urge for gentrification and tests of citizenship these exhibition spaces presented. The tenuous status of working-class, immigrant, and poor members of these audiences, people often with merely hopes of white citizenship, forced a comparison with the exhibit that can only place their membership in jeopardy. The spectacle of freakish whiteness on a slave's body posed a particular challenge to efforts of self-definition.

Scholarship on white Negro exhibitions is scarce and minimal. Winthrop Jordan's brief account of this phenomenon in *White Over Black* implies but does not explore the need of the philosopher to explain away blackness and somehow soothe the national tensions over slavery.[36] Only recently, in works investigating the nexus of gender and racial formation, have scholars turned their critical eyes toward the spectacle of the white or whitening African American body. In her work on the centrality of sentimentalized motherhood to the construction of liberal democracy, Eva Cherniavsky articulates the disruptive force of the albino African American body as it presents to Thomas Jefferson, in the text of his *Notes on the State of Virginia*, the conundrum of whiteness produced from the body of a black woman. The "dominant impulse" in Jefferson's work of natural history, she argues, "is plainly to occlude the white man's role in the degradation of the 'race.'" With this partially achieved, Jefferson can continue with his work to exclude the African American body from the formation of "republican womanhood."[37] Taking her cue from Cherniavsky's work, Dana Nelson shows the relationship between the white Negro exhibitions and the creation of what she calls "national manhood," a fraternal sense of "white" citizenship that erases political and economic inequalities and prepares these men for "market and professional competition." The racial instability of the white Negro is once again produced by the body of the African American woman. In addition to a reading of the white Negro display in Jefferson's *Notes*, Nelson surveys Benjamin Rush's speculations on the body of Henry Moss as it changes before philosophers and statesmen in a Philadelphia tavern. In each case, the whiteness in the African American body reflects "social anxieties about instability, chaos, and fragmentation" that require containment in the new Republic.[38] Both Nelson and Cherniavsky, by focusing their attentions on the female white Negro body, neglect the extensive and, for the most part, prevailing exhibitions of transforming male bodies and their effect upon their audiences. Generally restricting their discussions to the limited yet important philosophical dissertations of Jefferson and Benjamin Rush, these attempts to assay the importance of white Negro exhibitions have ignored the larger cultural context and influence of the white or whitening African American body.

In the following chapters, I will demonstrate the proliferation of the image of the white Negro in popular culture as well as its interpretation and implementation in works of literature. As Toni Morrison has argued for the "black presence [as] central to any understanding of our national literature," we are likewise haunted by a white presence, a shadow, a mimic that is equally central to any understanding of our culture.[39] For decades, the figure of the white Negro has proven a consistent obstacle to the attempts of racial science to fix difference in the skin. By necessity, these efforts to construct a rigid binary of black and white produce its antagonist, a figure that fits and defies both categories. The resulting narrative of white Negro exhibition exploits this collapse of definitions, providing for its audience a fantasy of racial transformation, the play of the image on the horizon, shimmering, a mirage or at least giving the effect of a mirage, under the influence of which, the closer a traveler seems to get, the more uncertain the vision.

At first this fantasy of transgressing bodies is not a psychological desire or envy of whites to turn or be black nor of African Americans necessarily to turn or be white; it is the desire for political and social concord achieved through homogeneity and the anxiety of that homogeneity produced through the hybrid body of the white Negro. This sense of agreement, of national unity, though, is never quite achieved. The figure of the white Negro pokes and prods the consciousness, worries the culture's dream-life, as a constant reminder of folly to those who adhere to a belief in distinct and immutable racial difference. The strain of restricting the white Negro through racial categorization aggravates the fissures and flaws in that faith and threatens to expose the fiction of whiteness.

The exhibition of white Negroes extends through generations of American culture. Whenever scientists, politicians, and writers defend or assault the boundaries of difference, the fantasy of racial transformation surfaces. Black dissolves to white. Spots materialize. Bodies are compared. In each appearance, the vocabulary of exhibition remains remarkably the same. Although I have tried to maintain a loose chronological organization to my account, I will often yield to the temptation to demonstrate the persistent influence of these images by drawing connections over decades and even centuries. The myths of miscegenation performed in Barnum's American Museum and on the stage of blackface theater, I will argue, emerge again in episodes of *Star Trek* and *Bewitched*, the script of exhibition kept whole over the broad span of time.

I begin my narrative of white Negro exhibition in the late eighteenth century, a moment when the extraordinary whitening body shifts in its audience's eye from a sport of nature to an object of philosophical and scientific speculation. Displays of African Americans with albinism and vitiligo proliferate in the exhibition spaces of the new Republic. The first chapter explores this phenomenon of white Negro exhibition and its role in the debates over the nature and origins of skin color as blackness emerges as the primary marker of racial difference. In particular, the chapter dwells on the Philadelphia exhibition of Henry Moss in the summer of 1796. His transforming body, seeming to grow visibly whiter during the weeks of his exhibition, offers the first major fantasy—and nightmare—of racial transformation. The natural philosophers who speculate on Moss's skin also use his body to narrow the parameters of whiteness and exclude the poor, immigrant, and laboring populations from its membership.

The legacy of Henry Moss continues in chapter 2, troubling the efforts of racial scientists to fix difference and inferiority in the slave's body. Threatened by the anatomical knife and the violence implied by exhibition, the body of the white Negro serves as a screen to project the anxieties of near-white peoples who aspire to the privileges of whiteness yet fear its denial to their vulnerable bodies. Gradually, the body of the transforming white Negro, what Barnum called the "Leopard Child" or "Negro Turning White," begins to represent the transgressive miscegenated body, the growing whiteness symbolic of an increasing fear of a population that escapes categorization through the erasure of difference. These exhibitions of racial characteristics in flux subsequently influenced Herman Melville, who in *The Confidence-Man* embraces the radical possibilities of the white Negro in his description of the rabble who view the Confidence Man's performance. Melville's figure of the "piebald parliament" undermines the constitution of a distinct and racially pure white body.[40] But the influence of the Leopard Child does not end with Barnum's exploitation of the black-and-white body. Its themes and tropes intact, the image of the nineteenth-century piebald child extends forward to the twentieth century and the spectacle of spotted sitcom children and bifurcated *Star Trek* aliens.

The third chapter focuses upon the hybrid body of the albino African American and explores the colonial origins of this figure, identifying its tendency to mimic and interrogate the whiteness of those whites who viewed it. Later, employed as a literary trope in the works of Edgar Allan Poe and, again, Herman Melville, the albino white Negro presents an implacable surface, a whiteness rendered disturbingly unnatural. In the twentieth century, African American writers appropriated the figure of the white Negro, seeing in its monstrous color a tool to defuse the primacy of whiteness and consequently exalt dark skin. In particular, novelists Chester Himes and John

Edgar Wideman produce albino white Negro central characters as problematic emblems of racial confusion. Ostracized by white and black alike, these exhibitions of the albino white Negro become inscribed with violence directed toward the black body, the bruises and welts rising conspicuously on the preternatural white skin.

The contexts of nineteenth-century white Negro exhibition—claims of racial superiority, scientific obsession with skin color, the curse of slavery—still affect present discussions of race. The fourth chapter demonstrates that influence by returning to the scene of exhibition. The early exhibitions created a template for later, mostly literary presentations of light-complected African American bodies. In this trope, originated by Charles Willson Peale and refined by P. T. Barnum, an audience, presumably white working class, views with fascination the appearance of whiteness on an African American body; the showman comments to the patron on the comparison of the exhibit's skin color to that of its audience, always to the detriment of the unknowing paying customer. This act of comparison places into question the binary of black and white as a malleable fiction. During the development of this trope in the passing narratives by African American writers, the formerly silent, placid body of the white Negro begins to move, to take control of its exhibition. The exhibitions before audiences who presume themselves white and therefore superior become more pointed, even vicious, as the body of the white Negro evolves into a weapon.

Finally, I will turn my attention to the transgressive and transforming body of pop singer Michael Jackson. Critics and social observers malign his apparently whitening skin as evidence of racial self-hatred. Public fixation on Jackson's body illustrates the continuing fascination with the figure that defies racial categorization. The chapter focuses upon Jackson's recent legal difficulties and the status of his altered skin as a body of evidence. His exhibition before the video cameras of the Santa Barbara County Sheriff, the rumored exposure of his bespotted penis for comparison to his young accuser's portrait, recalls the display of the white Negroes, the Spotted Children, the Leopard Boys who came before him. His efforts to manipulate his appearance and narrate the exhibition of his own body suggest greater possibilities for the construction of identity through the exaggeration of its artifice, an attempt to evade the whims of categorization and slip the bonds of essentialized race.

My chronology leaps, folds upon itself. In our collective fantasies, black bodies still turn white. The white Negro will have its sway. In the coming pages, as we witness Henry Moss, naked to the waist in the tavern at the sign of the Black Horse in Philadelphia, his skin scrutinized and probed by those men we call the Founding Fathers, we will also find his ghost in the King of

Pop as he narrates for us his humiliation, stripped for the camera, his body duly documented on tape. As the exhibitions continue to play out, the marvelous body of the Leopard Child still stuns and disturbs, blurring strict definitions of racial difference and provoking chimeras of boundaries trangressed, taboos defied.

So, we watch ourselves watch, our complacency as spectators troubled as the exhibition of the white Negro begins.

The White Negro in the Early Republic

A GREAT CURIOSITY

There is a man at present at Mr. LEECH's Tavern, the sign of the Black Horse, in Market-street, who was born entirely black, and remained so for thirty-eight years, after which his natural colour began to rubbed off. . . . The sight is really worthy the attention of the curious, and opens a wide field of amusement for the philosophic genius.

—Broadside tipped in Benjamin Rush's "Commonplace Book," 1796

White Negroes concerned Thomas Jefferson. Near Christmas of 1783, the manuscript of his *Notes on the State of Virginia* nearly completed, he sent letters of inquiry to Henry Skipwith and Charles Carter, owners of other Virginian estates, to ask about the presence on their plantations of any slaves with unusually white skin. As late as early February, a few short months before he would trundle the completed manuscript to Paris for private publication, Jefferson received accounts of slaves with skin drained of melanin, more than likely the result of albinism or vitiligo. The letters he wrote to his neighbors have not survived, but judging from the responses, he solicited intelligence on the quality of the white color, its manifestation, the effect of the whiteness on other faculties, the color of the parents, and, most important, the ability of the whitened slave to produce children.[1]

The letters supplied the data Jefferson apparently believed he needed to complete his survey of Virginia's natural products. In part, this catalog answers an earnest inquiry by François Marbois, the secretary of the French delegation in Philadelphia, who, on behalf of his government, requested each state to give an accounting of its history, boundaries, and by-products. Yet the opportunity of a survey inspired Jefferson to answer as well the theories of the European naturalists, especially the eminent Comte de Buffon, who declared that the insufficient American environment generated smaller animals and people, and in smaller numbers, than the Old World's presumably more congenial climate. The presence of the white Negro produced a more complex problem. The "domestic state," Buffon observes, alters the color of animals. The apparent whitening of the captive hog in particular "seems to mark the last degree of degeneration." By extrapolation then, African whiteness is also a sign of the degeneration brought on by the state of slavery.[2] Faced with the phenomenon of the white Negro, Jefferson did not simply have to defend the benefits of the North American climate; slavery—its institutions, its rationale, its dependence upon easily recognizable bodily difference—was also under attack. In *Notes on the State of Virginia*, Jefferson needed to demonstrate that the appearance of seemingly enfeebled white bodies in the slave population were singular events, not signs of a permanent and proliferating transformation.

In his report to Jefferson, Skipwith describes three sisters among his slaves whose skin is "a disagreeable chalky white." The sisters' parents, he is careful to point out, possess "the ordinary color of blacks (not jet)." Even though the whiteness in the slaves suffers in comparison to Anglo-Saxon skin, Skipwith still feels the need to address the threat of whiteness giving birth to whiteness and spreading to future generations.[3] He offers in the conclusion of his observation that "I know of no instance of this species generating together. Two of mine have generated with black's and each had issue female children of the ordinary complexion of light coloured negroes." The whiteness, he implies, does not transmit from parent to child. It remains safely within the borders of the afflicted slave's skin. In addition to the three slave sisters, Skipwith gives an account of white Negroes belonging to Captain John Butler and Charles Lee, of which Lee's receives the greatest attention: "[Mr. Lee] tells me his White Negro man slave was generated between a couple of negroes of ordinary colour and that he in every respect (the sex excepted) is like my own."[4] Dwelling on genealogy, Skipwith's letter indicates in Jefferson's inquiry an oblique fear of the potential for white Negroes to reproduce the disagreeable whiteness and dissolve the boundaries between the races.

Carter's less methodical letter largely confirms Skipwith's observations and once again restricts the whiteness of his slaves to a position that denies any affinity with, in Carter's eyes, the more agreeable color of the Anglo-Saxon. He describes one slave with poor eyesight and "a sallow white" skin with "a great many dark spots promiscuously scattered over it somewhat like the freckles on a white person's face but rather larger." Like Skipwith, he prominently addresses the production of offspring: "She has had a child by a true black, which had the complexion of the mother. The child lived but a few weeks."[5] In these accounts, Carter and Skipwith figure blackness as "ordinary" and "true," the sign of health and normalcy in the African body. On the other hand, the introduction of whiteness—the inheritance from the albino mother—dooms the unfortunate child, reassuring that whiteness will remain anomalous and not spread through the slave population.

The attempt in these letters to isolate whiteness in the slaves as abnormal and unnatural requires a description that differentiates the whiteness of the albino's skin from that of the viewer; otherwise, to condemn whiteness in the albino threatens the status of the normalized white audience.[6] With the incorporation of Skipwith's and Carter's accounts into *Notes on the State of Virginia*, Jefferson similarly employs terms to denigrate the quality of whiteness in the albino skin without the accompanying language that certifies the normalcy of black skin. Jefferson's textual exhibition of the white Negro reduces the white skin of the slave to a double anomaly: the black skin no longer ordinary and true, the white skin a result of abnormal processes rather than a marker of acquired privilege. Careful to isolate the anomalous whiteness, Jefferson attempts to eliminate as well the other potential cause for the lightening of African American skin—the sexual transgressions of the masters. He begins his passage on the white Negro with the blunt declaration that all white Negroes were "born of parents who had no mixture of white blood."[7]

For a long time, scholars discounted the *Notes on the State of Virginia* as a half-realized, prosaic compilation of data and facts. The presence of white Negroes in Jefferson's account of his home state is not an accidental, incautious glitch that somehow escaped from the editorial pen. Jefferson intends for his exhibition to carry political and philosophical weight. Recent scholarship has explored the conscious artfulness and argumentative intent of the text's structure. In this scholarship, Jefferson emerges as "obsessed by notions of design, system measurement, and style."[8] To elucidate the bounty within his state's borders and to argue for the essential order of nature on the North American continent, Jefferson utilizes charts of population distribution, lists of flora and fauna, tables of climate and militia membership, tallies of revenue, weights and measurements of livestock, taxonomies of Linnaean binomial nomenclature and popular names of plants and animals, catalogs of native tribes, an outline of state laws, a chronology of state papers, even a map of a cave. According to this critical narrative, the structure of *Notes* arises from philosophical tenet and personal need. In 1781, the time in which Jefferson claims to have written the bulk of the work, chaos threatened to overwhelm Jefferson's world: his daughter died, his wife became ill, the war had just come to Virginia, the approaching British troops had forced the government to flee Richmond, and, as governor, he faced the possibility of public censure by the legislature. The need for certainty and order also results from the national anxiety of a people winning a revolution but uncertain as to the inevitable changes that victory will bring. Seeking a panacea for flux, the rhetoricians of the period rely upon the natural world as a model for social construction.[9] The construction of taxonomies, as Christopher Looby argues, is "a rehearsal, so to speak, of social and political construction."[10] In this tradition, Jefferson's taxonomies in Query VI serve as a basis for national definition, a blueprint of natural hierarchy and social harmony. Yet into his representation of an orderly world, Jefferson purposefully places the disruptive figure of the white Negro.

When he incorporates the reports of the six white Negroes described by Skipwith and Carter into his Query VI, a scrupulous catalog of the state's flora, fauna, and mineral deposits, Jefferson admits that they do not belong among the rationally organized and carefully delineated Platonic essences. "I will add a short account of an anomaly of nature," he writes, "taking place sometimes in the race of negroes from Africa, who, though black themselves, have in rare instances, white children, called Albinos."[11] The white Negro is the only anomaly, the sole variation, he lists among the "Productions Mineral, Vegetable and Animal" of his query's title. Yet, unlike his extensive compendium of mammals, his mammoths, his defense of Native Americans, Jefferson curiously attaches no argument to his display of white Negroes. Seemingly not knowing what to do with them, he relegates the troublesome figures to a spot between his brief and dismissive accounts of the fishes and the insects, further diminishing their importance in the grand plan of his work. Even with the disclaimer, he chooses to display among the Platonic essences an extraordinary body, the residue of a world filled with wonders and signs, a figure whose oxymoronic label *white Negro* challenges the rational binomial nomenclature of Linnaean classification.

Scholars have never known what to make of the white Negroes in *Notes on the State of Virginia*. Most scholarship on Jefferson and race do not even mention his obvious fascination with the white Negro, choosing instead to focus upon his extended comments on slavery in Queries XIV and XVIII.[12] Taking Jefferson at his word, they have treated the exhibition at the end of Query VI as "an anomaly of nature," a harmless quirk or perverse afterthought in Jefferson's otherwise careful argument.[13] Even Winthrop Jordan, who devotes portions of *White Over Black* to Jefferson's views of slavery and to the white Negro phenomenon, offers little discussion of the importance of the white Negro to Jefferson's work.[14]

The presence of the albinos is curious, though. Given Jefferson's reputation as a methodical, logical, Enlightenment thinker, scholars have rejected the uncertainty introduced by inscrutable sports of nature. Jefferson, on the other hand, chose not to ignore the disruptive and the anomalous nor exclude them from his work. The presence of white Negroes was neither a mistake nor an inexplicable yet excusable whim of an otherwise rational mind. Jefferson, Mitchell Breitweiser argues, intended to render a world incompletely understood in order to inhibit the despotism of intellectual certainty. Although the philosopher can rationally comprehend the world, the omission of wonder is arrogance. Jefferson, with the figure of "the albino black," among other discrepancies in *Notes* Breitweiser names, "demonstrate[s] the enigma, prodigiousness, and incommensurability of the thing experienced."[15] This mystery is not permanently unsolvable; the natural philosopher will eventually set chaos to order through methodical philosophical pursuit. The prospect of slaves with white skin in particular, though, significantly fascinated Jefferson for him to disrupt the orderly surface of his extensive taxonomy in Query VI with a display of racial confusion. Jefferson presents the skin of slaves born white as a puzzlement unexpected by the reader and unexplained by the author yet discoverable through persistent inquiry.

Jefferson concludes his listing of white Negroes by adding what seems to be the catalyst for his interest and concern, a curiosity more inexplicable than those previously listed, a slave of his own, born black but with skin that over time has gradually grown white. He writes that, along with the albinos, "I may add the mention of a negro man within my own knowledge, born black, and of black parents; on whose chin, when a boy, a white spot appeared. This continued to increase till he became a man, by which time it had extended over his chin, lips, one cheek, the under jaw and neck on that side. It is of the Albino white, without any mixture of red, and has for several years been stationary. He is robust and healthy, and the change of colour was not accompanied with any sensible disease, either general or topical."[16] Jefferson has saved the most troubling white Negro for last. Unlike the albinos he listed in Query VI, whose whiteness is fixed and apparently congenital, this white Negro has vitiligo, a disorder that Jefferson cannot separate from albinism. The gradually whitening skin produces a greater problem to Jefferson than the stable surface of the albino. Skin that changes color erodes the belief in nature's fixity by erasing a supposedly indelible mark of inferiority. By challenging nature's fixity, the newly visible whiteness threatens social concord and hierarchy.

In order to mitigate this threat to the order of nature and society, Jefferson attempts to stabilize the revolutionary potential of the white Negro body by effacing the distinction between it and the body of the albino and reinforcing the difference between African and Anglo-Saxon skin.[17] He describes the color of the albino as "a pallid cadaverous white, untinged with red," reducing the albino, through this description, beyond the position of an analyzable living object of natural history to that of a dissectible corpse, apparently devoid of the warming and, to a small extent, humanizing blood that marks the proper whiteness of skin.[18] By lumping the gradually whitening skin of the person with vitiligo in with that of the albino, Jefferson effectively exiles his slave beyond the boundaries of nature to the realm of the nonthreatening, though still haunting, dead.

"THE HISTORY OF WHITE NEGROES"

In spite of his efforts to limit its effect, Jefferson's literary exhibition of his white Negroes spurred further display and discussion of the encroachment of white skin on the black slave body. The image of the African American deprived of blackness—slaves transforming, degenerating, possibly regenerating—fired the political imagination and insinuated its way into the debate on race as a disconcerting indicator of the fiction of whiteness. Introduced into an orderly accounting of natural history, a body in the process of transforming from black to white generated a fantasy of racial transformation, the possibility that biological essences were mutable, influenced by mysterious forces. We will find in the wealth of exhibitions that accompanied and followed Jefferson's dissertation on Virginian flora and fauna that the display of the white Negro affected the exhibition space, disturbing the solace and concord of a hierarchical nature staged in philosophical treatises and early museums. It is this challenge to natural philosophy and its construction of a disciplined universe I will focus upon first.

Before the American Philosophical Society in May of 1786, Dr. John Morgan presented "a motley coloured, or pye Negro Girl and Mulatto Boy."[19] Morgan reports the exhibition in the second volume of the *Transactions* of the society, taking great care to chronicle the quality of color and its distribution on the black body and investing the whiteness with the tantalizing possibility of an appearance of a different skin, one more acceptable to Morgan's audience. Unlike Jefferson, Morgan distinguishes between the color of the albino, "whose skin is altogether of a dead white color," and that of the toddlers he exhibits. He describes the infringing color of the boy's skin as "a beautiful lively white."[20] By creating a binary of the lively and the dead, Morgan invites a favorable comparison of skin color between the bespotted children and those of the society who gaze at their surface.

Morgan offers legal documentation of the authenticity of the children and their parentage, letters from a king's physician and a king's surgeon dutifully notarized by a lieutenant-judge at Grandterre, Guadeloupe. The papers confirm that both children are two years old and that both belong to a Mons. le Vallois of the West Indies. The testimony, the signatures, the official seals attest that the bodies of the children have not been doctored, so to speak. As he verifies the color transformation as a natural phenomenon, Morgan sufficiently restricts the whitening body of the girl, Adelaide, within African bloodlines, announcing it as "a well-authenticated fact . . . that she had a negro father and negro mother." Although Morgan discounts any infusion of white blood as he displays the spotted body of the girl and removes miscegenation from possible causes for the outbreak of whiteness, the young boy, Jean Pierre, poses a greater problem: he is born "of a negro wench named Caroline and of a white man, an European, whose name I did not learn." The mother bears similar white spots. The European father suffers from white spots as well, "a deeper white than his natural skin," as does the European's brother. Jean Pierre serves as a body of evidence, as it were, for a whole cluster of related cases of further whitening skin. Although Morgan never hazards the implication of a contagion afoot, the proximity of all these bodies suffering the same mysterious spotting weighs heavily in Morgan's presentation. Morgan tepidly attempts to put the burden on the reader to explain "what causes have produced those surprising phænomena and alteration of the natural color of their skin."[21] Like Jefferson, Morgan merely displays the bodies, offering up the toddlers as curiosities, *lusus naturae*.

Morgan immediately follows up his disavowal of explanation with a theory that embraces the philosophies of the imaginationists popular in Europe during the middle of the eighteenth century: external events, and their impression upon the minds of the mothers, must have caused the mysterious occurrence of their children's transformed skin. Under this theory, disfigurement results from the licentious behavior of the mother, which conveniently absolves the father of any wrongdoing.[22] By placing the sole blame upon the mother, Morgan removes the possibility that whiteness could spread among the slaves through the sins of their masters. Adelaide's mother "was delighted in laying out all night in the open air, and contemplating the stars and planets." Jean Pierre's great-grandmother "was frightened on having some milk spilled upon her." Morgan, however, does not explain how the fear of the great-grandmother has marked Jean Pierre's European father and uncle. The doctor ends his musing with a reprised equivocation that "every one will determine for themselves" the cause of the anomalous whiteness.[23]

Although Morgan hesitates to venture an interpretation of his exhibition, others among his readership were not so reluctant to employ his white Negroes for political purposes. The eradication of blackness offered hope to the abolitionist. Blackness served as the most prominent marker of inferiority. If slaves became white, the abolitionist logic went, then the masters would feel compelled to set them free. Morgan's account of his white Negro exhibition appeared the following year in the *American Museum*, a journal with a distinct antislavery agenda. The *American Museum*'s exhibitions of white Negroes coincided with an effort to end slavery. In other issues, the journal resurrected earlier white Negro exhibitions, even ones previously published in the *Transactions of the Royal Philosophical Society*, and displayed them alongside fictitious first-person slave narratives, pleas for the end of the slave trade, and numerous addresses from the Pennsylvania Society for Promoting the Abolition of Slavery.[24]

The flurry of white Negro accounts and exhibitions in the wake of Jefferson's earlier observations demonstrates the volatility of the figure. The white audience of the accounts began to replicate the exhibitions and to appropriate the body of the white Negro to serve their own philosophical agenda. The immediate readership of the *Notes on the State of Virginia* understood the importance of the white Negro as either a symbol of hope or a portent of social chaos. Two of Jefferson's early readers were David Ramsay, an early historian of the American Revolution, and the Reverend James Madison, president of William and Mary College and namesake cousin of the future president. Corresponding with Jefferson as he attended to his ambassadorial duties in Paris, both readers address his exhibition of white Negroes, but they employ them to different ends—one openly disputing the phenomenon of whitening black skin, the other proposing the eventual end of all blackness in North America.

Madison prefaces his discussion of gradually whitening skin by directing Jefferson's attention to the second volume of the *Transactions of the American Philosophical Society*, in which Morgan prominently exhibited the whitening skin of Adelaide and Jean Pierre. "I am well pleased," Madison writes, "that we have such a Repository of Facts." Although Madison directly follows this praise with an exhibition of whitening skin, the dark body he exhibits is not black. He presents to Jefferson an account by Ezra Stiles, president of Yale College, of "an Indian about 50, who for near two Years past, has been gradually whitening." Madison's fascination with whitening skin indicates a more-than-casual reading of *Notes on the State of Virginia*, the disturbance of Jefferson's white Negroes provoking his response. "The Complexion and Colour of his Skin," Madison quotes Stiles, "is even clearer and fairer than most white Persons with whom he has been compared." Unlike the vitiligo Jefferson observed in his slave, this affected skin compares favorably in exhibition, calling into question the status of his now-less-white audience. Stiles distinguishes the correct shade for white skin, as he sees it, in the altered surface of the Native American—"a clear English White with *English Ruddiness*."[25] As Jefferson has already pointed out, white skin is not truly white without a blush of red.

Even in the face of Morgan's exhibition of white Negroes in the *Transactions of the American Philosophical Society* and Jefferson's presentation in *Notes on the State of Virginia*—both of which he apparently read—Madison chooses to deny the possibility of metamorphosis in black skin: the transforming skin of the Native American "differs remarkably in the last particular from what the poor Black experiences.—It seems as if Nature had absolutely denied to him the Possibility of ever acquiring the Complexion of the Whites."[26] Nature's denial accompanies Madison's own. Through willful ignorance, he refutes Morgan's and Jefferson's exhibitions at the same time that he alludes to them, placing in apparent dispute the veracity of the whitening black bodies.

Rather than suffer the anxiety Madison expressed, David Ramsay saw hope in the transforming skin of the slaves. In May of 1786, he responds to the restrictions Jefferson seemed to place upon his white Negroes: "I admire your generous indignation at slavery; but think you have depressed the negroes too low. I believe all mankind to be originally the same and only diversified by accidental circumstances. I flatter myself that in a few centuries the negroes will lose their black color. I think now they are less black in New Jersey than Carolina, their [lips] less thick, their noses less flat. The state of society has an influence not less than climate." Ramsay interprets Jefferson's display of white Negroes as an expression of the hope that civilization will effect a change in the physiognomy of African slaves, an amelioration of their blackness that will allow for the end of their enslavement and their eventual incorporation into society. To this desirable conversion, though, Ramsay offers its antithesis: the "back country people," removed from the graces of civilization, who have grown as "savage as the Cherokees."[27] Although the white Negro benefits from such a comparison, Ramsay expresses a greater anxiety for the poor who, removed from societal and governmental influence, have grown wild. The changing skin of the white Negro requires the degenerating bodies of lower-class white homesteaders for comparison, which, narrowing the parameters of whiteness, identifies and isolates the threat of those who have taken themselves outside the boundaries of civilization.

Ramsay expresses a hope that dominates white Negro exhibition in the last decade of the eighteenth century: the eradication of blackness will alleviate the philosophical burden of slavery in a new democracy. Within that hope, though, are other anxieties over governmental stability and the unchecked behavior of poor and laboring people. The white Negro—the revolutionary transformation from white to black, the unnerving contradiction of whiteness enslaved—fired the political imagination and served as a handy metaphor for the effects of destructive phenomena that undermined a young nation's dreams of liberty. Josiah Meigs, the Connecticut Wit and publisher of the *New-Haven Gazette, and the Connecticut Magazine,* authored under the name Lycurgus a satiric editorial, "The History of White

Negroes." In his introduction, he glosses on the natural wonder of "a race of negroes in the middlemost parts of Africa, who are as white as snow." This appearance of an African with white skin stimulates in Lycurgus a philosophical reverie on the origins of blackness and whiteness. All humanity, all races, spring from the loins of Adam, he reasons. To explain the sudden transformation of the African in America, Lycurgus embraces the theories of the French naturalists. The white Negro results from a "degeneracy," environmental forces that seem to have created a slave with white skin. Captivity deteriorates the body.[28]

The metaphorical possibilities of this spectacle were not lost on the Connecticut Wit. In the aftermath of the Revolution and the early experiments with American self-government, concerns grew over the possible political and economic limitations placed upon the liberty of white citizens. A body degenerating under the oppressive hand of slavery proved a powerful image. In this potential transformation of an African American slave into a white person, Lycurgus foresees the degeneracy of free white Americans into slaves. The increasing national debt, he argues in the body of the essay, will in time make erstwhile citizens into "the most useful of all our domestic animals." The burden of paying the interest on the debt will fall to these citizens, especially laborers, who must pay the taxes "by the sweat of our white negro brows."[29] For Lycurgus, taxation is slavery, an oppressive condition that degenerates the bodies of those compelled to pay.

This mock monograph on racial metamorphosis explores the same political anxieties inspired by the scientific papers it lampoons. The appearance of the white Negro leads to apprehension about the revolutionary conversion of the laboring poor, a concern Ramsay voiced in his letter to Jefferson. Ripe for manipulation, the poor can become savages or slaves, enraged or pacified. "This transformation of men," Lycurgus warns, "takes place chiefly among the lower classes of people." As they begin to change, they "talk wildly" against the government, alienate themselves from the community, then finally subdued, "grow not only fearless of slavery, but fond of becoming victims of its chain."[30] The laboring poor in this fantasy of racial transformation are a dangerous population mutating into foreign matter that threatens political concord.

As it haunted exhibition spaces in the period directly following the American Revolutionary War, the figure of the white Negro consistently inspired fears of a world turned topsy-turvy. Black can fade to white; white can blacken. In the guise of Lycurgus, Josiah Meigs authors a display of white Negroes that links the exhibition of white Negro slaves to the fate of poor white citizens and, hence, the prospects of the Republic, a construction that Jared Gardner identifies as a "conflation of racial and national destiny."[31] The future, Meigs implies, depends upon the serenity of a uniform whiteness, one buttressed by an adherence to a rigid racial and social hierarchy.

THE DISPLAY OF "JAMES THE WHITE NEGRO"

In the late summer of 1791, on his wedding trip in Maryland, Charles Willson Peale, portrait painter and museum entrepreneur, encountered a slave named James whose skin had, over the course of years, turned white. Peale quickly gained permission from James's owner to paint a portrait of the curiosity, which he subsequently displayed in a local tavern to drum up business for his portrait-painting skills.[32] The exhibition before the tavern's clientele was a great success. "I painted his Portrait for my Museum," he later writes, "this I thought as valuable an acquisition that I did not begrudge my (late) trouble and expence (for) in traveling so far, (however) by amediately after this I get some portraits to paint."[33] Peale took advantage of the audience's familiarity with the spectacle. A comparison between transforming bodies—that of James and of the portrait—helped to advertise his wares, his ability to re-create life on canvas. The Portrait of James the White Negro first serves as a calling card, a sales sample. Later that fall in Philadelphia, Peale exhibited the portrait before the American Philosophical Society—where Morgan's exhibition of Adelaide and Pierre had taken place five years earlier—and, soon thereafter, among the natural history collections in his own American Museum.[34]

Peale is careful to stipulate his preference for the museum over the tavern as an exhibition space. Early in the eighteenth century, the tavern provided in its ideal form a congenial space for men from diverse social and political backgrounds to drink and mingle and find common ground. An institutionalized civility developed to overcome momentarily the distinctions between these heterogenous groups.[35] In spite of these efforts, close quarters still produced unease, especially among the tavern's more genteel clientele. Peter Thompson has argued that after the Revolutionary War, "Philadelphians of all ranks and backgrounds grew disillusioned with the mixed company previously typical of their taverns."[36] As a response to public demand, drinking establishments began to specialize and appeal to particular groups. The reputation of the tavern, at this time, was a step above that of the alehouse and the tippling house. This differentiation, this new hierarchy of once-communal public spaces, as Stallybrass and White see in the rise of the English coffeehouse earlier in the eighteenth century, derived from "a widespread attempt to regulate the body and crowd behavior."[37] Even as it was increasingly domesticated, the tavern, though, still carried the taint of sin. Distinguished by a mixture of peoples, from patricians to laboring people, and a variety of affairs conducted within its walls, from business negotiations to public auctions and exhibitions, the tavern at the end of the eighteenth century suffered from the stigma of unruliness and contamination. John Adams observes of the tavern that "the time, the money, the health, and the modesty, of most that are young and of many old, are wasted; [that] diseases, vicious habits, bastards, and legislators, are frequently begotten."[38] The social spaces of the museum and the learned society served as a sober antidote to the perceived anarchy of the tavern, civilizing the body and the body politic. The white Negro, its transformation hinting of the unruliness and rebellion, finds an appropriate home in the exhibition space of the tavern.

In "Account of a Black Man Turned White," a paper he presented before the American Philosophical Society and published in the *National Gazette*, Peale describes James with the same care a natural history practitioner would describe any specimen.[39] He details the slow disappearance of the blackness over the past thirty-two years as it shifts to "a reddish brown colour by degrees, and remains so about six months, [then] changes further and becomes white."[40] Like other exhibitors of white Negroes, Peale emphasizes the lineage of James. He carefully considers certificates of birth and ownership and the testimony that James had a white father, anticipating in his audience the anxiety over miscegenation. In a shorter account of James among the Peale papers at the American Philosophical Society, James identifies his first owner, Ignatius Bowman, as his father, a fact only implied in the account that made it to print.[41] In the published account, Peale also chronicles the bodies of James's wife and his children, "all black as negroes commonly are." One child, though, an infant he left behind with another wife and a previous owner, was "born with such white spots of hair on his head" that marked the beginnings of James's change in color.[42] The genealogy Peale traces from the slavemaster to the slave to the spotted slave-child, through implication, encourages speculation on the origin of white skin among the slave population and expresses an anxiety that the white spots may be the sin of the white father visiting the skin of the son and, possibly, the grandson in a subtle indictment of the institution of slavery.

Peale ends his account by musing over the quality of the whiteness, as he takes great care to record the exhibit's relationship to the audience of his portrait in the tavern: "His skin is of a clear wholesome white, fair, and what would be called, *a better skin*, than any a number of white people who were present."[43] James's "better skin" compares favorably to that of the tavern patrons, a crowd similar in composition to earlier audiences of white Negro exhibition. Peale's exhibition of his portrait puts into question the relationships between master and slave, exhibit and audience, while at the same time reinforcing those relationships. Although a wholesome white, his skin new and improved, James is still a white Negro and subject to exhibition. The exhibition of the portrait and his better skin permits James, through the gaze of the audience, to join them briefly, yet his status as an exhibit separates him from those who view him by making him a natural curiosity.

> . . . a revolutionary figure indeed.
>
> —Charles Sellers, on the *Portrait of James the White Negro,*
> *Mr. Peale's Museum,* 1980

The introduction of the *Portrait of James the White Negro* into Peale's American Museum in Philadelphia, a more formalized exhibition space with an explicit political purpose, disrupts the cultural work of its organized displays of a rational, hierarchical universe. In his American Museum, Peale attempted to reproduce what he called "a world in miniature," a representation of nature based upon the organizational logic of the Linnaean system, the Great Chain of Being revealed in displays of insects, stuffed animals, and, at the pinnacle of the chain, portraits of great men.[44] In Peale's museum, citizens of all occupations and classes met and mingled before the tableau of an orderly and harmonious nature, what might be called a democratic social space where social roles in the new Republic could rehearse.[45] Regulated and easy to decipher, the taxonomical displays reassured an anxious audience in the aftermath of the revolution that the old social hierarchies would not dissolve into anarchy.

By the time Peale placed the *Portrait of James the White Negro* among his exhibits, he had established his museum as one of Philadelphia's educational and cultural sites. Peale first advertised his museum, a large addition connected to his house, in 1786 as a "Repository for Natural Curiosities . . . classed and arranged according to their several species."[46] He moved the collection to the second floor of the American Philosophical Society in 1794, then, in 1802, the museum found its final home in the upper floors of the Pennsylvania State House. Peale saw his museum as a national resource; the display of natural history was "a NATIONAL CONCERN, since it is a NATIONAL GOOD."[47] In his advertisement for subscriptions to his museum catalog in 1795, Peale tried to sell the museum as "evidence of our progress in a department of science, whose successful cultivation has always been a characteristic mark of an advanced civilization."[48] To Peale, the museum was a display of republican pride, a source of national self-definition.

From the beginning, Peale attempted to create in his museum, through the display of natural history, a democratic social space. It was to be a site where his patrons could encounter the harmony and unity of nature, which he believed could encourage social harmony and unity: "One very important effect may be produced,—persons having different sentiments in politicks, being drawn together for the purpose of studying the beauties of nature, while conversing on those agreeable subjects, may find a concordance of sentiments, and most probably from a slight acquaintance, would think better of each other, than while totally estranged."[49] Peale intended the museum as a panacea for the national anxiety by erasing divisions and establishing a common identity. He had faith that, by demonstrating a stable, ordered nature, a "world in miniature," his museum could erase boundaries of class through instruction and establish a homogenous white citizenship. The museum was a "rallying point" where the "mixture of men . . . would become more sociable by being accustomed to see each other frequently . . . in the same pursuits of knowledge."[50]

Peale designed his museum and its exhibits to affect the behavior of his patrons, to instruct and civilize them by rehearsing the harmony and unity of nature. The framework of Linnaean classification stabilizes nature, fixes its apparent flux and chaos into an understandable grid that demonstrates uniformity and unanimity. Part of the instruction of natural history involves an understanding of the binomial nomenclature of the Linnaean system. In a 1790 broadside advertising the museum, Peale states his intent from the beginning to order his exhibits along the lines of Linnaean design, assigning each object of nature, each insect, bird, and quadruped, its fixed place in the space of the museum, a hierarchical representation of the earthly Great Chain of Being.[51] Before Linnaeus, Peale writes, the study of nature was reserved for specialists, those who could "remember all creation as it were in a Mass; jumbled together."[52] Linnaean binomial nomenclature makes the comprehension of nature more accessible, hence democratic: "Perhaps it is not possible for an individual to be so learned in the science of nature, as to possess a complete knowledge of all the objects of each branch; yet possessing the general principles of those systems which have been invented of late years, by several ingenious and learned men (with a view to facilitate the study of natural history,) he may, with a little application, acquire the knowledge necessary to know any object, although he had never seen it before."[53] The Linnaean system renders natural history accessible and transparent because it relies upon visible phenomena, the surfaces of things—the shapes, the inventory of parts, the colors—that, in Michel Foucault's words, "can be analyzed, recognized by all, and thus given a name that everyone will be able to understand."[54] By relying on sight as the ordering mechanism, natural history became a tool of democracy: it allows anyone to order nature. Since natural history is based upon visual phenomena and nature itself becomes delineated and defined in terms of visible similarities and differences, the democracy promoted by the space of Peale's museum manifested itself as a

visible display of domestic harmony and organization. Hierarchies were performed, then stabilized through performance.

Hazarding disruption, Peale purposely introduced the portrait *James the
White Negro* into the democratic space that was his museum. The presence
of the portrait challenged the rationality and the stability of the other
exhibits. The anomalous is so offensive to the idea of the natural history
museum space that, until recently, Peale scholars have largely ignored the
appearance of anomalies in his museum. Lately, though, in *Public Culture
in the Early Republic*, David R. Brigham has recognized the disruptive
potential of these anomalies in general—and *James the White Negro* in particular—to Peale's museum space. "Exhibits of albinism and changes in skin
pigmentation," he explains, "offered a view of racial difference that perhaps
was unsettling to Peale's audience: that the boundary between the races may
not be fixed and that the prevailing social order may not be stable."[55] In spite
of this observation, Brigham does not address the purpose behind con-
sciously unsettling the patrons in a space designed to pacify an audience with
its harmonious design. Like Jefferson, Peale presented his white Negro as an
enigma and positioned him likewise on the walls of his museum.

We may gain some idea of such positioning on the walls of the museum
of *James the White Negro* by reading Peale's 1795 *An Historical Catalogue of
Peale's Collection of Paintings*. Peale places the portrait deep in the "Miscel-
lanies" section of the catalog, separate from his portraits of illustrious men
and between a portrait of a young Philadelphia slave girl and the *Portrait of
a Man Dressed in Manner of an Otahetian Chief Warrior*. James occupies a
space between a girl, whose gender, in Peale's economy, reduces her significance, and a painting of ethnographic importance, not the portrait of a warrior but of a man dressed as one. James shares characteristics of both of these
paintings of liminal figures: the reduced social status of the girl, made worse
through slavery, and the status of an ethnographic curiosity of the man passing as a South Seas islander. Peale often placed the miscellany on walls at
the side of the displays, exiled from the taxonomic grid yet still under its
influence.[56]

The white Negro shifted from a central position in the exhibition space of
the tavern to the far reaches of the museum's well-regulated displays, exiled
yet still submitted to the intrusive gaze of the patrons. The members of
learned societies maneuvered the extraordinary body of the white Negro in
an effort to reduce its effect and to bring it to bear upon the nagging philosophical problem of slavery in a new democracy, a movement from carnivalesque wonder to medical specimen, from enigmatic sport of nature to
identifiable phenomenon that we will also see in the exhibition of Henry
Moss.

THE CULTURAL WORK OF HENRY MOSS

> Such is the history, so far as it goes, of the change of a negro to a white man—a change, which had Henry Moss happened to have been a slave, would have furnished an irrefragable argument for annihilating his owner's claim.

> —"Account of a Singular Change of Colour in a Negro,"
> *Weekly Magazine*, 1798

For several months in the summer of 1796, Henry Moss, a white Negro with vitiligo, exhibited his body in taverns in and around Philadelphia as well as before members of the American Philosophical Society, making his name, according to Charles Caldwell, "almost as familiar to the readers of newspapers and other periodicals (so frequently was it recorded in them) as was that of John Adams, Thomas Jefferson, or Madison."[57] Among the crowds of dignitaries and natural philosophers who crowded to see Moss, a curious President Washington witnessed the phenomenon of a transforming body.[58] According to an advertisement Benjamin Rush saved in his commonplace book, it cost a then-substantial fee of "one Quarter of a Dollar [for] each person" to view Moss body and his changing color, the same amount Peale charged to view the whole collection in his American Museum.[59]

Little is certain of Henry Moss other than the descriptions of his body. Accounts tend to conflict, contradict. Born in 1754 in Goochland County, Virginia, Moss was forty-two years old at the time of his display.[60] From various accounts of his exhibition, he appears to have narrated his own body, politely answering the questions of his audience.[61] Even though Samuel Stanhope Smith later declared that Moss had used the proceeds from his exhibitions to buy himself out of slavery, more contemporary accounts and advertisements declare him "freeborn."[62] During the Revolutionary War, he "served for six years in South Carolina as a soldier" in "a corps of pioneers," Virginian troops under the command of John Neville.[63] Appearing first in the July 13, 1796, *Aurora*, the advertisement for his exhibition announced "A Great Curiosity," an exhibition at "Mr. Kaufman's Tavern, the sign of the Bear" of a man "born entirely black" who after thirty-eight years "his natural colour began to wear off; . . . his wool also is coming off his head, legs and arms, and in its place is growing straight hair, similar to that of a white man."[64] This advertisement offers an early account of a white Negro that speculates on the relationship of blackness to whiteness, the chromatic hierarchy and hegemony. In this theory, whiteness serves as the foundational color for skin, and blackness, like soot or paint, seems to lie upon the white skin like veneer. If black skin is rubbed or worn down enough, the truer, whiter color will show through.

Groß Vater,
ein geborner Afeicaner.

Großmutter,
eine Indianerin.

Vater
Richard Moss,
ein in Virginien ge=
borner Schwarzer.

Groß Vater
primus ein geborner
Africaner.

Großmutter
Mary Lewis, eine trans=
portirte Irländerin.

Mutter
Hannah Lewis,
eine Mulattin.

Henry Moss.

Ein schwarzer Mann, der sich in einen Weissen verwandelt.

FIG. 5. Henry Moss, from *Americanischer und Land Calendar, Auf das 1797 Jahr Christi*. By permission of The Library Company of Philadelphia.

Moss told the curious the extent and variety of his family tree. In a report of his display published in a 1797 German-language almanac, the headlines proclaim his lineage in large type: his paternal grandfather was "an African," his grandmother "an American Indian"; his maternal grandfather was "the first child of an African," his other grandmother "an Irish immigrant" (perhaps an indentured servant); his father, Richard Moss, was "born black"; his mother "a mulatto."[65] The prominence of this genealogy suggests its importance to the presentation as assurance of the exhibited body's authenticity. He is a *real* black man; his whiteness is not his birthright. The prodigy is confirmed through lines of descent.

To convince his dubious audience further, Moss carried documentation to certify his character and his transformation. He offered this certification as an addendum to the advertisement, a presentation that implied no black person could turn white without the proper certification. The author of the certificate, Joseph Hall of Bedford County, testifies that he has known Henry Moss for "upwards of thirty years, the whole of which time, he has supported an honest character, in the late war he inlisted with me into the continental army as a soldier, and behaved himself as such very well, from the first of my acquaintance with him till within two or three years past, he was of as dark a complexion as an African, and without any known cause it has changed to what it is at present."[66] Unlike the body of the advertisement, Hall's testimony

does not risk speculation on the physical process of Moss's growing white-ness. To him, the transformation does not imply that whiteness lurks beneath the dark surface, waiting for external forces to wear it away.

Although there is no extant description of the process of Moss's exhibi-tion—where he stood or sat or how he displayed his body—the illustration of John "Primrose" Boby, "the Wonderful Spotted Indian," may offer some insight. John Boby, a West Indian of African heritage and a contemporary of Moss, showed his whitening body throughout England and Scotland but most particularly at Bartholomew Fair. In the illustration, Boby, his trousers rolled past his knees, peels back the purposely ripped opening of his shirt front as if he parts a stage curtain to reveal the mottled skin of his stomach. The exhibition is a dual striptease, the slow revelation of his unruly body, the even slower revelation of white skin.

In his exhibitions, Moss encouraged customers to touch him, to probe his skin. One writer described the sensation, that upon "pressing his skin with a finger, the part pressed appeared white; and on removal of the pressure, the displaced blood rushed back, suffusing the part with red, exactly as in the case of the European."[67] The account of Moss in Rochefoucault's *Travels through the United States of North America, the Country of the Iroquois, and Upper Canada* provides further understanding of the extent of Moss's display. Of the members of Moss's audience, Rochefoucault is the least concerned with the assumed scientific importance of Moss's body and, consequently, with the social and political ramifications of Moss's metamorphosis; he is most concerned with an accurate account of the spectacle. He describes the whiteness of Moss's "legs, thighs, arms, and hands," the spotting of his head and torso. Rochefoucault's intimate knowledge of Moss's body, though, ends at the genitals; however, Moss narrates for Rochefoucault that the whiteness has already "begun in them."[68] The description of the penis is the first instance of Moss's narration of what the viewer cannot see, which indicates that he exposed most of the rest of his body for exhibition. It is easy to imagine Moss with his trousers rolled up or removed, his shirt open or cast aside, only his penis clothed yet exposed in narration.

Moss's exposure to the curious in Philadelphia lasted until the first days of September. According to his last advertisement in late August, he had plans to exhibit next in New York.[69] Samuel Latham Mitchell, a prominent New York doctor, recorded an exhibition of Moss, possibly one that took place in that city. After the summer of 1796, we lose the trail of Henry Moss. Twenty years later, J. V. Wiesenthal, a ship's doctor for the USS *Independence*, records in the *New England Journal of Medicine and Surgery* the 1814 exhibition of an African American man "whose skin has nearly lost its native colour and become perfectly white." Although the unnamed man claims this "wonderful change commenced about four years previous"—the same time of transformation Moss gave to his Philadelphia audience nearly two decades before—the genealogy is clearly that of the most famous of white Negroes.[70] The exhibition of the transforming African American body, it seems, encouraged a bit of fraud. Mastering the art of ballyhoo, Moss, or someone trading on his fame, must have recognized the value of exaggeration—the idea of sudden miraculous change draws a better audience.

As with the surfaces of other white Negroes, the transformed skin of Henry Moss became a site for a debate over the origin and the possible cure, as it were, of black skin. Samuel Stanhope Smith, the most influential American philosopher of racial difference of his time, saw his theories alter before the body of Henry Moss. In 1787, nine years before meeting Moss, Smith presented to the American Philosophical Society his *Essay on the Causes of the*

Variety of Complexion and Figure in the Human Species, a work intended to explain skin color as a result of climatological and sociological influence. According to his initial theory, the heat of the sun turns white skin dark; those who dwell nearest to the equator possess the darkest skin. People closest to savagery—the ungoverned, the nomadic, the heathen—also have darker skins, since they expose themselves more to the elements. The summer sun peppers the skin of the fair and red-haired with freckles. So, Smith reasons, the skin of savage equator-dwellers likewise transforms, blackening the African with what he called "an universal freckle." In this early version of his theories, Smith sees in the skin of white Negroes only an anomaly and not a sign of climatic influence. Smith tersely discounts the whiteness of albinos as "the effect of some distemper." Even though he allows for natural processes to lighten skin, he reserves the majority of his text for the darkening of the complexion away from "the fair and the sanguine complexion" of Adam and Eve, the original couple. Aware of white Negro exhibitions and a faithful reader of the accounts, he obviously has yet to witness an African body in transformation. The white Negro, in his eyes, is merely "the accidental and diseased production of parents who themselves possess the full character of the climate."[71] Reduced to a sport of nature, the white Negro does not figure into Smith's theories. Sudden changes in skin color, and the threat they pose to societal stability, have no place.

In the summer of 1796, Smith entered a Philadelphia tavern to witness Moss unveil himself and tell the story of his transforming body. The growing patches of white, the fading blackness, clearly affected Smith's approach to complexion and changed his view of white Negroes. In the 1810 revision of his essay, Smith focuses upon the body of Moss to support his argument that the environment influences the pigmentation of skin and that, in the proper environment, black skin will revert to the original and ideal color that Adam's skin possessed. The universal freckle is gone. Whiteness no longer results from illness. He now proposes upper mobility between the races, especially that Africans, under the right circumstances, can become white. Smith highlights his belief by bringing the reader up to date on the progression of whiteness in Moss's skin: "I have been informed by respectable authority, that the whitening process was soon afterwards completed, and that, in his appearance, he could not be distinguished from a native Anglo-American." Moss has become "a clear and healthy white," but Smith is careful not to add him yet to the roster of the English-born.[72]

Smith's presentation of Moss's now completely white skin indicates the hope vitiligo presented to those who wished for an end to slavery. Smith describes the fading of Moss's black skin in almost symbolic terms: "This extraordinary change did not proceed by gradually and equably diluting the intensity of the shades of the black colour over the whole person at once; but the original black, reduced to spots, when I saw it, by the encroachments of the white, resembled dark clouds insensibly melting away at their edges."[73] To Smith, the whiteness appears to overwhelm the blackness, to exert a supremacy, the threatening "dark clouds" dissolving naturally, assimilating peacefully into the healthy white. The allegorical possibilities of a black slave turning white—the political potential—were not lost on Smith. The erasure of racial distinction appealed to his abolitionism and faith in a uniform, universal whiteness that would forestall future racial and class conflict.

Moss's spectacle and its latent political meaning inspired others to accompany accounts of white Negroes with an appeal for the abolition of slavery. The eradication of blackness held the promise of emancipation. Writing for the journal *Medical Repository* in 1801, Samuel Latham Mitchell announces the appearance of a new white Negro by rekindling memory of "Harry Moss" and his amazing transformation. The new Moss, a "young negro, named Maurice, aged 25 years, began, about seven years ago, to lose his native colour. . . . The change is not the dead white of the Albinos, but is a good wholesome carnation hue." The description of the whiteness as "wholesome" allows for Mitchell to make a strong political point directed, apparently, at newly elected President Thomas Jefferson, whose belief in separate origins spurred accusations of atheism from his opponents: "Such alteration of colour as this militates powerfully against the opinion adopted by some modern philosophers, that the negroes are a different species of the human race from the whites, and tends strongly to corroborate the probability of the derivation of all the varieties of mankind from a single pair." Mitchell concludes the article with a utopian vision of the end of slavery: "How additionally singular would it be, if instances of the spontaneous disappearance of this sable mark of distinction between slaves and their masters were to become frequent!" If black skin disappears, Mitchell argues, slavery disappears.[74] Even with their pragmatic, humanitarian intentions, the writers and philosophers who promoted the eradication of blackness advocated as well a removal of a troublesome group of people by purging the primary indicator of difference, the color of their skin.

To Moss's audience and Samuel Stanhope Smith's readership, the extraordinary body of Moss presented confirmation of the unity of the human species. Blackness concealed a common whiteness and the humanity it endowed. According to Winthrop Jordan, Smith's argument—and consequently Moss's exhibition—reconfirmed "the longstanding feeling that the most Negro thing about the Negro was his blackness."[75] To wash away or rub off the African's blackness removed the African and, therefore, the philosophical problem of slavery. If everyone were white, the reasoning goes, there would be no rationale of difference for one person to enslave another. A universal whiteness would make all men equal.

The pure, wholesome pallor of Moss's skin presented an ideal whiteness that few could match. Gradations of paleness grew apparent, especially among those whose work exposed them to daily doses of the sun. The exhibition of Henry Moss inspired Smith to narrow the parameters of whiteness further by comparing his skin to those of laboring people. Smith saw in the untransformed patches of Moss's skin an opportunity to distinguish the difference in skin color between the poor and the well-born, which he equated with the difference between the savage and the civilized, and to explain the natural origins of these distinct shades of whiteness. Moss, Smith noted, was "a labouring man, [and] wherever there were rents in the thin clothes which covered him there were generally seen the largest spots of black." Moss's transformation is not complete, Smith implies, because Moss, as a working man, still exposes his body to the darkening effects of the sun. Later in the *Essay*, Smith extends this theory to apply to the poor in all societies: "The poor and laboring part of the community in every country, are usually more dark in their complexion, more hard in their features, and more coarse and ill formed in their limbs, than persons of better rank, who enjoy greater ease, and more liberal means of subsistence. They want the delicate tints of colour, the pleasing regularity of features, and the elegant and fine proportions of the person so frequently seen in the higher classes. . . . The distinctions which subsist between the several classes of society become more considerable by time, after families have held, for ages, nearly the same stations." Skin color indicates a difference between the classes derived from exposure to the elements. Aside from the deleterious effects of the sun, the poorer and laboring classes develop a different physiognomy through indolence toward their young and a lack of cleanliness. Left to learn to walk by themselves, the unattended children develop deformities that "give them that gibbous form which is thought to be peculiar to the African race, but which is often seen among the poorest classes in other countries." The savage peoples, those beyond the reaches of civilization, experience an "entire inattention to the cleanliness of their persons," which "heighten[s] the disagreeable duskiness of their colour, and to render the features coarse and deformed." As an example of the effect of savagery upon the body, Smith turns to the observation of "the poorest classes in society, who are usually . . . distinguished by their meagre habit, their uncouth features and their dingy and squalid aspect."[76] The poor are as distinctively not white as the African or Native American.

In his observations, Smith collapses the oppositions of black and white, poor and rich, savage and civilized, dirty and clean, sick and healthy, contaminated and pure. To be poor, in a sense, is to be tainted—or at least darker—more savage, dirty, and sick. The "pale" American complexion, on the whole, does not compare favorably to the "red and white [of] the British, or the German." Smith blames the "tinge of sallowness" that infects the American whiteness on the heat, to which the poor expose themselves. Smith associates the darkness in skin color with the "putrid exhalations" of late summer that arise from the swampy countryside of New Jersey and Pennsylvania, an association encouraged, one imagines, by the recurring outbreaks of yellow fever in Philadelphia during the 1790s, including the great plague year of 1793, three years before the summer of Henry Moss.[77] To Smith, any variation from whiteness endowed by civilization is a disorder, a pestilence, a sign of ill-health and contamination.

Smith sees in the transforming surface of Henry Moss, naked to the waist at the sign of the Black Horse or the sign of the Bear, the powerful influence of the North American continent and the institutional network of a new democracy working in concert to remove the taint of blackness. The museums and the learned societies were civilizing agents, social spaces designed to turn rabble into citizens by disciplining the body. The danger of disorder still lurked in the emigration of citizens from the clean, safe streets of the towns and exposure of the body to the unhealthy atmosphere of the wilderness. Those who traveled beyond the influence of civilization risked becoming savage and, consequently, darkening their skins, tainting the purity of their whiteness. The threat is persistent to Smith, the "haggard, and diseased appearance" of the laboring classes to be mitigated only "by the arts of civilized society [and] by the continual intermixture of new colonies of emigrants from Europe with the natives of the country."[78] Smith associates disorder of the body with disorder in the body politic. The darkness in the skins of the white working poor and of the Africans, the indolence and savagery it represents to him, threatens civil order and social concord. The darker the skin, the greater the threat to civilization.

BENJAMIN RUSH AND COLOR AS CONTAGION

To Benjamin Rush, blackness had plague potential. When he viewed the exhibition of Henry Moss, presumably at the Black Horse Inn, he had recently witnessed the disastrous effects of a pestilence on civil order. In the summer and fall of 1793, Philadelphia suffered from a plague of yellow fever. By estimation, the epidemic killed more than five thousand, or at least 10 percent of the city's population, and threw the civil and federal government into turmoil.[79] Earlier that same summer, refugees, white and black, master and slave, poured into the city from Santo Domingo to escape the violence from slave uprisings. The proximity of the two events led some doctors to see the influx of foreign people, and their accompanying slaves, as a possible cause for the disease. Rush theorized that the pestilence most likely originated in the stench from rotting coffee discharged from the cargo hold of one of the refugee ships, a theory similar to Smith's virulent miasmas that arise from the swamps to infect whiteness. Although Rush maintained his theory, he found it difficult to avoid the correlation between the disorder of the slave revolts and the disorder of the yellow fever. A full year after the plague, Rush wrote that "a number of the distressed inhabitants of St. Domingo, who had escaped the desolation of fire and sword, arrived in the city. Soon after their arrival, the influenza made its appearance, and spread rapidly among our citizens."[80] By implying a post hoc relationship between the appearance of the illness and the influx of emigrants, Rush links the biological threat of the contagion with the societal threat of the slave rebellion.

Portentous connections between the natural world and political events were not foreign to Rush. On February 4, 1797, Rush wrote to Thomas Jefferson, the newly elected president of the American Philosophical Society, about events both natural and political. Rush reacts to Jefferson's report before the society of "the large claws and bones of the lion-kind animal," an extinct creature that provides, in Rush's view, a moral pertinent to recent events. These "tyrants of the forest," as Rush identifies the animals in his morality play, may have been "extirpated by a confederacy and insurrection of beasts of less force individually than themselves." Rush hopes for a likewise extermination of kings and "that the exhibition of crowns, scepters, and maces, like the claws and bones of extinct animals, shall be necessary to prove to posterity that such cannibals ever existed upon our globe!"[81] The extinction of the feudal system and the extinction of brutish power in the primeval forests both arise from natural processes, an evolution from savage to civilized. To Rush, exhibitions of the natural world, like those in Peale's museum, serve as object lessons, opportunities for political and national definition.

Later in the same letter, Rush describes another future exhibition that links political and natural processes: his intention to deliver a paper before the American Philosophical Society of particular interest to Jefferson. "I am now preparing a paper," he writes, "in which I have attempted to prove that the black color (as it is called) of the Negroes is the effect of a disease in the skin of the leprous kind." Rush's announcement acknowledges Jefferson's display of white Negroes in Notes on the State of Virginia. Derived from Rush's observations of Henry Moss's exhibition before members of the society, the paper encourages better treatment of African Americans yet "keeps up the existing prejudices against matrimonial connections with them."[82] People "known by the epithet of negroes" should be pitied, and maybe quarantined, for the pestilential threat they carry with them.[83] As with the theory Smith proposed, darkness of skin was a symptom of illness. In the white Negro, a body recovering from the contagion of color, Rush saw the threat and the solution to the social disharmony brought about by slavery and the foreign matter—the African body—that slavery had introduced.

Encouraged by Samuel Stanhope Smith's environmentalism—as well as by the exhibition of Henry Moss—Benjamin Rush embraces the idea of skin color as a symptom of the pure white body's contamination, a kind of leprosy that nature can cure with the aid of medical science. Rush suggests various possible antidotes to blackness: the friction from clothing, "bleeding, purging, or abstinence," fear, muriatic acid, and the juice of unripe peaches. Unlike Smith, though, Rush envisions the spread of blackness through intimate contact, extending the fear of miscegenation from the inheritance of the child to the infection of the spouse. Rush offers a second-hand account of a "white woman in North Carolina [who] not only acquired a dark color, but several of the features of a negro, by marrying and living with a black husband."[84] This leprosy, Rush proposes, is apparently a venereal disease generating from the licentiousness of the woman and the infectious potency of the black body.

After establishing his theory that disease causes blackness, Rush uses it to "destroy one of the arguments in favor of enslaving negroes." For Rush, the extraordinary body of Henry Moss serves as evidence of one of the "spontaneous cures of this disease" nature has visited upon black bodies, a "change from black to a natural white flesh color." If blackness is a disease, then white Americans should show compassion; yet expressing sympathy, they should keep their distance as well: "The facts and principles which have been delivered, should teach white people the necessity of keeping up that prejudice against such connections with them, as would tend to infect posterity with any portion of their disorder. This may be done . . . without offering violence to humanity, or calling in question the sameness of descent, or natural equality of mankind."[85] He places his faith in the removability of blackness as a means to ensure equality. Though removal can theoretically mitigate difference, the erasure of blackness, as witnessed in Henry Moss and other white Negroes, reinforces the importance of blackness as the primary marker of difference and as the greatest threat to social harmony in the Republic. Rush uses the surface of the white Negro to make his argument against slavery and prejudice; by doing so, he strengthens the argument against racial intermarriage in the name of quarantine.

A STUMP SPEECH AT THE AMERICAN PHILOSOPHICAL SOCIETY

Abluis Aethiopean: quid frustra.

—Latin proverb

Through the course of late eighteenth century white Negro exhibition, the image of the white Negro became a symbol for the instability of society and the threat of insurrection. As Jan Pieterse observes, the transformation of a person from black to white had long stood as a metaphor for absurd impossibility.[86] To "wash an Ethiop white," a common proverb throughout the eighteenth century, expressed the frustration that comes from vain effort: to scour away African blackness was a futile task.[87] With the exhibition of whitening African Americans in an age of revolutions, though, the image of the white Negro began to express the fear of social disruption. In the anxiety that followed the French Revolution and the rumored threat of the French invasion of the United States, George Washington associated the figure of a black man turning white with potential revolution. He feared that a foreign threat had infiltrated American borders. In a 1798 letter to William McHenry, then secretary of war, Washington expresses mistrust in the change of heart of "the brawlers against Government measures" who have recently joined the army. "You could as soon scrub the blackamore white," Washington challenges, "as to change the principles of a profest Democrat; and that he will leave nothing unattempted to overturn the Government of this Country."[88] Washington's employment of the proverb contradicts the fading blackness of Henry Moss that he witnessed just two years before, in essence denying the transformation as an impossibility, a heresy against the doctrine of fixed essences. The figure of the white Negro, a disruption in the fixed order of nature, serves Washington as a symbol of an untrustworthy transformation and an unimaginable rebellion in the hierarchies of the natural order.

The social and political aspirations of the poor and laboring peoples posed a threat to those institutions—such as museums and philosophical societies—that sought to fix social status and maintain the distinct character between the classes. As a perturbing revolutionary body, the figure of the white Negro continued to be associated with the threat of social disruption posed by the unruly masses. The various social strata blending and blurring found their correlative in the image of color slipping its banks and spreading from body to body. In his novel of manners, *Modern Chivalry*, Hugh Henry Brackenridge skewered the pomposity of the American Philosophical Society, a learned society that, in his eyes, had increasingly emphasized the presentation of insignificant curiosities by undeserving candidates rather than intellectual inquiry by the wiser elite. "There was, in a certain great city," he

writes, "a society who called themselves Philosophers. . . . There is no question, but there were in this body some very great men; whose investigations of
the arcana of nature, deserve attention. But so it was, there had been introduced, by some means, many individuals, who were no philosophers at all."[89]
The American Philosophical Society becomes emblematic for the disturbing
inversion of social hierarchies Brackenridge witnesses in the rest of society, a
body invaded by the lowly.

The narrator believes that merit and ability should determine a citizen's
position in society but that the strong egalitarian impulses within the new
country have rewarded undeserving opportunists who will connive their way
up from their natural status. Brackenridge, through the voice of his hero,
Captain Farrago, articulates this philosophy in terms of separate species with
distinct Platonic essences. In his mind, "everything ought to be preserved sui
generis; as nature makes no honourary animals; but all are of the species, or
take not the name; a bear is a real bear, a sheep is a real sheep; and there is
no commixture of name, where there is a difference of nature."[90] Brackenridge turns to the distinct articulation and arrangement of species as Peale
had displayed them, every creature to its assigned space in nature's hierarchy.
The greatest threat to the social space of the American Philosophical Society
is the nearly miscegenistic mixing of people with distinctly different natures
that identify them almost as different species. As representative of this social
threat, Brackenridge introduces to the exhibition space of the American
Philosophical Society the foreign bodies of an Irish laborer and an African
American slave.

Brackenridge first demonstrates the degeneration of the society by having
the most proletarian figure in the novel threaten to join. Captain Farrago's
Irish manservant and object lesson in societal flux, Teague O'Regan, having
found a large, dead owl, wishes through this offering to join the society. His
master worries that the introduction of the servant into the social space will
taint its purity. Farrago argues that the "fountain of honor thus contaminated
by a sediment foreign from its nature, who would drink from it?"[91] The dregs
of society, Farrago seems to say, must seek their own level. O'Regan's presence can only corrupt the exalted body of the philosophical society.

Captain Farrago, true believer in hierarchy and societal stability, discour-
ages O'Regan with a twofold threat: either the society of philosophers will
place him on exhibition, or, worse, they will ask him to present an academic
paper. The long-legged extraordinary body of the manservant may intrigue
the members of the society too much, "and when they have examined you
awhile, take the skin off of you, and pass you around for an overgrown otter,
or a muskrat; or some outlandish animal, for which they will, themselves,
invent a name." Exhibition, Brackenridge implies, necessarily leads to the

removal of skin, which becomes the body's sole signifier. Not relying upon the threat of exhibition to dissuade his servant, Farrago crowns his argument with the threat of paper presentation: "You will have to prove absolutely that Negroes were once white, and that their flat noses came by some cause in the compass of human means to produce."[92] Brackenridge yokes the scientific display of the African body—and in particular the body of the white Negro—with an acknowledgment of the threat to safety posed by exhibition. He also links the tenuous social status of Farrago's laborer with the disputed humanity of the African slave. Brackenridge conflates two extraordinary bodies—one an indentured Irish immigrant, the other an African slave.

The presentation of the African body in flux resurfaces in Brackenridge's next salvo on the American Philosophical Society, but for the presenter of the paper this time, he reaches further down the social ladder. A slave named Cuff finds a stone in the shape of a moccasin. When Colonel Gorum, Cuff's master, sends the stone to the American Philosophical Society, the society offers the colonel membership, which he turns down, logically arguing that the society should offer Cuff, as the finder of the stone, the membership. Enthusiastically, the society inducts the slave and eventually calls upon Cuff to deliver the annual oration. To Brackenridge, the image of the oxymoronic slave-philosopher in the democratic social space of the American Philosophical Society presents the chaotic culmination of extreme egalitarianism—a complete inversion of social hierarchy.

The presence of Cuff's body before the American Philosophical Society disrupts the exhibition space. He serves both as presenter before the body and the body on exhibition, the black skin that explains the origins of its own color. Cuff's speech turns Smith's theory of environmental influence on its head. Instead of establishing whiteness as the original color of humanity, the oration denaturalizes whiteness by making the original couple black: "Now, shentima, I say, dat de first man was de black a man, and de first woman de black a woman; an get two tree children; de rain vasha dese, and de snow pleach, an de coula come brown, yella, coppa coula, and, at de last, quite fite; and de hair long; an da fall out vid van anoda; and van cash by de nose, an pull; so de nose come lang, sharp nose."[93] The presence of a black body in the society's exhibition space immediately leads to a debate on the origins of black skin and an exhibition of the white Negro's disorderly body. Brackenridge parodies the exhibition of white Negroes before the American Philosophical Society and the scientific interest afforded those anomalous bodies by the society's members. Like these exhibitions of white Negroes, Cuff's presence provokes a comparison between the skin of the slave and the skin of the master. The oration naturalizes blackness, which gives Cuff the better, truer skin in opposition to the paleness of his philosopher counterparts.

Although Brackenridge purposely destabilizes the supremacy of whiteness, he exhibits the disorderly body to demonstrate the potential for disorder in the society around him.

In the spirit of satiric compromise, the narrator of *Modern Chivalry* presents a third, even more revolutionary theory on the origin of color. The theory he proposes directly lampoons Smith's attempts to argue for the unity of the human species. "There is no fact," he offers, "that has proved more stubborn than the diversity of the human species; especially that great extreme of diversity in the natives of Africa. How the descendants of Adam and Eve, both good-looking people, should ever come to be a vile Negro, or even a mulatto man or woman, is puzzling." The narrator reestablishes the superiority of whiteness by degrading the African, yet he challenges all of the standard contemporary theories of the origin of black skin: he discounts the mark of Cain for slaying Abel, the curse of Ham for looking upon Noah's nakedness, the environmentalism of Smith, as well as the influence of the mother's imagination. As a resolution to the debate on the origin of blackness, the narrator declares possibly the most offensive solution to Brackenridge's public—Adam and Eve as a mixed race couple: "I am of opinion that Adam was a tall, straight-limbed, red-haired man, with a fair complexion, blue eyes, and an aquiline nose; and that Eve was a Negro woman." With the image of the original interracial couple, Brackenridge returns to Jefferson's anxiety of whiteness produced from the African female body, an alteration in color that derives from the hushed transgressions of the slaveowners.[94]

Obviously, as Emory Elliott has pointed out, the narrator does not necessarily speak for Brackenridge, nor does Captain Farrago.[95] Although the targets of Brackenridge's satire may be easy to recognize, no one character serves as his voice. Grantland S. Rice argues that the shifting moral center of the novel—found alternately in the voices of Farrago, O'Regan, and the narrator—"points to the danger of the omniscient narration" expected by the reading public, the despotism of a singular voice of reason.[96] Brackenridge slips easily from skin to skin, undermining their authority, and his, as he speaks through various characters. The slipperiness of his characters, the proto–confidence men who manipulate identity for personal gain, is not as threatening to Brackenridge as the equally arbitrary taxonomies dictated in post-Revolution rhetoric and social spaces. Like Jefferson's introduction of enigmas to undermine intellectual certainty, Brackenridge lampoons the authority of the American Philosophical Society by exhibiting the figure of the white Negro, the challenger to strict racial categories, as a symbol of this slipperiness.

Addressing the removability of skin color, Cuff's oration is an act of racial ventriloquism that prefigures the stump speeches of blackface theater.[97]

Intimidated by the prospect of the oration, and at a loss for words, Cuff begs his master for help. Colonel Gorum furnishes Cuff with the general text of the speech. The inversion of the origin theory generates from the white master, and the voice of the master speaks through the slave. Brackenridge, wearing now the skin of Cuff, satirizes the American Philosophical Society, and all origin theories, in black dialect, placing the black body on exhibition.

Brackenridge employs these tales of origin and their fantasy of racial transformation to skewer the pomposity of natural philosophers. White begetting black, black bleaching to white, little mulatto Cains and Abels, all upset the notion of discrete racial essences and alter the exhibition space, just as did the bodies of James and Henry Moss presented before the American Philosophical Society. The manipulations of the exhibitor upon the display of Cuff—the script of the master that speaks for the otherwise silenced exhibit, the dialect of the narrator that reduces the slave to absurdity—reveal another sinister aspect to the exhibition space: the exposed body is subject to the whims of the showman as well as to the prying eyes of progressively intrusive scientific inquiry. The need for philosophers and scientists to standardize the hierarchy they required of nature and establish unalterable biological essences threatened the bodies that resisted this regimen. Exhibition is a dangerous proposition, and the presentation of a whitening body as an anatomical specimen instills a mortal fear in those audience members uncertain of their status—poor, laboring, and immigrant peoples with hopes of citizenship yet equally vulnerable to exhibition and medical scrutiny. In the next chapter, focus will shift away from the effect the transforming body of the white Negro had upon the exhibition space to what the piebald figure represented to those who witnessed the exhibition.

CHAPTER TWO

Barnum's Leopard Boy

THE REIGN OF THE
PIEBALD PARLIAMENT

A NEGRO TURNING WHITE!

He is said to have discovered a weed, the juice of which changes the Colored Skin to White! His person, as may be seen, is rapidly undergoing that change.

—Advertisement for Barnum's American Museum,
New York Atlas, August, 11, 1850

Color vexes Thomas Jefferson. Darkness conceals, withholds, masks. Black skin resists scrutiny. "Are not the fine mixtures of red and white," he asks in *Notes on the State of Virginia*, "the expressions of every passion by greater or less suffusions of colour in the one, preferable to that eternal monotony, which reigns in the countenances, that immoveable veil of black which covers all the emotions of the other race?"[1] Next to this vision of a uniform, impenetrable blackness, Anglo-Saxon skin becomes easily read, the emotions close to the surface and available for observation. By secreting expressions of feeling and intent, blackness endangers the safety of the white community. The figure of the white Negro, which should seemingly relieve the problem by lifting the veil of black, does not soothe Jefferson's anxiety. As discussed in the previous chapter, the perceived pure color of the white Negro, the telling flow of blood apparently absent from the skin, frustrates Jefferson as an enigma and therefore provides no solution. Momentarily, in Jefferson's philosophical musings on the nature of racial difference, color separates from the skin, suspended, as it were. Autonomous as a mask, the blackness hinders the policing across racial and even class boundaries.

In Jefferson's philosophy, the camouflaging properties of color provide the primary barrier to the emancipation of slaves and their potential incorporation into free society. As he continues with his observations, the metaphor of the veil—a thin, gauzy wrapping over the skin—quickly dissolves, replaced by a drive to seek out difference between and beneath the layers of dermis.

"The first difference which strikes us is that of colour," he writes. "Whether the black of the negro resides in the reticular membrane between the skin and scarf-skin itself; whether it proceeds from the colour of the blood, the colour of the bile, or from that of some other secretion, the difference is fixed in nature."[2] Indelible, irreparable, color defines the distance between the European and African and hints at the possibility of separate species. The gulf firmly established in his mind, Jefferson fears the universal emancipation of the slaves in North America and the violence he believes inevitable. The passions he imagines inherent in the black body—the "want of forethought," the male lust for African females (as well as the threat to white womanhood this ardency implies), the bestial wantonness of the African female, the lack of imagination in the African mind—these enumerated differences, unchecked, will necessarily lead to "convulsions which will probably never end but in the extermination of the one or the other race."[3] In this apocalyptic prophecy of racial violence, color is the sticking point, the emblematic obstacle to peaceful assimilation. The distressing difference that lies at the surface, like the emotions Jefferson believes to be concealed, now recedes from the gaze, avoiding easy observation, settling beneath the surface in the flesh, the fluids, the tissues.

Dissatisfied that African skin will not yield the knowledge he sought, Jefferson understands the next logical, intrusive step: to delve beneath the surface, to apply scalpel to skin and remove it to unveil the secrets of racial difference he hopes to uncover. The proof of inferiority that Jefferson believes dwells beneath the skin requires submission to "the Anatomical knife, to Optical glasses, to analysis by fire, or by solvents" to delineate difference.[4] Properly applied, the tools of rational scientific observation will peel back layers of surfaces until they will reveal the seat of difference and expose it to the gaze of the inquiring philosopher. In his anxiety over the violent end of slavery, Jefferson anticipates the eventual necessity for the dissection of African American corpses.

> Learned authors and skillful anatomists, have passed their lives dissecting the bodies of men and animals in order to prove that I, who am now writing, belong to the race of Ourang-Outangs.
>
> —Pompée-Valentin Vastey, 1817.

Just as the extraordinary body disturbs the democratic spaces of the philosophical society and the natural history museum, the exhibition space affects the body labeled for display. Reduced to a scientific and public curiosity, the body in the museum becomes an object of speculation, dehumanized and consequently exposed to the whims of the natural scientist, the prying eyes, the probe, the scalpel of the anatomist. In his *Notes*, Jefferson rehearses the process that takes the racialized body from its confinement as a lesser grade in the hierarchical natural order to its inevitable atomization at the hands of scientists and medical professionals who wish to pinpoint the body's essential difference. This deadly process articulates the threat that exhibition posed to the individual on display as well as to those among the audience equally vulnerable to public scrutiny: in particular, the near-white poor, laboring, and immigrant peoples.

The democratic impulse that valorizes easy visual recognition of natural phenomena reinforces the status of skin color as the primary marker of racial difference.[5] Faced with the possible erasure of color that the figure of the white Negro presents, the natural philosophers and medical practitioners of the early Republic sought to define more physiological markers of variation and to bring hidden sources of difference to the surface. Intrusive experimentation toward the end of the eighteenth century and into the nineteenth began to replace observation at a distance. Doctors of medicine introduced the anatomical knife to the arena in order to make visible the invisible processes of color and other physiological differences. This shift in the mode of scientific inquiry brought about a more abrupt and violent representation of the removal of color: instead of encouraging nature's processes, the anatomist could use the knife to slit the aberrant skin like a zipper and remove the organ whole. In these morbid investigations into the nature of the African American's apparent difference, the white Negro surfaces and resurfaces, continuing to confound the inquiries of those who seek to define the boundaries of race.

Although never placed under the knife, Henry Moss suffered from increased interest and more invasive scrutiny as he made his journey from public house attraction to scientific curiosity. Removed from the tavern space, he willingly submitted himself to the medical gaze. The natural philosophers of the American Philosophical Society, no longer satisfied with neutral, passive observation of the white Negro's extraordinary body, began to test the skin, to poke and prod, to measure with calipers and apply solvents to accelerate the process of the encroaching whiteness and uncover the origins of black skin. The body of the white Negro, as with those of other liminal figures on display, suffered increasingly greater dangers as philosophers turn into anatomists and exhibitors attempt to reveal the processes of racial difference to an interested public.

Benjamin Rush apparently never ventured beneath the skin of Henry Moss; nevertheless, Rush still speculated on the anatomical processes of color at work beneath the surface in violent and invasive terms. "The destruction of the black colour," he writes, "was probably occasioned by the absorption of the coloring matter of the *rete mucosum*, for the pressure and friction it is well known aid the absorbing action of the lymphatics in every part of the body." Rush's desire for the destruction of black skin finds hope in the implicit violence of external pressure and friction. The speculation of the processes beneath the skin suggests anatomical knowledge derived from dissection, knowledge Rush can only surmise from his reading. He recounts efforts of other natural philosophers to destroy skin color through bleeding and purging. He tells of one doctor who "discharged the color in the black wool of the negro by infusing it in the oxygenated muriatic [hydrochloric] acid."[6] The display of white Negroes encouraged discomfiting experimentation to accelerate the processes of lightening skin color. Although Rush has to satisfy himself with speculation from external observation, he hopes to encourage the destruction of "this disease of the skin."[7] In these fantasies of racial extermination, Rush implies that the natural philosopher can only uncover the secret of the white Negro's transformation through the removal of the skin itself.

> O Lord! wilt Thou bestow upon the Vice President a double portion of Thy grace, for *Thou knowest he needs it.*
>
> —Rev. Jedidiah Champion, public prayer for Thomas Jefferson, 1796

During his presidential campaigns in 1800 and 1804, Jefferson's suggestion that Africans may have sprung from a separate creation met with accusations of atheism. God intended for a radical distinction between human and animal; an inferior race arising from an inferior, nonbiblical Adam and Eve muddied the waters to the point of heresy. These allegations of heterodoxy placed the philosopher-president at the radical extreme of racial theory.[8] As scientific inquiry met the nineteenth century, though, those medical practitioners who wished to distance Europeans from African darkness answered Jefferson's call for invasive investigation. To defend the immutable difference between black and white, master and slave, these racial scientists and comparative anatomists worked to prove polygenesis, the idea that each of the world's races had a separate origin.[9] Black was always ever black and white ever white. No change over time, no crossing boundaries. Of course, the white Negro frustrated polygenesis. The transformation of Henry Moss suggested a common Anglo-Saxon ancestor for all humanity. To address the haunting whiteness, racial scientists—and even the early evolutionists who followed—eventually put scalpel to skin and sought a deeper darkness.

As a medical investigator of this new generation, Charles Caldwell, Rush's young protégé, refused to restrict himself to mere observation. In his 1855 autobiography, he chides Samuel Stanhope Smith for the brevity and superficiality of his observations of Moss's tavern exhibition. Instead of confining himself to the casual display of the tavern exhibition, Caldwell secured the services of Henry Moss for his own personal surveillance and suffered him to undergo experimentation. "Anxious to know as much of his case as possible," he boasts, "I took him in some measure under my care, procured for him suitable lodging and accommodation, induced many persons to visit him, kept him under my own strict and constant observation, and, by his permission, and for a slight reward, made on him such experiments as suited my purpose." Like Rush, Caldwell never submitted Moss to the anatomical knife, yet he still sought an understanding of biological processes beneath the surface by drawing out color through other, less invasive means. He records that he first drove Moss "to excite, by exercise, a copious perspiration, that I might ascertain, by suitable tests, whether the fluid perspired, by the colored portions of the skin, was *itself* colored."[10] Caldwell saw in the sweating body of Henry Moss, huffing and puffing in the doctor's quarters, an opportunity to isolate and distill the stuff of difference, a liquid blackness that could be expunged with the appropriate application of hard work.

Satisfied that color does not leech from the body in warm weather, Caldwell eventually deduces that the imagined membrane that holds the coloring matter, the *rete mucosum*, must therefore have been absorbed, receding from the surface and the gaze into the body, leaving only "the bloodless whiteness of the *cutis vera*."[11] By casting the newly white skin as morbidly bloodless, he denies Moss the healthy sanguine complexion of the Anglo-Saxon and thereby permanently exiles him from white membership. As a white Negro, Moss cannot become white. He is merely formerly black.

Caldwell neglects to list the other experiments he performed on Moss's skin, yet he offers that Moss was "unusually sensitive to heat, cold, and friction."[12] It is not unreasonable to assume that some of the doctor's experiments involved the artificial application of these elements upon Moss's skin, along with daily measurements of his growing patches of white. Although Caldwell failed to find the source of Moss's mysterious whiteness, his experiments and observations began the relocation of the white Negro body from a philosophical conundrum to a series of measurements recorded in a scientist's notebook, the body anatomized and reduced to so much data.

This new cabal of racial scientists required a more invasive and threatening gaze as the need for anatomical studies in medical education grew more evident and the legal restrictions upon dissection of the dead relaxed.[13] To assess racial inferiority, these scientists literally sought out the skull beneath the skin. In his books *Crania Aegyptiaca* and *Crania Americana*, Samuel George Morton attempted to delineate difference in cranial capacities between the races by measuring white pepper seed into the brain pans of individual skulls. Through his observation of a handful of skulls collected from medical school dissections and the grave robbery of archaeological sites, Morton declared in graphs, charts, and prose the essential superiority of the Caucasian intellect and the pitiable smallness of the African brain.[14] As a result of what he considered irrefutable empirical evidence, Morton asserts that the "social position" of Africans in Egypt "was the same that it now is, that of servants and slaves."[15] To undermine the efforts of those natural philosophers who wished to demonstrate the kinship between the races through the removal of the veil of blackness, Morton casts aside the skin entirely as the seat of difference.

By the middle of the nineteenth century, scientists began to dissect the bodies of dead slaves to uncover the secrets of racial difference and to subdue the disruption caused by the exhibition of white Negroes. In an 1851 address before a medical convention in Louisiana, Samuel Adolphus Cartwright out-lines "the anatomical and physiological differences between the negro and the white man," differences he declares "more deep, durable and indeli-ble . . . than that of mere color." Color was problematic to the racial scientist: it altered and shifted in the body of the white Negro; it diminished over time and between generations in children produced from interracial unions. After his declaration of color's superficial insignificance, Cartwright immediately presents the white Negro male as a straw man—the primary evidence of unity between the races—in order to discount its importance by establishing the whiteness as an anomaly. "In the albino the skin is white," he first offers, only to counter that "the organization is that of the negro." Like Caldwell and Jefferson, Cartwright collects white and whitening black bodies under the term *albino*, now a designation for an understandable medical curiosity with definable symptoms. He proceeds to probe beneath the surface of the white Negro, essentially casting aside the skin to uncover differences that reside "in the membranes, the muscles, the tendons, and in all the fluids and secretions." He narrates and synthesizes the various efforts by other racial sci-entists to dissect the black body beneath the white skin, rendering it a collec-tion of parts, each of which signifies the distance between black and white. Color, now insignificant in the skin, has seeped into the membranes, organs, and ganglia; even the brain is now "tinctured with a shade of the pervading darkness."[16] The bones, in contrast, are whiter and harder, the neck shorter, the legs bowed, the feet flat, the skin thick. Blackness carefully reaffixed to the skin of the slave, Cartwright depicts the African American as a separate creation, a creature somewhere between human and animal.

The anatomical eye of the racial scientist, the gaze that sought to render visible the disorderly flesh beneath the surface of the skin, attempted to regu-late the body by resolving it to a mechanism of classifiable parts. This anatomic intrusion to mitigate the revolutionary potential of the white Negro body threatened as well the near-white and nonwhite body politic. In its quest for fundamental blackness, the anatomical knife endangered the near-white bodies of the poor, working-class, and immigrant populations. The figure of the white African American, however, continued to lurk beneath official oversight within the channels of vernacular expression on the pages of Southwestern humor, in the working scripts of blackface theater plays and songs, and in the exhibition spaces of the popular museum. As the debate among racial scientists necessarily sank beneath the skin in an effort to take difference bone-deep, the body of the white Negro, increasingly imperiled, served in popular discourse to undermine endeavors of scientists to affix racial and class difference to the body.

CUTTING UP A NEGRO

The efforts of the racial scientist to contain the white Negro body resulted in part from the more general exertions of the anatomist to know, and thereby control, the most intimate inner workings of the body. In order to pursue this knowledge and control, the doctors of medicine needed corpses, which were in short supply. According to popular belief and legislative action, dissection was a deliberate violation of the body's sanctity and, throughout the eighteenth century, a punishment delivered upon the bodies of those convicted of murder.[17] As a result of this public distaste for dissection, body snatchers and medical students surreptitiously dug up the recently buried, focusing their attentions largely upon those whose graves were the least guarded—the poor, the indigent, the immigrant, and the African American communities. Even as the laws prohibiting dissection relaxed, the threat to the bodies of working-class, immigrant, and African American populations increased. The living also felt the threat, concerned that their marginal status might target them as potential medical specimens. In spite of longstanding cultural objections against the violation of the dead body, the increasing professionalization of medical doctors socially raised the person with the scalpel at the same time as the scalpel increasingly endangered those people most vulnerable. Michael Sappol argues that in the eighteenth and nineteenth centuries, "plebeian men and women saw the anatomical appropriation of dead bodies, especially their bodies, and claims to authority over the body generally, as an attack. . . . [T]hey regarded the taking, surveying, mapping, and cutting open of bodies for the profit of the profession and individual professors as an act of professional enclosure," a way for the new class of doctors to set themselves apart.[18] This anatomical invasion and appropriation of the popular body by medical professionals materializes in

nineteenth-century literature as a violent violation of the dead through dismemberment and mutilation.

In the nineteenth century, works of southwestern humor articulate the
implicit and explicit threat all members of the scientific and medical communities posed to lower-class, immigrant, and African American people.[19]
Henry Clay Lewis, writing as Madison Tensas, the "Louisiana Swamp Doctor," reflects upon the importance of anatomical examination from the point
of view of the scientific observer and underscores the intention to reduce the
medical subject to a docile, even dead, body. In "Stealing a Baby," the
Swamp Doctor, at this time a young medical student, reduces all of humanity to a mere collection of analyzable parts, to sinew, bones, and tissue.
"When I met with persons extremely emaciated and finely developed," he
muses, "my anatomical eye would scan their proportions, and instead of paying them the usual courtesies of life, I would be thinking what glorious subjects they would be for museum preparations or dissection." Lewis links
anatomical examination with the threat of death, a possible outcome if the
narrator's scientific interest goes too far. Those ill and indigent, "consump-
tive people and orphan children" housed in asylums and fully aware of their
tenuous status, cast a leery eye at this young anatomist. Lewis acknowledges
the anxiety experienced by the poor, the sick, and the working class, but he
also extends the threat to other classes. The Swamp Doctor's anatomical gaze
renders all bodies extraordinary and vulnerable to his knife, including the
well-born and the fit. During a romantic kiss, he even reduces his well-born
intended to so much viscera, a potential experiment in reanimation: "Instead
of floating into ecstasies of delight, my anatomical mind would wonder
whether, even in death, electricity, by some peculiar adaptation, might not
be able to continue their bewitching suction."[20] The Swamp Doctor's
necrophilic reverie, the disembodiment and rape of his virginal bride-to-be,
evokes the sense of intimate violation, the horrifying taboo breached by the
idea of dissection in the mind of the public.

In spite of his initial musing, the dissection of the wealthy never manifests
in Lewis's work. In particular, he reserves the anatomical knife and eye for
the vulnerable African American body. Madison Tensas steals a black baby
dead and abandoned in the morgue, its mother "so black in the face that I
would have suspected foul play," establishing in the body of the mother a
correlation between blackness and violence received.[21] In other works of
humor, anatomists heap abuse on black bodies. In "Cutting up a Negro
Alive," by Marcus L. Byrn, the good doctor David Rattlehead decides to try
out a set of new medical instruments on the "brain-holder" of an African
American slave he assumes dead. The instruments, insufficient against the
slave's "tough skin," prove useless. Rattlehead resorts to "an old rusty saw," an

action that reminds him of "the old dissecting room in the college." Much to his chagrin and disappointment, the slave revives with a groan, "his head cut to the bone all around." To the doctor, the violence he enacts upon the black body "is all that saved him."[22] The doctor's rationalization of his near-fatal mistake echoes a popular argument in favor of slavery: the African needs the firm hand of slavery in order to ensure health and well-being.

As a medical curiosity and a threat to the efforts of the racial scientist, the white Negro is particularly exposed to the horrors of the anatomical knife. The whiteness of the figure, at once desired and feared, serves as a temptation for the acquisitive anatomist, who establishes ownership of a desirable commodity and deprives the African American of the potential of white membership through removal of the skin. At the separation of the white skin from the African American body—now rendered a black body according to Cartwright's observations—the anatomist employs the skin to frighten those at the outskirts of whiteness, the poor and working class, who usually suffer in the comparisons with the white Negro. In "The Curious Widow," Lewis presents the white Negro as a frightening, pallid document that haunts the Swamp Doctor. Still a student of anatomy, the Swamp Doctor plays a trick upon his working-class nosey landlady by slicing off the face of a dead hare-lipped white Negro, rolling up the paper-thin dermis in an oilcloth, and stuffing it into a coat pocket for her to find as she rummages through his belongings.[23]

The white Negro, now figured as a horror, becomes especially vulnerable to the mythical anatomist, its disfigurement suitable for skinning and display as a fright mask. Lewis identifies the corpse as "one of that peculiar class called Albinoes, or white negroes." To defuse the potentially revolutionary nature of the white Negro, Lewis reinforces its status as a freak—"one of the most hideous specimens that ever horrified sight," he writes—by endowing the figure with additional deformities, including a "cleft extending half way up his nose externally" and a "pair of tushes projecting from his upper jaw."[24] Like the racial scientists who served as his mentors, Lewis derogates the white Negro, casting aside its formally exalted status as a philosophical phenomenon by giving it other disfigurements.[25] He enacts upon the white Negro body the desire of the racial scientist to depict the African American as a beast with tusks, a nearly demonic, grotesque figure.[26]

Even so reduced, the true horror of the white Negro, its revolutionary nature, continues to dog the Swamp Doctor. Although he intends the document of the albino to cure the curiosity of his landlady through fright, he cannot get the white image out of his own mind. "I endeavoured to sleep," he continues, "but that hideous face, which we had locked securely in a trunk, kept staring at me through its many envelopes."[27] The racial scientist, even in the moment of confining and repressing the threat of the white Negro, cannot escape its haunting effects. It peers through its containment, now denied of both voice and body yet still articulating the anxieties of the color line.

Inherent in the display of the white Negro is its comparison to members of the near-white poor and working classes who view the display, and the Swamp Doctor's practical joke is no different. From the beginning of the story, the Swamp Doctor attempts to reduce craniometrically the status of the landlady and her offspring, whom he describes as "the happy mother of a brace and a half of daughters" with "diminutive skulls." His hope is to cure her transgressive behavior, break her down with the face of the albino, and make her "a good landlady."[28] Yet even at the height of the Swamp Doctor's own anxiety over the presence of preternatural whiteness, the revelation of the white Negro does not put her off. Instead, the landlady compares the frightful appearance to that of her drunken husband, an association that recalls the comparisons of the nation's founders, the white Negro possessing a superior appearance to that of the near-white poor and working class. Instead of suffering the terror of white skin from an African American body, she embraces the comparison and undermines the anatomist. As Lewis links the white Negro to the working class, he attempts to equate the two near-white figures, their fates somehow joined in the popular mind.

HUMBUGS, BUMPKINS, AND IMMIGRANTS

The callous removal of white Negro skin—its display as a fright, as a sport of nature—reminds its audience of the violence possible at the hands of scientists seeking to defend the borders of whiteness. Those hopeful populations at the fringes of white membership felt the prick of the anatomical knife. Medical students robbed the unprotected graves of the poor and working class to provide their schools with corpses for dissection and display. As a consequence, paupers, laborers, and new immigrants feared the possibility of their own definable bodily difference. Since natural history museums too often featured the anomalous specimen—the too tall, the too thin, the too dark—the working-class and immigrant patrons began to imagine the indignity of their own bodies skinned and stuffed before a paying public.

The growing anxiety toward exhibition and the violence it threatened found their expression in the white Negro and other nonesuches and neithernors—composite figures, almost literally amalgamated, seemingly cobbled together in the museum space out of binaries rendered distinct as male/female, human/animal, white/black. The border of the binary, delineated and demarcated, began to dissolve in the body of the nonesuch and, as a result, threatened the bodily integrity of the museum-goer. The figure of the white Negro, along with other members of its liminal fellowship, expressed and exacerbated the anxiety of uncertain status of those among the underclass. At the same time, the figure served a middle class that utilized the display of the nonesuch, the muddied middle ground between two distinct essences, to cast aside with derision nonmembers as extraordinary bodies worthy only of exhibition as anatomical curiosities.[29] Excluded from genteel white society, the poor and immigrant classes became white Negroes.

In works of American humor, figures at the borders of citizenship experience the threat of exhibition that comes from nonmembership, their bodies depicted as anomalous, excessive, bestial, by those authorities who would dismember and display them. In George Washington Harris's tale "Sut Lovingood Escapes Assassination," Sut visits New York and takes a "skeer" in a restaurant, where he encounters P. T. Barnum, "the man what shows the dead snakes and frogs." Barnum, at the height of his fame as a museum proprietor and exhibitor of humbugs, observes the strange, anomalous figure of Sut and, in order to put a scare into him, jokingly threatens him with exhibition. Barnum discusses with his dining companion the possibility of "presarv[in'] his perposhun in stuffin' him . . . as a speciment of the 'Ramus Scrambleusimus,' the only wun ever kotch."[30] Through application of Linnaean binomial nomenclature—"Ramus Scrambleusimus"—Barnum renders Sut an analyzable object of natural history. The objectification necessarily entailed in exhibition dehumanizes Sut and threatens him with the potential violence associated with scientific analysis: murder, evisceration, dissection, and taxidermy. Showman, entrepreneur, purveyor of humbugs, Barnum is a threatening figure, a bogeyman that embodies the fears of uncertain social status and the threat of violence that accompanies that uncertainty.

Even though Sut recognizes Barnum's joke, a "pussonel skeer" overtakes him.[31] Barnum's joke—the placement of Sut outside of recognizable natural history and humanity, presenting him as a nondescript and a freak—expresses a greater societal anxiety toward the natural history museum and the culture of exhibition. Sut's tenuous status as a backwoodsman, a member of the Jacksonian rabble on the outskirts of genteel society, places in question his status as a citizen and as a member of the human race.

Barnum's American Museum did not imitate the rational plan of Peale's collections. It did not seek to re-create the harmony and hierarchy of nature that Enlightenment philosophers hoped would inspire social concord. Still, Barnum maintained his museum as a democratic social space where patrons could discern and judge visible phenomena. In his version of the museum space, he encouraged the patron to participate actively in detecting the difference between the constructed humbug and the natural object. Barnum's humbugs were part of what Neil Harris has termed the exhibitor's "operational aesthetic." Together, they performed a beneficial social function: they "trained Americans to absorb knowledge . . . [and] to examine for literal truth."[32] Like Peale's museum space, Barnum's American Museum served as an educational mechanism, a test for Yankee citizenship, but it was a test that the patron could fail. Passive observers, the gullible rubes who accepted all the exhibits at their face value and could not separate the real from the counterfeit, exposed themselves to the perils of exhibition.

Barnum took personal pride in the flood of humanity the American Museum attracted, some thirty-eight million in the twenty-three years of its existence, from Bowery b'hoys and g'hals to Irish immigrants, country folk visiting the city, the growing urban middle class, and visiting dignitaries like Prince Albert and the first Japanese delegation in 1860.[33] In spite of his professed country store origins, he aspired to gentrification. In 1845, he announced in his playbills, "No Admittance for FEMALES OF KNOWN BAD CHARACTER, or other improper persons."[34] From the museum's beginnings, Barnum struggled to establish his museum as a socially acceptable venture in the face of a clientele that tended toward the rowdy Bowery crowd. "By dedicating his Museum to entrepreneurialism, temperance, domesticity, and Christianity," Bluford Adams explains, "he targeted a core of middle-class patrons and their 'respectable' working-class allies."[35] In 1865, Barnum bristled at the accusations in the *Nation* that his patrons consisted of the "worst and most corrupt classes of our people."[36] In his response, he defends the necessity to "popularize" the museum through the mishmash exhibition of "whales, giants, dwarfs, Albinoes," among other freaks and curiosities.[37] To maintain middle-class respectability for himself and his museum, Barnum renounces the extraordinary body as he publicly spurns the lesser of his patrons who still throng through his doors.

Even according to Barnum, rural and immigrant classes, those outside of the middle-class gentility to which Barnum aspired, suffered most in his museum space. Barnum was ambivalent toward the near-white Irish immigrants, who, in his writings, oscillated between valued patrons and intolerable annoyances. Even though "Irish peasants were mocked as preindustrial primitives," Adams points out, "assimilated Irish Americans were invited to take their place among the Museum's loyalists."[38] In one of the more famous passages in his 1869 autobiography, *Struggles and Triumphs*, Barnum, faced with ever-increasing mobs of Irish immigrants who poured into his museum only to stay the day, hangs a sign at the back exit that reads "To the Egress." The immigrants, not comprehending the meaning of the sign, believe the passage leads to a new exhibit. Barnum recounts their puzzlement in Irish dialect: "The Aigress . . . sure that's an animal we haven't seen."[39] Unable to

IRISH EMIGRANT.

Patrick, (just landing.) "BY MY SOWL, YOU'RE BLACK, OLD FELLOW! HOW LONG HAVE YE BIN HERE;"

Nigger, (imitatng the brogue.) "JIST THREE MONTHS, MY HONEY!"

Pat. "BY THE POWERS, I'LL GO BACK TO TIPPERARY IN A JIFFY! I'D NOT BE SO BLACK AS THAT FUR ALL THE WHISKEY IN ROSCREA!"

FIG. 7. Cartoon of "Irish Emigrant," from *Diogenes, Hys Lantern.* By permission of The Library Company of Philadelphia.

negotiate the democratic social space successfully, the immigrants find themselves on the outside, exiled by their own ignorance. Barnum reduces the gullible immigrants to an exhibition in his life story, the butt of his joke.

The comparison between Irish and African American bodies grew out of economic competition: in the cities of the Northeast, the newly arrived Irish and the free African Americans often competed for the same low-wage jobs. The exhibition of the white Negro challenged the status of Irish immigrants in particular, who in popular parlance were described as "niggers turned inside out."[40] Both the Irish and the African American were identified by "simian" features; the African American was sometimes called a "smoked Irishman."[41] An 1852 political cartoon depicts an Irish "emigrant" so frightened by the African American body, which he assumes turned black by the New World climate, he decides to return to the Emerald Isle. "By the powers, I'll go back to Tipperary in a jiffy!" he exclaims. "I'd not be so black as that fur all the whiskey in Roscrea!" The fantasy of racial transformation—from white to black or black to white—creates a nightmare for the immigrant who aspires toward gentility: the person who accompanies the lowest rung on the social ladder, the person with whom the immigrant competes for work, can somehow become more white and leap to acceptability while the immigrant can darken, consequently marked as a social pariah. The presence of the white Negro threatens the body of the immigrant by leaving it behind as extraordinary and unassimilated.

The concept of the "operational aesthetic" attempts to define Barnum's intentions for his museum experience, yet it falls short. He might have wished for his patrons to decipher intelligently the fraud behind Joice Heth, the Fejee Mermaid, and the Woolly Horse, but aside from determining the veracity of exhibits, patrons still faced the ambiguities presented by these figures. Barnum's missing links and composite figures presented challenges to fixed hierarchical binaries. These hybrids of oppositions—of human and animal, male and female, black and white—openly interrogated the status of Barnum's customers. To view the bearded lady asserted and challenged the gender of the patron. To gaze at the white Negro asserted or withheld the racial membership of the near-white population who flocked to the American Museum. Like those earlier spectacles, Barnum's exhibition of the white Negro helped test the whiteness of an audience frequently made up of near-white Irish immigrants and unsophisticated rural roughs who the still prominent racial theories of Samuel Stanhope Smith considered less white.

BARNUM'S LEUCOETHIOPIAN DIASPORA

> The tall giant woman made her best bow; the fat boy waddled out and kissed his hand; the "negro turning white" showed his ivory and his spots; . . . the Albino family went through their performances.
>
> —Barnum on Prince Albert's 1860 visit to the American Museum,
> *Struggles and Triumphs*, 1866

For years, Barnum offered his aspiring near-white patrons a never-ending parade of white Negroes: Leopard Children, Albino Families, Negroes Turning White. He presented them most frequently on a platform with his other performers labeled freaks, available to the public for twelve hours a day, with an hour sometimes for a midday meal. The intentions of these exhibits, like the displays of other extraordinary bodies, were ambiguous at best, often varying from exhibit to exhibit. This mercurial quality reflected an attempt to address the needs and anxieties of divergent and changing audiences. Throughout the decades of the American Museum, Barnum's white Negro resonated in the public imagination, enough for Barnum to bring the exhibition back time and again and reinvent the figure with new staging and fresh fictions. Using the earlier exhibitions of white Negroes at English fairs as a template, Barnum gradually reinscribed the marvelous with a new narrative, incorporating the efforts of racial science to stifle the revolutionary body while at the same time developing a language to tap into the popular desire for racial transformation. In the process, and in the context of his concocted humbugs, Barnum undermined the supposed fixity and naturalness of racial difference. To an audience educated in the uncertain veracity of his exhibits, color, as a marker of difference, became at once fluid and fraudulent.

The British exhibitions of John "Primrose" Boby and George Alexander at the English fairs proffered the whitening bodies as simple yet exotic artifacts, curiosities collected from the colonies, ne plus ultrae from elsewhere. The showmen who presented them let the skin speak for itself as a marvel from God's creation. Barnum began with the fact of the body with albinism or vitiligo and the premise of the white Negro as a natural marvel from the tropics, then built upon the narrative, aggrandizing the presentation by renovating the staging and the dress as well as contriving elaborate and often false histories, thereby exploiting the expectations of the audience and manipulating their responses to the white or whitening African American body.

Most prominent and ubiquitous among Barnum's white Negro exhibits was what he often called "Leopard Boys" or "Leopard Girls," bodies seemingly split between black and white that did not overtly exploit the fantasy of transformation so much as they emphasized a profound permanent hybridity. Like Henry Moss and James the White Negro, these children were marked by vitiligo, the large patches of white across their dark faces and torsos branding them as extraordinary bodies. Before the museum crowd, the display of the Leopard Children stressed the revelation of their bichromatic bodies. In a Mathew Brady photograph taken in the 1850s, a Leopard Girl, lounging in a chair, wears a dress that bares most of her shoulders and her legs, her black skin and white spots exposed to observation. In a second photograph from that session, the girl stands, the straps of the dress pulled off her shoulders to reveal unhindered the dappling of her upper torso, a chaste striptease that hinted at further speckled regions. The exhibition of these children demanded that they expose their skin by often wearing costumes that showed their limbs and midriffs. In the Charles Eisenmann photographs of Ashley Benjamin, a Leopard Boy who exhibited in Philadelphia and New York in the 1880s, this mode of display becomes clear. In all of his photographs, Benjamin wears an exotic circus leotard with leggings cut high up on his thighs and a large circular opening in the front that bares his torso from chest to abdomen. In the Eisenmann photographs of John Wesley Nash and the Anderson siblings, other youngsters with vitiligo, the dress is reduced even further: brief shorts that reveal all that contemporary propriety would allow.

FIG. 10. John Wesley Nash, photograph by Charles Eisenmann. By permission of the Becker Collection, Syracuse University Library, Department of Special Collections.

FIG. 11. John, Maria, and Rose Anderson, photograph by Henshel. By permission of The Harvard Theatre Collection, The Houghton Library.

Can the Ethiopian change his skin, or the leopard his spots? then may ye also do good, that are accustomed to do evil.

—Jeremiah 13:23

The term *Leopard Child* worked two ways. Most obviously, the moniker pointed to the biblical rhetorical question that serves to teach of the immutability of separate natures. Specific to Barnum's display, a person born with black skin should always remain black. But the exhibit teased to contradict the proverb and biblical authority, the ever-whitening skin seeming to challenge the attempts of racial science to fix racial difference and to confine Africans to the position of a separate species. True to his fashion, Barnum offered ambiguity, quandary; he poses the question of race to his audience. Can a Leopard Boy truly change his spots, or are they everlasting? Is his white skin a humbug, or is it his black skin that deceives? Barnum presented the white Negro as an enigma, a call for a definition of categories that confuses any attempt to fix the categories of race.

Leopard. Child. The two elements of the term also rendered the afflicted exhibit a beastlike hybrid.[42] Like the centaurs and minotaurs of ancient Greeks, creatures formed from transgressive trysts between beasts and maidens, the bichromatic child hinted of taboo sexual practice.[43] As a result, the showman equated miscegenation and bestiality in the piebald figure, a sinful commingling of separate, incompatible species.[44] The suggestion of a leopard father and a human mother insinuated the more domestic coupling of a black father and a white mother, the child then a bastard of rape, the troubling outcome of black men forcing themselves upon white women, or worse, a love child, the consummation of a welcome interracial assignation.

Like the Leopard Child, the miscegenated body of the mulatto produced a confusion of categories that undermined the attempts of racial scientists to verify discrete black and white essences. In answer to the whitening slave body, these theorists and defenders of racial difference tried to establish the mulishness of the mulatto, exhibiting the figure as a sterile hybrid of distinct species to convince a worried white public that a biracial body cannot survive if it cannot reproduce new, whiter bodies. To argue the threat of amalgamation, Josiah C. Nott claims that the hybrid mulatto is "a degenerate, unnatural offspring, doomed by nature to work out its own destruction."[45] Imagining a racial apocalypse, he infers that race mixing will lead to the mutual extinction of black and white. Yet at the same time as it epitomized the impossible hybridity of separate species, the thriving body of the Leopard Child refuted the sterility that should result from this supposed incompatibility.

To moderate the revolutionary nature of the display, the showman still worked to distance the Leopard Child from domestic political concerns.

Fantastic staging and costumes embellished the ballyhoo of alien hybrids from Africa by further suggesting exotic, barbarous origins. Barnum and his dime museum descendants most often presented boys and young men with vitiligo as primitives, arming them, as the Eisenmann photographs demonstrate, with spears and machetes. As he presented all of his racial grotesques, Eisenmann placed the white Negro subjects in outdoor settings to define them as feral, brutish.[46] In their portraits, the hair of Ashley Benjamin and the Anderson siblings is spectacularly coifed, the remaining black hair shaved away to emphasize the white forelock; the resulting Mohawk serves as shorthand for the aboriginal. The barbaric props, the strange costuming, the grotesque hairdos, all enhanced the appeal of the Leopard Child, enticing patrons with dreams of the savage, the taboo. In a sense, to cast the white Negro as a jungle exotic mitigated the threat of racial transformation, yet by tapping into a public unease about miscegenation, the Leopard Child hinted at a nightmarish world peopled by halflings and half-breeds.

In advertisements and biographical pamphlets, Barnum often pitched the figure of the white Negro as a foreign agent, a found member of a lost or decimated tribe. Robert Bogdan attributes these exaggerated narratives to "a time of intense world exploration and Western expansion."[47] The English colonial project, which brought the whitening African body to England as spoils from the nation's far-flung possessions, translated well into the domain of Manifest Destiny, a policy that promised the formation of empire and the pursuit of national material wealth. A belief in "a distinct, superior Anglo-Saxon race," Reginald Horsman argues, sustained both British imperialism and American Manifest Destiny.[48] Articulating the fantasies of burgeoning American colonial aspirations, the published narratives of Barnum's exhibitions welcomed the whitening African American body from the jungles of Martinique or Madagascar. Only in rare cases was the body a domestic product, which foreclosed audience speculation about interracial escapades and master/slave rape. Barnum's literature of his white Negro exhibitions offers the figure for consideration as a separate race that marvelously and immaculately generates from African parents, an extensive leucoethiopian diaspora.[49]

In most of these potentially revolutionary exhibitions, Barnum was careful to contain the white or whitening African body. The advertisements of these acts assure the patrons that beneath the white skin lie "every other feature and characteristic of the real African."[50] The 1860 playbill that announced the arrival of "2 Albino Girls with their Black mother" attests with emphasis that "it is impossible for any person to look upon them without seeing, unmistakably, that these girls now offered for exhibition are *White Negroes* without one particle of any other than pure African blood, though *their skin*

FIG. 12. "Albino Children with their Black Mother and Black Sister," lithograph by Currier and Ives. By permission of The Harvard Theatre Collection, The Houghton Library.

and hair are white as the purest snow." Although it affirms the easy accessibility of empirical evidence in the manner of a democratic social space, the Barnum proclamation echoes the contemporary voice of racial science that difference resides now no longer certainly in the skin but in other physical features and, even more particularly, in the blood.

Not surprisingly, the exhibitors of white Negroes began to adapt the discourse of racial science to their own ends. The endorsements of the scientific establishment lent not only veracity to a potential humbug, they also added an educational note to the proceedings. Although the intrusion of scientific discourse is largely credited with the eventual demise of the dime museum and the freak show, the testimony of physicians, Bogdan explains, was "generally used as part of the status-enhanced presentation."[51] A large portion of the 1860 pamphlet *History of Rudolph Lucasie*, the father of "The Albino Family," is dedicated to the long history of scientific interest in "Albinos, Leucoethiopes, or White Negroes."[52] A broadside publicizing a "Novel Concert by Four Snow White Negro Boys," an act that played both the American Museum and Boston Museum stages in the 1840s, incorporates no less than three "Certificates of eminent Medical practitioners" from Boston that "testify to the facts" and endorse the boys as "objects of great interest to the curious or scientific." After thorough examinations of the boys, the doctors verify the African American parentage and authenticate their possession "in eminent degree all the characteristics of the *Leucoethiopes* (white negroes,) viz. a pearly white skin, white hair, and pink pupils of the eyes, together with all the features of full-blooded negroes." This scientific testimony diminishes the whiteness to the status of a medical anomaly. The specter of racial intermixture lingers in the coda of one doctor's testimony: the boys "are not to be mistaken for or confounded with mulattoes." Lurking in the rhetoric of the physicians is the fear of unbounded sexual relations between the races.

Like the natural philosophers and racial scientists before them, Barnum and other exhibitors of white Negroes concentrated on the genealogy of the children, emphasizing the unalloyed blackness of the parents to soothe fears of amalgamation as a cause for the persistent whiteness. "The Four Snow White Negro Boys" have parents *"Black as Jet."* One of the doctors quoted on the broadside goes to great lengths to establish the parentage of the boys, the father "a negro," the mother "a negress . . . subject to . . . periodical variations of color." The pamphlet accompanying the London exhibition of Clem Foster, another white Negro who exhibited in Barnum's American Museum, offers a romantic account of his savage origin in the jungles of Martinique, his birth announcing a change of fortune in a battle with a rival village. Clem's mother and father, the chief of the village, are "black as it is possible to find a negro."[53] The blackness of the parents assures the audience that the whiteness is anomalous, contained, an indicator of a new race, maybe, but not of membership among Anglo-Saxons. In an 1860 magazine advertisement, Barnum presents a tableau of two white Negro girls accompanied by their mother who holds their baby sister. The familial scene is further framed by other Barnum exhibits, including the hydrocephalic "Aztec Children" and the "What-Is-It?," another hydrocephalic man presented as "a mixture of the wild native African and the Orang Outang."[54] The advertisement places the white Negro girls within two intersecting contexts: the dark-skinned mother and sister help constitute the whiteness of the girls as they also establish their "black" lineage, and the two freak exhibits reduce the status of the girls to that of racial grotesques, hybrid figures that challenge the museumgoer to discern whether they are black or white, human or animal. The obsession with genealogy, with undiluted blackness, betokens a struggle to contend with the horrors of racial transformation and especially with the whitening of bodies through miscegenation.

Barnum's freaks, his composite figures, Rosemarie Garland Thomson explains, "confounded classification systems that organized collective cultural perceptions."[55] The white Negro, whiteness on an African body, blurred the boundaries between black and white, African and European, and clouded the professed distinction between the races that rationalized the perpetuation of slavery. The stress placed upon genealogy in the advertisements for white Negro exhibitions indicates an overriding concern with the confusion of categories brought about by racial intermixture. Visibly divided into

FIG. 13. "The Wonderful Albino Family," lithograph by Currier and Ives. Courtesy of the National Library of Medicine, Bethesda.

FIG. 14. "Novel Concert by the Four Snow White Negro Boys," poster. Courtesy, American Antiquarian Society.

black and white, the parti-colored body emerged in the public imagination of the nineteenth century as a handy symbol of this cross-racial transgression.

Published in 1835 by genealogist Jerome B. Holgate writing under the name of Oliver Bolokitten, *A Sojourn in the City of Amalgamation in the Year of our Lord 19—* is the first work of American fiction to treat miscegenation as its central issue.[56] This Swiftian fantasy takes Bolokitten into a future where the government tyrannically enforces racial intermarriages in an effort to ensure social concord. The satiric centerpiece of the novel is a white Negro exhibition: the display of a black and white figure complete with a printed "biography of the wonderful man." The title page of the biography bears the pedigree of white Negro exhibition in the form of the epitaph of George Alexander, the spotted child presented at Bartholomew Fair. In "The Memoirs of Boge Bogun," Holgate transforms the body of the piebald white Negro into an allegory of racial animosity. Born of a white mother and black father, Bogun narrates the "intestinal" war that results from his mixed parentage, the "differently complexioned particles" sharing "a mortal hate."[57] Holgate devotes several chapters to this conflict, the numerous generals, the myriad battles over the head, the liver, the spleen. Peace is not achieved until the white general slays the black king and the body settles into its segregation—the top half white, the bottom black.

As a living embodiment of the hope and fear produced by the growing whiteness of slaves, the images of the Leopard Boy and the fantasy of the Negro Turning White surface in the most extreme rhetoric of the debates over abolition. In 1864, the Emancipation Proclamation on the books, two Democratic journalists, David Croly and George Wakeman, anonymously authored the satiric political pamphlet Miscegenation, palming it off as a Republican manifesto for the blending of the races. The authors foresaw a utopia where "the most perfect and highest type of manhood will not be white or black, but brown, or colored," a racial transformation that darkens rather than lightens.[58] As a response to these accusations, Theodore Tilton, the radical abolitionist and editor of the New York Independent, disavows in his editorial "The Union of the Races" any promotion of racial intermixture, yet he believes in its inevitability, offering the observation that "the African-tinted members of our community will in the future gradually bleach out their blackness." This image of the amalgamated white Negro, "growing paler with every generation" until "[he] will at last completely hide his face under the snow," submits a fantasy of racial transformation also embodied by the exhibited albino African American.[59]

Converted into a symbol of amalgamation, the Leopard Child supplied a ready vocabulary of racial transformation—the growing patches of white on dark skin, the challenge to racial science, the troubled speculations of the gawking white and near-white public. When literary efforts turned toward the child of miscegenation, writers mined the tropes of freak show displays to use in their arguments against slavery, segregation, and other forms of racial prejudice. The piebald body in the museum suggested that the eyes were too unreliable to isolate black from white or master from servant. The display toyed with the possibility of liberation from prejudice, of freedom from surveillance, yet as a distinctively marked extraordinary body, the spotted surface of the Leopard Boy also expressed the threat of exposure experienced by the African American with skin light enough to pass as white.

In his 1857 *The Garies and Their Friends*, Frank J. Webb explores the fates of two African American families affected by the violence of color prejudice in antebellum Philadelphia. At the core of the novel are the contrasting coming-of-age stories of two young free men of color—the dark-skinned, middle-class Charlie Ellis and the nearly white, wealthier Clarence Garie. Through good-natured pluck, intelligence, and a little help from sympathetic friends, Charlie eventually overcomes the obstacles of racism to rise in the world and finds happiness in his African American community. The light-complected Clarence, though, suffers from the quandary of his near-whiteness. He is called a "white nigger."[60] He is kicked out of school when a neighbor informs the teacher of the child's blackness. Spurred on by a jealous cousin who wishes to inherit the Garie family lands, rioting Irish thugs murder Clarence's white Southern aristocratic father for the sin of miscegenation. That same night, the trauma of the evening's violence kills the mulatto mother in childbirth. To shield Clarence from further prejudice, the executors of his father's estate elect to conceal his origins. Webb characterizes this decision as a betrayal of race that ultimately condemns the child to an adulthood of paranoia.

Already labeled a white Negro, the now-grown Clarence Garie finds his fear of public exposure materialized in a nightmare image of the Leopard Child. He becomes engaged to the daughter of a wealthy Virginian plantation family, but the weight of his secret has drained his skin of color, his albino-like complexion "without a particle of red to relieve its uniform paleness." Before he can reveal his race to his fiancée, Anne Bates, she recounts a prescient nightmare that threatens their relationship and checks his revelation. In her dream, the couple walks blissfully together until a "rough ugly man" touches Clarence's face. This contact causes him to break out in "loathsome black spots."[61] The image of the transformed Leopard Boy melodramatically foreshadows Clarence's eventual unmasking by the son of the man who plotted the death of the elder Garie, the secret blackness rudely unveiled. In a conscious allusion to Barnum's display of children with vitiligo, Webb explores the dilemma of biraciality, the passer tantalized by the privileges given to whiteness yet painfully aware of the act of racial treason. Bearing the burden of anxiety and guilt, Clarence the Leopard Child grows even "paler" until he passes away, shunned by the white citizens among whom he yearned to walk and exiled from his darker loved ones.

Spots mark the freak, the body suspended between black and white. The fantasy of racial transformation, even when it manifests as an expression of utopian hope, leaves the body naked to prying and condemning eyes. Later,

in the second half of the twentieth century, fueled by the Civil Rights movement and a popular desire for racial harmony, the legacy of Henry Moss, the
Leopard Children, the antimiscegenationist rantings of Oliver Bolokitten
lived on in the aspiring radicalism of a television sitcom. On Christmas Eve
in 1970, the television show *Bewitched* broadcast "Sisters at Heart," an
episode written in large part by the tenth-grade English class at Thomas Jefferson High School in Los Angeles, a group of inner-city schoolchildren
mentored by a staff writer of the show. The episode concerns the interracial
friendship between Tabitha, the four-year-old magical daughter of a witch
and a mortal, and Lisa, an African American girl of the same age who never
again appears in the series. Sharing a mutual fondness, the girls express a
wish to be sisters. When a rude, bigoted playmate tells them that they cannot
be sisters since they do not share the same color skin, Tabitha casts a spell to
achieve this goal, turning the two girls into a kind of hybrid: Tabitha aug-
ments her white skin with half-dollar-size dark brown polka dots and adds to
Lisa's dark complexion half-dollar-size white polka dots, all perfectly circular
and uniform. By implication of the makeup, the two girls have actually
exchanged patches of skin to share now a dermis and an identity. They
become sisters of the skin, literally amalgamated.

A sitcom conceived, in part, with a social conscience, *Bewitched* began
with a premise of miscegenation, a relatively safe fantasy of a "good" witch
and a mortal marrying, having kids, and dealing with the secret of the wife's
passing and the fear of mortal prejudice. This premise was not lost on the
inner-city high school students. According to Barbara Avedon, the staff writer
who guided the students' efforts, one student explained that the show interested him because it was about "a mixed marriage."[62] In the students' collec-
tively written teleplay, the amalgamated bodies of the two spotted girls briefly
threaten to expose Tabitha and her mother, Samantha, as witches passing as
mortals. Through their televised tale of passing and the threat of exhibition,
the students confirmed the persistence and potency of the spotted child as a
symbol of miscegenation.

BURNT CORK AND "DE MALGAMATION"

The child's play of the large, round, uniform spots strongly registers the
artifice of the makeup. The employment of a piecemeal blacking and whit-
ing up to signify a racial transformation insinuates the tradition of blackface
theater and the minstrel stage. Recent criticism of minstrelsy has focused
upon the unalloyed racism of the blackface mask. In one model of
minstrelsy's development, Eric Lott identifies minstrelsy as "a socially
approved context of institutional control" that "continually acknowledged

and absorbed black culture even while defending white America against it."[63] Susan Gubar, who embraces Lott's reading, attributes the appeal of blackface performance—as well as other "racechanges," as she calls them—to "the dynamics of white guilt," the haunting of the so-called white population "by the killing fields of their history." The wearing of the blackface mask, she writes about minstrelsy in American cinema, is plainly and simply "a symbolic rite of scapegoating, the flip side of lynching."[64] This critical denunciation of the minstrel show still manages begrudgingly to acknowledge that blackface theater, in Lott's words, "demonstrates the permeability of the color line."[65]

Although the racism of blacking up cannot and should not be denied, lost in this critical flagellation is the ability of the blackface mask to unsettle categories, confound containment, and trifle with the discrete essences sought by racial science. Early blackface theater, W. T. Lhamon Jr. argues, "developed distinct responses to 'amalgamation'—not by attacking but by enacting miscegenation."[66] Like the playful polka dots that surface on a television sitcom, the makeup of early blackface theater also sported with racial identity and its slipperiness, employing burnt cork and greasepaint to represent the miscegenated body in a way that echoed the exhibition of white Negroes.

In published and working actor's scripts, images of racial transformation and the piebald body draw upon the revolutionary nature of the white Negro to elude the constrictions of racial scientists and the violence of potential exhibition. Utilizing the surface of the white Negro body to theorize the origins of racial difference, philosophers and doctors discussed the blackness of Africans as a color laid upon the original whiteness, a skin equally removable and applicable through natural forces: difference is displayed in the skin, color can be cast off and, therefore, laid on. Obviously, this physical removal of the skin color might not have had a direct effect on the application of cork to the white Negroes of blackface theater, but the plays and parodies of that theater often displayed a keen interest in the anatomical experiments and speculations of the burgeoning racial science.

Recent criticism has explored the complicated set of cultural circumstances that gave rise to the popularity of the blackface mask in the nineteenth century. Blackface theater can trace at least partial ancestry to the folk rituals of northern European common peoples, nonracial mummery that challenged authority through inversion.[67] Translated to North America, these rituals and their implied critique of authority were embraced and assimilated by the population of disenfranchised and disempowered young working-class men in their struggles against the efforts of policing by the merchant and elite classes.[68] The application of blackness, the enacted fantasy of racial transformation, was as much an expression of solidarity with what these youths identified as another alienated group as it was an expression of anxiety over tenuous social status.[69] Concerned as well with the fantasy of racial transformation, white Negro exhibitions developed alongside of blackface impersonations, often confronting the same audience and criticism. Blackface theater embraced the same fantasy of racial transformation and the threat of social chaos this transformation presents, happily engendering a world of protean identities and uncertain essences.

Early blackface plays addressed the implied violence of exhibition and the incursions made by doctors and scientists to qualify and fix racial identity. In particular, Thomas Dartmouth Rice's 1835 blackface minstrelsy play, *The Virginny Mummy*, satirized the perils of exhibition and scientific investigation. In the play, a young man in love hires a free man of color, Ginger Blue, to impersonate an Egyptian mummy in order to impress the scientist guardian of the young man's fancy.[70] The guardian plans to learn the secrets of the ages by resuscitating what he calls "this degenerate race of mankind."[71] The performance mirrors the efforts of racial scientists to contend with the Egyptian body and appropriate the pyramids and the Sphinx as Caucasian achievements and not African. Early in the 1840s, racial scientist Samuel George Morton measured the cranial capacity of mummy skulls to establish ancient Egyptians as "originally peopled by a branch of the Caucasian race," but with the advent of "Persian dominion . . . the varied inhabitants of Europe, Asia and Nigrita poured into the valley of the Nile, abolishing in degree the exclusiveness of caste, and involving an endless confusion of races."[72] Josiah Nott incorporated Morton's findings into his theory that "the civilization of Egypt is attributable to these Caucasian heads" and that gradual racial intermixture eventually reduced the empire to "barbarism."[73]

In anticipation of these theories of racial origin, the young man in love disguises Ginger by essentially changing his race. He not only beshrouds the free man of color in wrappings, he applies coats of "white, black, green, blue and a variety of colours" to his already corked-up skin. To induce the desired racial transformation, he layers on identity, mixing it up, amalgamating then parodying mongrelization. In the application of paint, though, Ginger sees an opportunity to sustain the metamorphosis. He asks the young man to "put plenty of turpentine wid de white paint so it wont rub off. I like to make em believe I'm white man too." Although this request reinforces the primacy of white skin, the joke of the transformation indicates an understood fluidity of racial identity and implies its basic fraudulence.

Placed in a box, instructed to remain still and "silent as death" for the exhibition, Ginger understands the price of passing as an Egyptian pharaoh: he must play dead and subject himself to the potential violence that visits the exhibited body. The servants of the museum proprietor each attempt to dismember parts of Ginger. The Irish servant tries to remove Ginger's toe to send back to his wife in the old country. The artist wants to cut off a finger "to keep as a curiosity." The maidservant sticks her finger in his mouth to check his teeth. Exhibition exposes the body of Ginger Blue to potential violation—probing, experimentation, dismemberment. The immigrant, the artist, the maidservant, and the scientist all fail in their attempts to violate the body of the ersatz mummy, because Ginger Blue rebels by refusing to mind and remain still as an exhibit. He consistently subverts their efforts by escaping the box into which he has been forced, turning the orderly museum space into chaos and, through his disruption, undermining the scientist's experiment.

A standard of blackface theater, *The Virginny Mummy* enjoyed further versions and revisions as it continued to engage the tenets of nineteenth-century scientific racism. In the original Rice script, the doctor fusses over the method of the elixir's injection, whether to "bore a hole in his head," "open an artery," or "sew up his mouth, and lance him in the back of his neck." In the Byron Christy version of the play, performed in the 1850s, the threat of violence refers even more directly to racial science as the scientist proposes to perform with a hammer and chisel "a boring experiment" on Ginger the Mummy, then, in a slight change of mind, considers to "knock out his eye and see if he has any brain." The fascination with the mummy's brain pan alludes to the work of Samuel George Morton and his intensive study of his Golgotha of skulls.[74]

One of the final jokes of the Rice script involves the threat of interracial marriage. In the same soliloquy in which he threatens the exhibited body of the free man of color, the scientist announces his intention to offer the hand of his daughter to Ginger the Pharaoh. Already a figure of miscegenation by virtue of his painted, parti-colored body, Ginger registers the absurdity of his pretend hybridity and acknowledges the threat of his secreted black body. In an aside to the audience, he comments, "Dats what de missionary call de malgamation." The joke of amalgamation may have addressed the anxieties of the audience, but the humor of Ginger's commentary also relies upon an irony that registers the absurdity of those concerns, an absurdity not lost on the first audiences of blackface theater in the integrated areas of the Five Points section of New York, where Rice grew up. Two decades later, southerner William Bobo witnessed an interracial gathering in a Five Points basement, a dance with "a few males and females, black, yellow, and white," what he called "a piebald party," and condemned the neighborhood as an "outlandish and heathenish portion of the city."[75] In this stew of peoples, blackface theater first developed and entertained. This attraction for mixed and mixing groups of people—"piebald charisma," as Lhamon terms it after

Bobo—found its reenactment on the early blackface theater stage. The image of the piebald body—a white man blackened with cork, further amalgamated with additional layers of greasepaint to produce a synecdoche of miscegenation—resonates in this piebald audience as a talisman against those who would regulate its behavior, including the missionaries who would try to civilize and uplift the rowdies of Five Points.[76]

Blackface theater continued to offer figures in piebald makeup that directly referred to the exhibition of white Negroes and connected these piebald figures to miscegenation. These displays of artifice undermined the authority of the racial scientists who strove to fix racial difference into a rigid dichotomy of black and white. Rice's 1843 parody *Otello* pursued the miscegenation theme of the original play further than contemporary serious productions were willing to go. Nineteenth-century reviewers, commentators, actors, and audiences all attempted to contend with the controversy of the interracial relationship. Two of the most famous Shakespearean actors of the day, Edmund Kean and Edwin Booth, tempered the blackness of their makeup to produce a less African Moor.[77] Reacting to contemporary performances of Shakespeare plays, John Quincy Adams pronounces that the "great and moral lesson of Othello is that black and white blood cannot be intermingled without a gross outrage upon the law of nature."[78] In Rice's parody, the "gross outrage" of the play's miscegenation finds its object lesson: the Moor and Desdemona have a child. Desdemona presents the boy to Othello. "Behold this pledge," she announces as she points to the boy's face, "your image here is seen/Not this side love, the other side I mean." Desdemona's declaration, as well as the stage directions, indicate a bifurcated makeup, blackness—Othello's image—and whiteness split down the middle of the boy's face. For comic effect, the child may have entered the stage with the whiteface makeup visible to the audience, only to display the corked-up side upon Desdemona's direction. Like Bolokitten's Boge Bogun, the visually amalgamated boy embodies the joke (and concern) of racial amalgamation as well as the myth of a world split into black and white, the maintenance of the segregation reduced to a laughable artifice.[79]

> Are you blind, Commander Spock? Look at me! Look at me! . . . I am black on the right side. . . . Lokai is white on the right side. All of his people are white on the right side.
>
> —Commissioner Bele, *Star Trek*, 1969

On the nineteenth-century actor, parti-colored makeup—visibly divided between black and white like the extraordinary body of the Leopard Boy—signifies a miscegenated body. The political potency of the bichromatic body to depict the transgression of racial transformation lasts well into the twentieth century in other blackface performances, bringing with it the old theories of mulishness and racial incompatibility. In *Black Like Me*, John Howard Griffin darkened his pigmentation in order to "pass" for a month as an African American. The publication and promotion of the magazine article, which he would expand into the best-selling book, created a stir among the segregationists in his hometown of Mansfield, Texas, who viewed his "passing" as a betrayal of his race. One morning, as Griffin tells it, a reporter from the *Fort Worth Star-Telegram* called to tell him that the townspeople were burning him in effigy on Main Street. To symbolize his sin and their outrage, the mob attached his name to "a dummy, half black, half white."[80] Re-created in Griffin's account, the piebald body—symbol of miscegenation and the transgression of "blacking up"—becomes a symbol of racial hatred, a fetish of civil violence.

In its episode "Let That Be Your Last Battlefield," an allegory on the destructiveness of racial prejudice, the television show *Star Trek* uses stark black and white greasepaint to create a bichromatic alien species. Split vertically between pure blackness and unadulterated whiteness, the line of absolute demarcation falling evenly down the middle of the forehead, along the crest of the nose, dividing the lips, the chin, the neck, the species arbitrarily determines racial difference and hierarchy by the distribution of the color: blackness on the right side of the body indicates superiority. Lokai, a member of a slave race from Cheron, a planet from the southernmost part of the galaxy, seeks asylum on the *Enterprise*, as he has been pursued for fifty thousand terrestrial years by Bele, a member of the master race and a commissioner of the Committee of Political Traitors, for leading a slave revolt on his planet. At the end of the voyage to Cheron, in which the racial conflict nearly destroys the ship, Lokai and Bele take the chase to the planet's surface, where they discover that a race war has devastated the planet and annihilated its population. The surveillance of the *Enterprise* officers pursues the piebald men as they play out a spectacle of rage and futility.

In an early scene that echoes the speculations of nineteenth-century racial science and the exhibition of white Negroes, the crew members of the *Enterprise* pause over the unconscious body of Lokai to theorize about the origin of skin color in the hitherto unknown species. Faced with a body bisected into black and white, Captain Kirk, First Officer Spock, and Medical Officer McCoy initially render the body extraordinary, a singular "mutation," a dermatological condition that deserves further scientific scrutiny. Color stymies the explorers. "You are certain, doctor," Spock asks, "that this pigmentation is the natural condition of this individual?" At a loss after a careful examination of the body, the doctor replies in exasperation, "I can't explain him." Kirk speculates enigmatically that the coloring has resulted from some "dramatic conflict." The conflict to which he refers is the racial struggle between black and white contemporary to the series; however, this fixation on skin color and the apparent incompatibility of black and white in the same body reinforces assumptions of nineteenth-century racial theorists, the warring particles that plague the parti-colored Boge Bogun revived for the science-fiction utopia of sixties television. In a later scene, still in pursuit of a theory of origins, Spock postulates that the species once "must have been monocolored." The otherwise logical Spock's inexplicable and oddly illogical assumption resurrects the idea of the piebald figure as a symbol of racial hybridity and the essential insolubility of black and white.

The racial science of our past haunts our imagined future. As with nineteenth-century white Negro exhibition and the makeup practices of early blackface theater, the partial blacking up of white actors to portray an alien species leads to commentary and speculations about skin color and its origins. The piebald body also allegorically represents a piebald body politic—in this case, one imagined as equally split between black and white and in conflict. The episode clearly warns that racial hatred inevitably results in mutual self-destruction, yet Spock's theory of a miscegenated body recalls as well the assumptions of nineteenth-century racial theorists that the hybrid, the mulatto, is inherently violent and doomed to extinction.

THE PIEBALD PARLIAMENT

By the middle of the nineteenth century, racial scientists strenuously discarded the idea of black skin lightening through any natural means aside from miscegenation. Charles Caldwell, in *Thoughts on the Original Unity of the Human Race*, his book-length rejection of Samuel Stanhope Smith's theories, sought to nullify the importance of the white Negro. He argues that the "African race has never, within the memory of man, or the reach of history, been changed by climate into the Caucasian." Instead, the reputed erasure of blackness in slaves results from illness. "Disease renders him pale, as it does the Caucasian," Caldwell counters. "Remove him to a climate unfavorable to his constitution, and with the loss of his health and vigor, he will lose somewhat of the depth of his glossy black." To illustrate this theory of depletion, Caldwell once again resurrects Henry Moss to recast him as an unfortunate ex-slave who temporarily suffered from disease of the skin. Like the color of Jefferson's white Negroes, Moss's skin in this exhibition becomes "a *dead chalky whiteness*." Having thereby reduced the status of his anatomical exhibit to that of a cadaver, Caldwell then presents a magically retransformed body before an imagined audience of his dumbfounded scientific rivals. "And, to the utter disappointment of Dr. Smith and his followers," he proclaims, "when Moss at length recovered his health, his original complexion returned, in its full depth, and he was again as complete an African as the country contained."[81] By inventing a mysterious reversal of the vitiligo, Caldwell cancels the revolutionary effect of Moss's first exhibition in Philadelphia. The improbable restoration of Moss's color is crucial to Caldwell's racial assumptions. To establish the fixity of racial difference, the threat of the white Negro must be temporary and curable.

In spite of these efforts to discount racial transformation, popular culture kept the figure of the white Negro alive and on display, converting it into an emblem of possibilities, of social unsettlement, of escape from rigid categories of race and class, a potential counterattack against the threat of banishment from white membership. As the presence of slavery in a democracy threatened to tear a country apart, the idea that the blackness of slaves could somehow fade away increasingly fascinated an anxious public. In August 1850, during the summer of the Great Compromise and the Fugitive Slave Law, Barnum presented in his museum space a black man who, by virtue of an elixir distilled from a mysterious weed, performed a slow striptease of color, daily fading shade by shade into whiteness. Named the "Negro Turning White," this figure made a lasting impression on Barnum's museum-going public who daily visited the museum to see the metamorphosis.[82] Six years later, when bankruptcy forced Barnum to relinquish control of the American Museum, the *New York Herald* listed the Negro Turning White in the company of his greatest humbugs: Joice Heth, Tom Thumb, and the Feejee Mermaid.[83] In his autobiography, sixteen years after the exhibition, Barnum proudly quotes from "Barnumopsis," a parody in verse that commemorates in part the initial and lingering cultural impact of Barnum's man with the weed:

> And last, not least, the marvelous Ethiope,
> Changing his skin by preternatural skill,
> Whom every setting sun's diurnal slope
> Leaves whiter than the last, and whitening still.[84]

Grouped with the museum's most famous frauds and exaggerations, this spectacle of racial transformation carries hints of the humbug, itself a parody bearing the suggestion of dissolving blackface and the absurdity of endless fading until whiteness itself becomes a folly.

The Negro Turning White was a different white Negro exhibit for Barnum. Gone was the foreign origin, the jungles, the native superstitions. He was a less-exotic display, an American of color gradually removing color, designed to soothe the anxiety of difference as he also performed the cultural work of normalizing whiteness. To some of Barnum's audience, though, he also represented an incursion on the privileged space of white manhood. William Northall, in his theatrical memoirs, expresses the anger induced by the white Negro: he writes that Barnum's "fat boys . . . reached the climax of everything that was disgusting in the way of human monstrosities; but he has lately added a spotted negro, whom it is said, in the bills of the day, has discovered a weed by which he can in process of time change his skin from tawny-hue to lilly-white. These spotted negroes are common in the South; and white spots are attributable either to absorption of an original deficiency of the middle skin or rete mucosum. . . . It is said that the ignorance of the audience is the actor's salvation. The ignorance of the public, who rush to see the spotted nigger, is the reason why he has not had his head broken of his impudent assumption."[85] Northall tries to refute the racial transformation of Barnum's exhibit by first describing it as a monstrosity, then by employing the clinical language of racial science. But the Negro Turning White, who, even according to Northall's own attempts to explain away the encroaching whiteness, cannot help his condition, finally dissolves Northall's facade of dispassionate scientific objectivity into a violent snit of ad hominem vituperation. The impudence that Northall imagines of the white Negro's "assumption" to whiteness attests to the threat the figure posed to white membership. Regardless of Barnum's obscure intentions, his exhibition of the white Negro at a time of national crisis was interpreted as a political attack on the presumed fixity of racial difference that propped up the institution of slavery.

The indeterminacy of the Negro Turning White enthralled. Audiences—white and near-white, poor and patrician—converged to witness the attempt at the erasure of racial characteristics, a compromise of sorts between white and black that inevitably satirizes racial science at the same time as it retrieves skin color as the primary marker of difference. At some point during the exhibition, though—when cork-black led to bronze or swarthy blended to cream—identities began to slip, become confused, uncertain. As the border between black and white started to dissolve, it began to beg the question: when does whiteness begin? The operation at work, the mechanism of the humbug was no longer the concern, but the question of color and hierarchy still loomed. With status unmoored, the exhibition left the near-white audience thwarted, unsatisfied in its quest for a definable whiteness.

As the exhibition of racial transformation stymied aspirations for whiteness, the confusion that resulted from observing a black body turned white opened the door to other possibilities. The white Negro stood as a reflection of what its near-white audience longed for as well as what they feared themselves to be. Yet, humbug or not, the transforming body suggested the opportunity for multiple constructed identities, the illusion of race—and, as a consequence, maybe class and gender as well—donable as clothes and makeup. For the hopeful citizen, the ability to shift membership willfully through conspicuous racial transformation could become a means to escape the indignities and the violence of exhibition and to manipulate the policing gaze. Early in *The Confidence-Man*, a novel of slippery identities, Herman Melville presents a long manifest of the diverse humanity that make up the passengers of the steamship *Fidèle*:

> Natives of all sorts, and foreigners; men of business and men of pleasure; parlour men and backwoodsmen; . . . Fine ladies in slippers, and moccasined squaws; Northern speculators and Eastern philosophers; English, Irish, German, Scotch, Danes; Santa Fé traders in striped blankets, and Broadway bucks in cravats of cloth and gold; fine-looking Kentucky boatmen, and Japanese-looking Mississippi cotton-planters; . . . slaves, black, mulatto, quadroon; modish young Spanish Creoles, and old-fashioned French Jews; Mormons and Papists; . . . hard-shell Baptists and clay-eaters; grinning negroes, and Sioux chiefs solemn as high-priests. In short, a piebald parliament, an Anarcharsis Cloots congress of all kinds of that multiform pilgrim species, man.[86]

Not unlike the crew of the *Pequod* in *Moby-Dick*, the *Fidèle*'s human cargo represents a microcosm of what Melville viewed as an amalgamated American society. Rendered piebald in a distinct allusion to white Negro exhibition, his passenger list comprises a mosaic of human difference: presumed-white, nonwhite, near-white, a population revolutionary in its lack of segregation and, like the audience of Barnum's transgressive Negro Turning White, audacious enough to sit in judgment upon the potential citizenship of others. In the long tradition of white Negro exhibitions, a near-white crowd such as the multitude of the *Fidèle* requires a jet-black performance to secure its citizenship and fears the snow-white display that would inhibit its aspirations. As a fetish of racial transformation, the white Negro necessarily haunts the first quarter of *The Confidence-Man*, posing the same political threat to its audience as Barnum's Negro Turning White.[87]

Melville is careful to prepare the deck of the *Fidèle* as an exhibition space for the unsuspecting piebald parliament. In the novel's opening scene, a wanted poster "offering a reward for the capture of a mysterious imposter" foreshadows the performance of the Confidence Man as a humbug spectacle that promises to work out and further complicate the fictions of identity. The crowd treats the poster as "a theatre-bill," which announces a contest of discernment, "a careful description" of the imposter challenging the audience to seek him out for prize money (3). Rather than a simple challenge to identify the outlaw in the crowd, the avatars of the Confidence Man present a racial performance that, in the manner of white Negro exhibitions, threatens the identity of those who view it. Manipulated by the aggrandized exhibit, the uneven relationship between the display and the audience reverses. Like Barnum's patrons, the piebald parliament stands ready to judge the humbug of white Negro performance in a contest for white membership, yet in spite of their yearnings, they do not distinguish themselves in contrast to the white Negro. Unassimilated, the diverse humanity of the passenger manifest have essentially become piebald, which retrieves the figure of the white Negro from freak show exile and normalizes it. Like Barnum's Leopard Children and their audience, Melville's piebald parliament is a population of uncertain status, pitched between whiteness and blackness. They serve as spectators who, like patrons before the humbugs of the American Museum, attempt to see through the various masks of the Confidence Man. In Melville's version of the operational aesthetic, the true nature of the exhibition—humbug or genuine, black or white—is impossible to determine.

As an early manifestation of the Confidence Man, "a grotesque negro cripple" works the crowd on the deck of the boat, shuffling and japing for pocket change, banging on his tambourine like an outcast from a minstrel show. Black Guinea, as he is identified, re-creates the theatrical contest between exhibit and audience that Barnum promoted in his white Negro exhibits. The crowd cheers on his antics, literally feeds him coins by tossing them into his open mouth, but two men loudly doubt his performance. A curmudgeon customshouse officer denounces him as "a sham, got up for financial purposes" (12). A panhandling "fellow limper," who competes for sympathy and money from the same crowd, declares Black Guinea "some white operator, betwisted and painted up for a decoy. He and his friends are all humbugs" (14). In response to the challenge, the crowd gapes at Black Guinea and tests the veracity of his display, finding themselves "sole judges in the case," who "could not resist the opportunity of acting the part: not because it is a human weakness to take pleasure in sitting in judgement upon one in a box, as surely this unfortunate negro now was, but that it strangely sharpens human perceptions" (12–13). Subject to the democratic activity of observation, of definition through visible markers of difference, the display of Black Guinea is a dangerous endeavor, as are all exhibitions. To emphasize the peril of racial performance, Melville compares the efforts of the piebald parliament to divine the true identity of Black Guinea to the "truly warning spectacle" of an Arkansas lynch mob (13).

The temptation is to imagine Black Guinea a white operator corked up, banging his tambourine, speaking in stilted minstrel dialect. Eric Lott, reckoning the collective response of Melville's readership, asserts that "we realize with a jolt that this is probably a blackface performance; the attentive reader recognizes another of the confidence man's disguises."[88] Like a member of the piebald parliament, such a reader—confident, so to speak, of the Confidence Man's genuine (white) appearance—falls prey to hubris. Although the performance of Black Guinea derives from blackface minstrelsy, it is a mistake to attribute any particular racial characteristics to the Confidence Man, whose identity neither the audience nor the reader ever truly uncovers. Marking the importance of this uncertainty, Carolyn Karcher argues, "Black Guinea, who may after all be only a white masquerading as a black, incarnates the Confidence-Man's joke on America: that the phantasm of race . . . may not exist except in the white mind. Even more subversively, Guinea's masquerade indicates that there is no way of ascertaining whether he is black or white."[89] Liberatory as that indeterminacy is, the piebald parliament seeks to pin down the essence of Black Guinea, to assert his exaggerated stereotypical blackness as it would qualify an oppositional whiteness. Neither black nor white, the Confidence Man relies on the confidence of the near-white audience in its ability to detect the markers of racial difference and its vain need to fix blackness to the body of Black Guinea to establish its white citizenship.

At first, the presence of Black Guinea appears to help constitute the whiteness of the piebald parliament. Melville compares the "shuffling" of Black Guinea into the crowd to "a half-frozen black sheep nudging itself a cozy berth in the heart of the white flock." This comparison momentarily maneuvers the formerly piebald parliament, a mass of diverse nationalities and skin colors, into unadulterated whiteness, yet the uncertainty his performance induces among the passengers confounds any comparison. If he is some white operator who can shift identity through the mere application of color, then whiteness, denaturalized by the performance, loses its stability. As with blackface theater and white Negro exhibition, the prospect of racial transformation fosters theories of skin color and its origin: in this case, the effects of climate. When "a purple-faced drover" asks him where he sleeps at night, Black Guinea responds, "On der floor of der good baker's oven, sar." The drover sees the opportunity to sport with Black Guinea's appearance and, as a result, unknowingly establishes his tenuous whiteness. "What baker, I should like to know," he asks, "bakes such black bread in his oven, alongside of his nice white roll, too?" (11). When Black Guinea answers by pointing to the sun, he undermines the drover's attempt to fix difference by raising the possibility of racial transformation: the sun has baked him, just as it can bake, and has baked, his piebald audience.

For the ensuing manifestation of the Confidence Man, Black Guinea reemerges on the deck of the *Fidèle* as a white man wearing a crepe widow's weed. The performance of "the man with the weed" intimates that other exhibition of racial transformation, the slow metamorphosis of Barnum's Negro Turning White by the virtue of a mysterious weed. Melville's allusion to Barnum's 1850 attraction illuminates the impact of skin transforming from black to white in the exhibition space, its troubling indeterminacy, its challenge to the arrogance of white supremacy. The piebald body, fluctuating and evasive before the museum crowd, dismantles the surety of racial science and erodes the barriers between black and white.

Barnum's Negro Turning White, a cousin of his bichromatic Leopard Child, embodies a world troubled by a segregation of color yet still safe from the potential disruption of a multiracial, multiethnic United States. At bottom, the piebald parliament reveals itself as an imposture and a contradiction: Melville declares the passengers piebald, split into categories of black and white, but he has presented as well a "multiformed" humankind with endless variation in appearance. By placing the image of a piebald humanity at the end of his passenger manifest, he demonstrates the absurdity of the black-white binary and the institutions it helps enforce. At a time when racial scientists dissect the African American body in order to establish and fix its fictive inferiority, Melville's Confidence Man, neither black nor white nor necessarily anything in between, frustrates the construction of racial difference through easily identifiable markers by using the revolutionary body of the white Negro against itself, rendering racial boundaries not only fluid but a humbug as well.

The Double Bind of the Albino

"L E S S   N I G G E R   A N D   M O R E   N I G G E R   A T   T H E   S A M E   T I M E"

But first, let me tell you about these other two strange creatures you see before you! Very strange indeed! Not only are they pygmies from the heart of deepest Africa, . . . they are "albinos," weird creatures in whom normal pigmentation does not exist! In fact, this is why we are able to bring them to you today. They were rejected by their fellow tribesmen because of this strange condition!

— Harry Lewiston's ballyhoo, as told to Jerry Holtman,
Freak Show Man, 1968

U nlike the chromatic fluidity of the piebald white Negro, the color of the albino African American is fixed and complete. Pale patches do not appear on dark skin. Black men do not turn white. While lacking the striking hybridity of the Leopard Child, the albino still manages to embody the binary of black and white, at the same time straddling yet defying racial categories. In a sense, this preternaturally white figure enacts the end result of racial transformation, representing an apparently thorough repudiation of dark skin. This manifestation of flawlessly white skin does not promise white citizenship, though. In the imagination of the audience and in the theories of the racial scientists, the ghost of blackness remains. Kinship with the piebald white Negro aside, the pale body of the albino African American converts through exhibition into an exotic ideal of whiteness, the necessary twin of an African blackness in its invented extremity. The spectacle of the albino African American suggests, and often demands for display, the spectacle of its dark opposite.

Prior to his shuffles and grimaces before Melville's piebald parliament,

Black Guinea has his bleached antithesis, a sham whiteness to match his sham blackness. The opening sentence of *The Confidence-Man* announces the arrival of "a man in cream-colours," whose peculiar paleness is no less an artifice than his other manifestations. "His cheek was fair," Melville writes of this opening act, "his chin downy, his hair flaxen." He wears a hat of "white fur . . . with a long fleecy nap" to further accentuate his pallid appearance (3). As the chapter ends, the piebald parliament directs its scrutiny toward this pale body as "his flaxen head drooped, his whole lamb-like figure relaxed, and . . . lay motionless, as some sugar snow in March . . . with its white placidity" (6). This vision of exaggerated snow-whiteness contrasts with the vision of exaggerated blackness to follow in Black Guinea. As much a racial performance as Black Guinea's minstrel spectacle, the display of the man in cream colors has deep roots in the exhibition of African Americans with albinism.

Melville frames this initial display of whiteness by the man in cream colors in theatrical terms that echo the freak show exhibition of the albino body, where the whiteness of the display and of the audience suffered challenges and redefinitions. At the moment this white figure performs his gestures, the crowd collects around the reward poster for the Confidence Man, reading it as "a play-bill" (3). Even though scholars have correctly identified Black Guinea as a reference to blackface theater performance, they have yet to acknowledge the whiteface performance in the opening chapter, thereby consecrating the white body as a more natural one: a presumed base whiteness upon which to layer darker shades.[1] Inextricably linked, the man in cream colors and Black Guinea are part of a distinct theatrical sequence, a purposeful movement from the extreme white of the albino to the equally extreme black of the stage Negro.

Since the audience on the *Fidèle*, as well as the readership of the novel, expects whiteness—even the unmitigated whiteness of the albino's complexion—neither suspects the possibility of contrivance in the figure of the man in cream colors, the probable presence of white makeup and flaxen wig. His anomalous unadulterated whiteness, though, still draws the attention of the crowd that forms his immediate audience. The "shrugged shoulders, titters, whispers, wonderings" of the crowd mark the white figure as, "in the extremest sense of the word, a stranger," separate from the diverse shadings of the piebald parliament and therefore worthy of its observation (3). Although his whiteness isolates him from the other passengers, his apparent disability—he is deaf and mute—solidifies his status as a freak, an extraordinary body. As we will see in more contemporary albino characters later in this chapter, hearing impairment, muteness, and even feeblemindedness have long been part of the mythology of albinism, a doubling of affliction intended to isolate the white figure.[2] Confronted by his "peculiar inarticulate moan, and a pathetic telegraphing of his fingers," members of the piebald parliament marvel at the silence of the pale figure (6). His whiteness is surprisingly reticent and resistant to the stubborn speculation of the crowd that surrounds him and, interestingly, a readership that presumes to detect and decipher the manifestations of the Confidence Man. By introducing the title character of *The Confidence-Man* in the terms of albino exhibition, Melville exploits the naturalized quality of whiteness and its impediment to scrutiny. As a result of his exaggerated pale complexion, the man in cream colors reduces the unsuspecting piebald parliament that views him to an insufficient near-whiteness and, in the process, dramatizes the absurdity of such racial constructions.

The Confidence Man's movement from whiteface to blackface echoes the intimate connection between albino display and minstrel performance and their equal reliance upon the binary of extreme blackness and extreme whiteness. In 1843, the blackface minstrel troupe the Harmoneon Family Singers, which would soon become the Boston Harmoneons, performed the first half of their concerts "with whitened faces and flaxen wigs," dubbing themselves the "Albino Minstrels" and the "Albino Family."[3] Dale Cockrell argues that this whiteface performance parodied the staid, morally uplifting concerts of the then-popular white Hutchinson Family Singers, the albino makeup representing a purity of rectitude that ran counter to the audience's expectation of blackness and its gleefully derogatory chaos and good-natured fun.[4] By associating the Hutchinson Family Singers with albino exhibition, the Harmoneon Family Singers rendered the act's moral decency unnatural, even freakish. In conjunction with the later blackface portion of the program, the original whiteface presentation of the Harmoneon Family Singers reproduced whiteness as a racial performance, an identity as fluid and applicable as greasepaint. Surviving playbills of the Harmoneons indicate maintenance of this split bill yet remove the white makeup, lose the references to albino exhibition, and hence absorb the parody of whiteness and its assumption of moral purity: from 1846 to 1851, bills advertise concerts by the Harmoneons "as Whites and Blacks," the first half performed without makeup as "Citizens," the second in blackface as "Ethiopians." Its satiric display of moral decency now in earnest, the albino whiteness of the Harmoneons transforms into a sober exhibition of white citizenship.

As evidence of the tenuous nature of racial difference, the exhibition of albino African Americans had a kinship with blackface minstrel performance and, at times, incorporated its staging. In 1844, as the faux-albino Harmoneon Family settled into the Boston Harmoneons, the Lowell Museum hosted a genuine white Negro exhibition, "unrivaled musical entertainments" by "The

FIG. 15. "The Four Snow-White Albino Boys," lithograph by Thayer and Company. Courtesy, American Antiquarian Society.

Four Snow-White Albino Boys, Born of Negro Parents"—two albino African American brothers partnered with two other albino African American brothers in a spectacle of melodic merrymaking and racial disorientation.[5] A lithograph used to advertise the concert shows the boys in a classic minstrel arrangement: the middle children playing fiddle and banjo, the end children, like the minstrel show's endmen, playing tambo and bones. As with the performance by the bogus "Albino Family" of the Harmoneon Family, these two sets of albino brothers offered a moral family entertainment. A broadside for the concert guarantees "the strictest attention to propriety and decorum, and that nothing that has the slightest tendency to immorality will be permitted." As with the Harmoneon Family performance, the pure "snow-white" skin of the albino betokens a minstrel performance scrubbed clean of blackface, the order of the white body displacing the contaminating chaos of the black.

The minstrel show staging of "The Four Snow-White Albino Boys" does not nullify their status as medical curiosities with the potential to expose the fragility of racial difference. Medical testimony dominates the advertisements for the concert as doctors endorse the authenticity of the white bodies, thereby further isolating the whiteness and limiting its production. Early in 1844, one set of brothers—Peter and Charles Manner, eight and ten years old, respectively—were exhibited at the Boston Museum sans tambo and bones. During the course of their exhibition, they submitted every day from nine in the morning to nine at night to examinations by members of the Boston medical community, as well as other museum patrons. The broadside for the later concert announces that the young performers "will be introduced to the audience" in order to "remove any doubts that may exist of the boys being what they are represented." The advertisement encourages further scientific scrutiny. "Medical gentlemen should visit them," it coaxes, "as they may never be favored with another opportunity of testing, to a like extent, the correctness of the assertions, the descriptions, or the theories, of those who have written largely and learnedly on the color of the different races of men, and the causes which tend to change it." As the act moved from the museum space to the minstrel stage, the draw of "The Four Snow-White Albino Boys" remained the whiteness of their skins and its potential impact on racial theory. The bodies of the four small albino boys provided living specimens of the obstacle to the efforts of racial scientists to demarcate and fix racial difference.

The exhibition of "The Four Snow-White Albino Boys," like that of other albino African Americans, relied on the polarities of racial difference: the spectacle of pure whiteness depended upon the audience's expectation of pure blackness. The same broadside advertising the boys attests that their "*skin* and *hair* are as white as snow" even though "they are of two Families *all of whom*, with these exceptions, are *Black as Jet*." In the exhibition of albino African Americans, the bodies of the seemingly normal parents were likewise displayed and rendered extraordinary for their contrary blackness. During the fall of 1860, on the eve of the Civil War, Barnum exhibited "Two Albino Girls," who, according to an American Museum playbill, were "white as the purest snow." The same poster bill establishes the father and mother as "perfectly black Africans." The advertisements and the exhibitions created between the parents and the children a purified opposition of jet-black and snow-white. These displays emphasized the inexplicable production of whiteness out of blackness, which, to an audience of near-white laborers and immigrants, allegorized a frustrated yearning for unqualified white membership. Seizing upon the already well-established fascination with the white Negro, Barnum and other museum entrepreneurs exploited this ambition for greater social status through pale complexions and instilled greater dread of its possible achievement. This figure of inherited whiteness invested the possibility of citizenship bestowed upon an African American child with the growing anxieties over the potential for passing eventually resulting from generations of miscegenation.

Eighteenth-century natural philosophers tended to view albinism and vitiligo as the same condition, yet as the nineteenth century progressed, the white body of the albino in the space of the natural history museum began to distinguish itself from the hybrid body of the assimilating Negro Turning White and from the piebald audience that viewed the body. Fixed, congenital, and complete at birth, the whiteness attributed to the albino did not permit the fantasy of social mobility or the hope of transformation for those exhibited; in this case, the body suffered an additional stigma, not of blackness removed but anomalous, even contaminating, whiteness layered on. Even stigmatized, the seeming purity of the whiteness still placed the status of white museum patrons in jeopardy by contrasting a more utopian hue to their now less-than-white pigmentation. As a result of this apparent defiance of the African body, the surveillance of the transgressive whiteness in the museum intensified out of a need to fence off the albino as ineffectually white.

THE ALBINO POLAR GOD

The European fascination with the albino African body began with the Portuguese explorations of the African coast, expeditions largely inspired by dual dreams of religious conversion and material gain. The economic motive of these early European explorations encouraged a rationalization for the acquisition of raw materials and the subjugation of the peoples who occupied this prized real estate. Dark skin distinguished the African, and, in the covetous eyes of the explorers, that darkness rendered the native alien. Yet in this heart of darkness, white bodies appear. In his seventeenth-century account of the Jesuits and their forays into geographical regions and encounters with darker-skinned peoples new to European eyes, Balthazar Tellez coined the term *albino* to name those natives with inexplicably white skin.[6] Abdul JanMohamed has observed that the useful presumption of racial difference led to theories based upon "the manichean allegory": a series of binary oppositions that transform superficial physiological differences into signs of moral and metaphysical inferiority.[7] Darker skin pigmentation quickly becomes black, as opposed to white; evil, as opposed to good; savage, as opposed to civilized; emotional, as opposed to rational; and so on. In this context, the spectacle of white skin on a "black" body initially confounds the efforts of the colonial project to establish racial difference by challenging the imagined binary of black and white.

Much as the fascination with white African bodies first arises from European colonial efforts to rationalize the often violent acquisition of materials and territories, it also derives from an impulse to transform the African, to change habits and encourage religious conversion, to colonize the "black" body with a semblance of whiteness. The result, in the eyes of the colonizer, is not a white body but, according to Homi Bhabha, "a reformed, recognizable Other, as a subject of a difference *that is almost the same, but not quite.*"[8] Bhabha's colonial mimic performs the manners of the colonizers, wears their clothes, appropriates their beliefs, and speaks their language with the proper accent. In spite of the coercion of the colonizer, Bhabha's mimic retains some, if minimal, agency. Along the coasts of Africa, the first European explorers came face to face with their chromatic doubles, African bodies seemingly already reformed to pure, near-European whiteness. As with the colonial mimic of manners, this chromatic ambivalence, its mimicry, its mockery of the white body, weakens the confidence of the colonizers by directing scrutiny to their own insufficient whiteness.

The albino African American, though, has no agency in the exhibition space, no control over the presentation or its reception. Unlike Bhabha's mimic, the white Negro makes no attempt to parrot or parody "white" manners. In the public spectacle of the albino, a challenge to whiteness bedevils the audience; nevertheless, the albino never strives to pass as white. Like Melville's man in cream colors, the albino African American body is mute. Others speak for the silent white body, give the ballyhoos, write the histories, testify to the scientific plausibility of whiteness where only blackness should exist. The mimicry, the mockery of the white Negro, generates not within the pigmentless bodies of the albino Africans but within the minds of the colonizers who need to see the blackness in the African body to establish their own whiteness and, consequently, their superiority. The body of the albino African defies the manichean allegory, the stark binary of racial difference necessary for the colonial project.

In *The Narrative of Arthur Gordon Pym of Nantucket*, Edgar Allan Poe offers a nightmare landscape for the colonial and commercial aspirations of his characters. The eponymous narrator stows away on a whaling brig and witnesses in the ship's mostly white crew the worst of human behavior–greed, murder, cannibalism. Both black and white members of the crew take part in a violent mutiny, slaughtering those loyal to the captain, casting others overboard to drown. The survivors of the attack eventually quell the mutiny only to suffer through a hurricane that sets the ship adrift with a quickly exhausted supply of food. Faced with imminent starvation, even the narrator participates in the murder of a shipmate and helps to eat him. At the end of this doomed voyage, after his rescue by a commercial vessel, Pym encounters an exaggerated embodiment of the colonial manichean allegory: pure "black" bodies of natives that lead eventually to the pure "white" body of the tale's final ghostly image.

Poe frames the latter half of his narrative as a colonial encounter between Americans who seek profit and South Seas islanders whom the Americans consider childlike and superstitious. The schooner *Jane Guy*, Pym's savior, sails "for any cargo which might come most readily to hand," exploring islands primarily to exploit resources and find new markets.[9] The land they discover, an island named Tsalal, confirms their colonial expectations of darkness, ignorance, and savagery. In the spirit of this sortie of commercial imperialism, Poe reduces the natives, even the island itself, to the nadir of the manichean allegory: a profound, unrelieved, pervasive blackness. Reminiscent of the language of white Negro exhibition, the inhabitants are more than dark—they are "a jet black" (189). To complete the extremity of their difference from the crew of the *Jane Guy*, even the islanders' teeth are black (238).

As representations of irredeemable blackness, the Tsalalian islanders express a pronounced aversion to all things white. Pym observes that "we could not get them to approach several very harmless objects—such as the schooner's sails, an egg, an open book, or a pan of flour" (192). This seemingly natural antipathy between black and white articulates popular segregationist philosophy, an understanding that the two colors, the two races, cannot coexist. In 1830, to promote the cause of sending slaves back to Africa, Henry Clay expressed his belief that black and white have no affinity for each other. "By the very condition of the relation which exists between us," he wrote, "we are enemies of each other."[10] The islanders' repulsion from innocuous white objects, though, seems not to extend to the whiteness of the crew's skin. Through Pym's biased perspective, the islanders "appeared to recoil" from the supposed whiteness of the crew, yet in the rest of the narrative, the crew's complexions, obviously sullied and darkened over the months of exposure to the sun and sea, never observably daunt the islanders (190). The natives do not avoid the crew the way they apparently do other, more distinctly white objects; neither do they show any reluctance to trade or communicate.

The extent of the islanders' blackness raises the possibility, even likelihood, of exaggeration. As a consequence, this potential humbug leads to a suspicion that Pym embellishes as well the whiteness of his crewmates.

Teresa Goddu tentatively argues that Pym's strict adherence to the binary opposition of black and white, the stark blackness and its accompanying whiteness, "could actually work to expose the artifice of race."[11] As white Negro exhibition fabricates a purity of whiteness and blackness, so does Pym's biased account of the islanders. Dana Nelson goes as far as to pronounce Pym's racial classifications "arbitrary": even if we can suspend our disbelief enough to "grant Pym the 'blackness' of the Tsalalians, we know that 'whites' are not *white*."[12] In other words, exposure to the sun after months at sea precludes any possibility of pale skin surviving on the body of the narrator and his fellow Americans. It is the colonialist bias of Pym's mind that imagines dark skin as jet-black. Growing from a need for polarized markings of racial difference, the blackness of the island of Tsalal and its inhabitants allows Pym and his shipmates to define themselves as white and, through the conversion of allegory, as civilized, moral, and superior to the islanders in technology and intellect.

As he constructs his vision of blackness and whiteness, Pym clings to a belief in a contrast in morality between the islanders and the explorers, an indefensible assumption given the atrocities committed by the mostly white crew of his first ship—the mutiny, the murder, the eating of human flesh. Even as the narrative shifts to the island of Tsalal, Poe takes pains to undermine the presumed moral superiority of whiteness. The captain and the crew of the *Jane Guy* attempt to exploit the islanders commercially through conscious deceit and guile. The "jet-black" islanders prove not amenable, though: they revolt and kill the crew, an action no more violent than the earlier transgressions by the Americans. After the islanders bury alive the delegation from the *Jane Guy* and subsequently kill the remaining crew members who guard the ship, Pym and his shipmate Dirk Peters find themselves the lone survivors. In the wake of the islander victory over the colonizers, Pym hypocritically denounces them as "among the most barbarous, subtle, and bloodthirsty wretches that ever contaminated the globe" (205). The savagery and duplicity of Pym and his companions dismantle the allegory between immorality and blackness. In his haste to construct racial difference upon setting foot on Tsalal, Pym forgives and forgets prior and current sins.

Now firmly lodged in Pym's mind, the extreme blackness of the islanders works to extend white membership to those who might otherwise not be considered. Peters, Pym's companion throughout two-thirds of the tale, begins the narrative as "a half-breed Indian" and a "hybrid," essentially a racial freak with features as exaggerated as the Tsalalian islanders (43, 102).[13] In the shadow of the mutiny, Pym describes his distorted features: "Peters himself was one of the most purely ferocious-looking men I ever beheld. He was short in stature—not more than four feet eight inches high—but his limbs were of the most Herculean mold. His hands, especially, were so enormously thick and broad as hardly to retain a human shape. His arms, as well as legs, were bowed in the most singular manner, . . . His head was equally deformed, being of immense size, with an indentation on the crown (like that on the head of most Negroes), and entirely bald" (84–85). In this first impression, Pym reduces Peters to an extraordinary body, distorted, grotesque, apelike in the racial difference assigned to him, a description that portends the grotesqueness of the islanders. In spite of these inauspicious beginnings as a racial freak, Peters achieves a conditional and temporary white membership at the expense of the islanders by the end of the tale. The islanders' "barbarous" behavior and "jet-black" color, as they fit Pym's need for physical contrast, repositions Peters's racial membership in Pym's mind. Pym declares Peters and himself "the only living white men upon the island" (212). In Peters, Poe offers an object lesson in the tenuous conditional nature of white membership, a citizenship that can be bestowed and withheld with equal ease. Upon his return to American shores, Peters loses his temporary whiteness and regains the mantle of "half-breed" (43). Denied white membership once more, Peters suffers a legal status so diminished that Pym cannot even use his testimony to support his incredible claims.

This new fluid racial status affects Pym as well. Pym imagines the crew of the *Jane Guy* as the absolute embodiment of whiteness, but his encounter with a more purified and intimidating figure of perfect whiteness at the end of his narration exposes his less-white body to transformation from white to black. Escaping the black island of Tsalal, Pym, his companion, and a cowering, captive islander find themselves in a harrowing white landscape, when "there arose in our pathway a shrouded human figure, very far larger in its proportions than any dweller among men. And the hue of the skin of the figure was of the perfect whiteness of snow" (239). This final white image has proven problematic for Poe scholars, who have tended to view the figure positively, an object of desire rather than one of fear: the Great White Mother ready to embrace Pym back to the Great White Womb; the White Goddess of Arthurian and Celtic legend; the political sanctuary of a purified white country.[14] Instead of a soothing reassurance of white supremacy, the display of a refined, utopian whiteness frustrates European expectations of indigenous blackness. Without a dark aboriginal complexion, the binary of black and white threatens to invert and challenge the formerly white body with moral and intellectual inferiority. As Bhabha writes of colonial reformation of manners, the mimicry of whiteness is "at once resemblance and menace," inducing a proprietal fear of appropriation.[15] Like the exhibition of white Negroes, the idealized, albinotic figure that looms before the travelers in this *oceana incognita* provides the antithesis to the "jet-black" islanders, a nightmare of whiteness that imperils the previously white Pym and Peters with the chaos of uncertain racial status.

WHITE UTOPIA

For his fantasy of an unsullied Antarctic whiteness, Poe drew upon the radical theories of John Cleves Symmes, who proposed a hollow earth open at the poles.[16] The final nightmare of whiteness, the towering shrouded figure at the end of Pym's narrative, has its menacing counterpart in a fictional travel narrative long attributed to Symmes. In 1820, an anonymous author published *Symzonia, a Voyage of Discovery, by Captain Adam Seaborn*, a first-person fictional account of the captain's journey into the interior of the earth by sailing through a large hole at the South Pole.[17] Instead of Poe's devious jet-black islanders, Seaborn discovers a whiteness in the aboriginal population that challenges not only the quality of pigmentation of the captain and his crew but the assumption of Anglo-Saxon moral and intellectual superiority as well.

The desire to venture beyond the poles is rooted in colonial avarice and market capitalism. Symmes himself tried to sell the dream of an expedition to the Antarctic to young men hungry for the material benefits of exploration. In 1818, he issued a circular seeking "one hundred brave companions" to help him discover the inner world, "a warm and rich land, stocked with thrifty vegetables and animals, if not men."[18] From the beginning of his fictional narrative, Captain Seaborn establishes the commercial motives behind his "voyage of discovery . . . to a new and untried world."[19] He imagines his excursion to the center of Earth will "open the way to new fields for the enterprise of my fellow-citizens, supply new sources of wealth, fresh food for curiosity, and additional means of enjoyment; objects of vast importance, since the resources of the known world have been exhausted by research, its wealth monopolized, its wonders of curiosity explored, its every thing investigated and understood" (13). Seaborn yokes together the yearning for scientific knowledge and the lust for wealth, a connection made in other narratives of exploration. The impulse that drives him "to discover a region where seals could be taken as fast as they could be stripped and cured" is not that far removed from that which rues the missed opportunity to acquire the "skin and skeleton" of a polar bear–like beast "for the examination of the learned, and the benefit of Scudder's Museum," a predecessor of Barnum's American Museum (30, 70).

Seaborn has imperial ambitions, a patriotic intention to establish trade, acquire lands, and exploit the natives. Shortly before the opening at the South Pole, he comes upon an uncharted continent, of which he takes "possession . . . in the name and on behalf of the people of the United States of America" (73). In the tradition of the early European explorers, he performs the traditional ritual of possession, posting a legal document, a "manifesto" that declares his ownership of "land never before . . . seen by any civilized people, having been occupied for the full term of eighteen days by citizens of the said United States, whether it should prove to be in possession of any other people or not, provided they were not *Christians*" (73–74). Seaborn operates at this moment a legal apparatus intended to validate colonial acquisition. The proclamation relegates those inhabitants who may not understand the mechanism to the status of ignorant "savages." Since, from the perspective of the explorer, they cannot comprehend the process of acquisition, the native peoples do not appropriately possess the land. Columbus and others who followed him in the early European incursions in the Americas performed rites of eviction, what Stephen Greenblatt calls a "compact anthology of legitimating gestures," that metaphorically canceled the presence of non-European peoples.[20]

When Seaborn states his intention "to open an intercourse with a new world and with an unknown people," he expects to come upon darker-skinned peoples he will identify as black in order to prepare them for their exploitation through commercial trade (96). Instead, he encounters on the inside of this hollow Earth inhabitants whose extremely fair complexion mimics and ultimately mocks Anglo-Saxon aspirations to whiteness. He observes in his meeting with their leader that "the sootiest African does not differ more from us in darkness of skin and grossness of features, than this man did from me in fairness of complexion and delicacy of form" (108). The would-be colonizer finds himself in an exhibition of bodily difference, his skin placed next to one of those he calls an "Internal." As a result of this comparison, he declares ominously, "I am not a white man" (110).

In this moment of bodily comparison, a spectacle that inverts the expected outcome of colonial contact, Seaborn's complexion transforms, grows "dark and hideous" in his own eyes (107). As a consequence, and in adherence to the colonial construction of polarized racial difference, the expected dark skin of native peoples transforms in the narrative into superior whiteness. The conversion of European whiteness to blackness accumulates the trappings of the manichean allegory, rendering the captain bestial in the eyes of his inquisitors. The new darkness of Seaborn's skin, he observes, affects the scrutinizing Internal, who, it appears to him, is "in doubt whether it was a mortal or a goblin that stood before him" (107).

The theory of skin color and its origin proposed by Seaborn's narrative follows the model of Samuel Stanhope Smith: poor physical and moral conditions darken the complexion. The natives at first mistake Seaborn for a

Belzubian, a neighboring rebellious people whose name is a telling conflation of Beelzebub and Nubian, the fallen angel and the African. The Belzu-
bians were once fair like the Internals, yet the "influence of their gross
appetites and of the climate," the chief Internal explains, "causes them to
lose their fairness of complexion and beauty of form and feature. They
become dark coloured, ill favoured, and mis-shapen men, not much superior
to the brute creation" (132). Like Smith and Benjamin Rush, the white
natives associate dark pigmentation with disease and declare Anglo-Saxons "a
contaminated race, descendants of a degenerated people" (150). Under this
theory, racial difference is not fixed; whiteness comes from clean living. The
Internals, though, opt not to reform Seaborn's black body: as Rush suggested
upon viewing Henry Moss's body, they choose to quarantine their shores and
exile blackness in an attempt to keep the white body pure.

Embedded in Seaborn's narrative is a criticism of colonialism and its
abuses. The captain desires to colonize the Symzonians, as he has named
them, to establish commercial trade unilaterally beneficial to his interests. In
the course of his tour of the land and its abundant resources, he surreptitiously
pockets a handful of pearls, an act for which Seaborn shows no remorse. When
he speaks again with the leader of the Internals, Seaborn tries to impress him
with an account of the superior character of his people only to condemn them
in the telling. He praises his country's commercial endeavors and boasts of
their military prowess. The vainglorious catalog of American achievement
marks Seaborn as a pariah in the eyes of the Internal. Fearing contamination
from his corrupt dark body, the leader banishes Seaborn and his kind with an
admonition directed toward "an inveterate selfishness" of Anglo-Saxons. The
rebuke carefully elaborates upon this fatal flaw in national character—listing
the greed, the deceit, the rapacity, the misplaced pride—until it finally
addresses and condemns the sins of commercial imperialism. The white leader
chastises Seaborn and his people for "the practice of injustice, violence, and
oppression, even to such a degree as to maintain bodies of armed men, trained
to destroy their fellow-creatures." This propensity for violent oppression, he
notes, results in the institution of slavery, human bondage "for the purpose of
procuring the means of gratifying [American] sensual appetites." The leader
continues his diatribe against commercial imperialism by explaining that
Seaborn and his degenerate kind "were inordinately addicted to traffic, and
sent out [their] people to the extreme parts of the external world to procure, by
exchange, or fraud, or malice, things pernicious to the health and morals of
those who receive them, and that this practice was carried so far as to be supported with armed ships" (196). This censure of colonialism condemns the
enterprise that brought Seaborn to the interior world and casts as evil the rituals he performed to take possession of "Seaborn's Land."

In spite of his instruction, Seaborn does not experience an epiphany of cultural relativism on the white island. He does not see the error of his ways. As the acme of beauty, the white body is still atop the chromatic hierarchy; the black body still represents physical and moral degradation. Since the sermon from the leader of the Internals fails to convert him, Seaborn leaves Symzonia to continue his pursuit of wealth through the ecological exploitation of the Antarctic waters and his patriotic acquisition of lands for his country. He packs his ship with "one hundred thousand seal skins" (216). He performs "the important ceremony of taking possession of the islands for the United States, by hoisting the stripes and stars upon them in the usual manner" (218). This lack of virtue and self-knowledge does not go unpunished. Seaborn's addiction to "traffic" results in his own exploitation at the hands of unscrupulous lawyers and merchants. His agents at port, who would sell his acquired booty, run off with his profits. The end of his narrative leaves him a defeated and destitute man, dreaming yet of new excursions to the utopia of perfect whiteness.

Through the exhibition of an aboriginal white body, the author of *Symzonia* aims a challenge at the moral and physical supremacy of Anglo-Saxon whiteness and the philosophies that support the exertion of that supremacy—namely the greed and selfishness of capitalism. This morality tale offers some insight into the flights of fancy inspired by the exhibition of white African American bodies. Magnified by the illusion of missing blackness, the whiteness of the African American body with albinism stimulates dreams of colonial acquisition and nightmares of resistance. The moment of encounter with an aboriginal white body returns the gaze of the audience to its own imperfectly white bodies. Although the white bodies of the Symzonians are immune to Seaborn's imperialist efforts, the white bodies in the narratives of white Negro exhibitions offer a more tranquil fantasy of whiteness extended into new territories, an exotic whiteness that reassured the audience of the aesthetic supremacy of the complexion. Seaborn's narrative presages later transformations and permutations of white Negro exhibition. The anomalous beauty of white children appearing in black families eventually extrapolates into white utopias produced in the heart of Africa or Asia Minor, imaginary white enclaves already colonizing the dark continents, outposts ready-made for assimilation into the European colonial project.

THE BEAUTY OF WHITE MOORS

These surprising curiosities were brought to the notice of Mr. Barnum in Amsterdam, Holland, where they were creating a great furore about a year ago, since which time he has been in treaty with them to induce them to visit America, and give the people of this country an opportunity to see the greatest wonder of the world, a family of White Negroes, or Moors.

—Broadside, American Museum, 1860

In 1860, Barnum presented to his museum audience a Danish family by the name of Lucasie as "The Albino Family," a group he advertised as "White Negroes, or Moors" brought from Madagascar by way of Amsterdam. As proclaimed in hyperbolic, bold capital letters in their 1860 *History of Rudolph Lucasie*, both the father, Rudolph, and the mother, Antiana, were born "of PERFECTLY BLACK PARENTS, of African descent." The account offers for comparison Antiana's siblings, "three brothers and four sisters, all of whom are black; have curly black hair, or wool, thick lips, flat noses, and all the other peculiarities of the African race, indicating beyond the possibility of doubt, their pure African descent." The story of Rudolph Lucasie reads like an aborted captivity narrative: the white body kidnapped by superstitious natives. According to the tale, the crew of a Portuguese merchant ship witness on the shores of Madagascar "a number of negroes in the act of carrying off an Albino of about five years old."[21] The narrative neither stipulates nor hypothesizes the intent of these natives, but the conceit of colonial contact between white European merchants and darker-skinned savages mines a rich store of imperial anxieties and fears about so-called natural antipathies between black and white. Through the abduction of the young Lucasie's white body, the colonial merchants and those white American Museum patrons who witnessed "The Albino Family" and read their account could imagine the threat to their own white bodies posed by Africans and African Americans: the violence of incorporation and corruption, whether through conversion, miscegenation, or cannibalism.

The appearance of "The Albino Family" on the freak platforms of Barnum's American Museum not only caused the patrons to marvel at the white skin of black Africans, it required the audience to determine the Africanness of the Lucasies' other features—the extraordinary white shocks of long kinky hair, the apparent broadness of the noses—in order to establish the veracity of Barnum's claims. To further convince or confuse a skeptical audience, an "Account of Albinos, Leucœthiopes, or White Negroes" serves as an appendix to the *History of Rudolph Lucasie* and places the exhibition of "The Albino Family" in the context of racial science, where the whiteness of the white Negro exhibit requires the search for other indicators of difference. These other racial markers complicated the hopes of the near-white audience for admission into white membership through skin color alone. For those patrons who understood the true operation of the exhibit, Barnum's

F I G . 1 6 . Rudolf Lucasie and family, photograph by Mathew Brady. By permission of The Meserve Collection, National Portrait Gallery, Smithsonian Institution.

display and ballyhoo of "The Albino Family" rendered this vain search for physiognomic difference absurd: the Lucasies are Danish, not African. The white complexion endowed by albinism afforded a slippage that allowed for the whitest of Barnum's exhibits to pass as "black."

The history and genealogy of "The Albino Family" changed following the American Civil War. With emancipation, the anxieties generated by the black body in slavery were now moot, yet the threat of a purified whiteness still remained. In the 1869 version of his *History*, Rudolph Lucasie is no longer the product of African parents but the potential victim of native superstition and their antipathy for white skin. Removed from this edition of the narrative are references to any African heritage. The young Rudolph is now orphaned, "born of European parents at Iranque, on the east coast of the island of Madagascar."[22] Antiana likewise sheds her African ancestry. Curiously, though, the *History* maintains its extensive "Account of the Albinos, Leucœthiopes, or White Negroes," a vestigial reminder of their former condition, a narrative of racial science and white African bodies now divorced from the actual exhibition.

Once a synonym for white Negro, the term *white Moor* underwent a shift in definition after the Civil War, parting whiteness from the African body and exalting it. Although Barnum advertised "The Albino Family" as albino white Negroes and white Moors, the *History of Rudolph Lucasie* makes a slight, yet important, distinction between the two designations: "Generally, the Albinos are incapable of procreation: the White Moors not so."[23] The Lucasie children served as proof of distinguishing fertility. The white Moor, under the new rubric, signified a distinct people of superlative whiteness racially separate from black Africans—a dream of Anglo-Saxon purity. The promotion of albino Europeans as exotic manifestations of exemplary whiteness derived in part from the exhibition of women called "Circassian Beauties," white slaves supposedly rescued from Turkish harems, indigenous white bodies delivered from the clutches of dark bodies.

Circassia, the mythical white utopia, carried some importance for racial theorists. In the eighteenth century, Johann Friedrich Blumenbach, prominent German anatomist and father of craniometry, found in one human skull obtained from the region of the Caucasus Mountains characteristics he had idealized as particularly German. By the virtue of this one Teutonically perfect skull, he located the home of human origin in the central Asian mountains and coined the term *Caucasian* to forge the direct link between the German people and the tribe of the Circassians.[24] Throughout the nineteenth century, the romance of a perfectly white eastern European people continued to reinforce the supremacy of whiteness. In *Moby-Dick*, Ishmael embraces the aesthetics of pure whiteness to illustrate the preeminence of

Manila rope for sailing. "Hemp," he explains, "is a dusky, dark fellow, a sort of Indian; but Manilla is as a golden-haired Circassian to behold."[25] The advent of the Crimean War spurred further images of exotic eastern European whiteness and tales of the dark-skinned Turk abducting perfectly white Russian Eves and enslaving them in the pasha's harems. The resulting literature of abduction fed upon the erotic lure of sexually available white women threatened by dark Turkish male bodies that somehow mirrored domestic American fears of miscegenation.[26]

In 1856, Barnum sent his agent, John Greenwood, to acquire Circassian Beauties from the slave markets of Turkey. Faced with the ethical dilemma of actually buying a white woman for display, Barnum proposed a kind of conversion of contract. In a letter to Massachusetts legislator David K. Hitchcock, he speculates that he will have to purchase the Circassians, "then give them their freedom and hire them, making contract through U.S. Consul."[27] Under this conversion of contract from slave to wage worker, the Circassian Beauty moved from the private exhibition space of the harem to the public space of the American Museum, technically free but in some ways equally confined and under the scrutiny of leering male patrons. Barnum was cagey about the success of this particular venture, but he includes in his 1866 autobiography a curious account of Greenwood passing as a Turkish slave trader in order to gain access to the slave market, where "he saw a large number of Circassian girls and women, some of them the most beautiful beings he had ever seen."[28]

Shortly after he had published this account of white slavery, Barnum offered his first Circassian Beauty—Zalumma Agra, "the Star of the East." Although Barnum presented her as a Circassian saved from the auction block, she was most likely an exhibit concocted to satisfy the public imagination of perfect, yet foreign, whiteness—a woman rumored to have hailed from Hoboken, New Jersey.[29] Zalumma Agra, and the many exhibits her appearance inspired—Zoe Meleke, Zana Zenobia, Zuleika the Circassian Sultana, Zumigo the Egyptian, Millie Zulu, Miss Fatima—underwent exotic modifications, attired in peasant dresses with scalloped hems and fringes or embroidered with flowers. Later, to capitalize further on the erotic lure of the harem slave, the costuming shrank to scanty boudoir displays with short pants and form-fitting bodices. The crowning feature of each Circassian exhibit was the hair, washed in beer, teased out to kink and frizz into what was essentially a large Afro.[30] The ethnic kink supplied a visible bridge between the normalized, exalted whiteness that conferred citizenship and the distinguishing marks of racial difference that facilitated slavery. The emancipated white body still bore the evidence of its dark-bodied captivity.

The racial uncertainty of the albino found a home in the vogue for exotic

FIG. 17. Zalumma Agra, the Star of the East. From author's collection.

FIG. 18. Zoe Meleke, photograph by Charles Eisenmann. From author's collection.

whiteness. The lesson of Barnum's "Albino Family" and their transformation from white Africans to unsullied white Moors prompted the singular racial makeup of these new exhibitions of unmitigated whiteness. In the 1870s, "Miss Ettie Reynolds, the Madagascar Lady," exhibited in Barnum's Traveling World's Fair. *The History of Miss Ettie Reynolds* carefully composes the boundaries of her white allure: "She is of the purest type of blonde known in the world, and belongs only to a race of people called 'fair,' and found only upon the Island of Madagascar. Some have called the people belonging to this very beautiful race, white Moors. But no one has yet, I think, been able to give positively, their origin, or tell why these persons (of all the races that have inhabited this globe) have been blessed of heaven with such distinctive, peculiar and attractive marks of alluring beauty." The Barnum ballyhoo returns to Africa to reclaim a source of pure whiteness. To maintain this fantasy of origins, the history must refuse her status as an albino, which would reduce her to a medical condition and deny her Circassian-like beauty. In a section entitled "What She Is Not," the history proclaims that "she is positively not an Albino; for while possessing some of the prominent characteristics of the Albino . . . she belongs to a time honored and ancient race, while the Albino does not belong to a race at all, but to a class." She retains the symptoms of albinism–the pamphlet acknowledges her "long, beautiful white hair," her eyes "pink in color and constantly rolling about from side to side in an extremely restless manner," her near-blindness in daylight—but through a disavowal of the disorder, she can be presented as "very rare and much more of a curiosity than any Albino possibly could be."[31] This appeal for a new white ethnicity indicates a diminished public interest in the albino body as a sport of nature and at least a suspicion on the part of the museum entrepreneur that pure racial whiteness was more marketable.

As the nineteenth century came to a close, even the body of the albino African American suffered from the flagging interest of museum and circus crowds. The loss of cultural currency in the aftermath of emancipation, as well as the surfeit of white African bodies in the anxious decade prior to the Civil War, directed the scrutiny of the public away from the spectacular white body of the albino and toward the more prevalent and equally transgressive white body of the mulatto. Some of the remaining exhibits held to the prescribed mythology of Barnum's "Albino Family." Fearing whiteness, black natives targeted albino infants for sacrifice before their rescue by Europeans. Unzie, "the Australian aboriginal beauty," was advertised this way in the 1890s.[32] In an attempt to revive audience curiosity for the white African body, the owners of some circuses and dime museums dyed the hair of albino African American women and dressed them in oriental costume to pass as Circassian Beauties.[33]

FIG. 19. "Miss Ettie Reynolds, the Madagascar Lady," photograph by Charles Eisenmann. By permission of The Harvard Theatre
Collection, The Houghton Library.

Efforts to reclaim the beauty of the albino and, to a limited extent, restage
the exhibition of white Moors have recently rematerialized. In a 1998 photo
spread in *Life*, fashion photographer Rick Guidotti presents glamorous
images of young men and women with albinism in an attempt, according to
the magazine's blurb, to open "our eyes to [its] beauty."[34] Entitled "Redefining Beauty," the photo spread of well-dressed and well-coifed young people is
a part of a larger project Guidotti is pursuing with the backing of the
National Organization for Albinism and Hypopigmentation (NOAH) to give
albinism a human face. He has plans to photograph people with albinism
from around the world—a world congress of whiteness, so to speak. The sub-
textual fantasy of this project, though, is to erase racial difference through the
display of white bodies. In the history given on the project's website, the idea

FIG. 20. Albino Circassian Beauty. By permission of the Becker Collection, Syracuse University Library, Department of Special Collections.

germinates from a chance encounter with a teenage girl at a bus stop. "She was stunning," Guidotti explains. "Her physical characteristics crossed all cultural and racial boundaries, yet never had been included in any beauty standard."[35] Guidotti's assertion is a bit shortsighted, though. The beauty of albinos has a long history. He has merely recast the slipperiness in the bodies of fashion models.

WHITE NEGRO, WHITE WHALE

> THE ALBINO FAMILY, from Madagascar, consisting of Husband, Wife, and Child! . . . The LIVING WHITE WHALE, from the coast of Labrador, is an extraordinary specimen of the great monsters of the deep.
>
> —Broadside for Barnum's Aquarial Gardens, Boston, 1860

In all of the history of albino exhibitions and the attempts by showmen and writers of travel narratives to bestow utopian perfection and beauty on the whiteness of albino skin, such whiteness still disturbed those who viewed the nineteenth-century exhibition of albino African Americans. Members of the American Philosophical Society associated the complexion of albino African Americans with death. In his *Notes on the State of Virginia*, Jefferson labeled the whiteness of his albinos "cadaverous" to defuse the revolutionary potential of racial transformation.[36] To distinguish the complexion of those African Americans transformed by vitiligo, philosophers who yearned for the skin of slaves to shed its difference described the color of albinos as "dead white."[37] Extolling the transforming skin of Henry Moss, Benjamin Rush called the whiteness of albinos "morbid" in comparison.[38] Along with this restrictive association with death, which deprives the African American with albinism of kinship to the living, the albino has suffered as well from a cultural affiliation with the satanic that persists to the present day. In 1819, Ludwig Gall, a German traveler, recounts the exhibition of "a white Negro" in Peale's museum. Demonstrating the ambivalence of the albino figure, Gall counters a presentation of utopian white beauty with a description of the eyes that deprives the exhibit of humanity. "His teeth," he writes, "are of the most beautiful ivory, his skin as delicate and white as the petals of a lily, his long, silky hair as white as alabaster. But the dull, fire-red eyes are repulsive—eyes that distinguish this person from others." He then reflects on the portrait of "The Beautiful Albiness," whom he mistakes for the mother of the boy he has just seen: "I cannot recall having seen such a beautiful woman in real life. . . . But what is beauty without a soul, for which you search the fire-red eyes in vain?"[39] Another bit of superstitious apocrypha from albino lore, the red eyes render the beauty's whiteness unnatural, demonic. Under the withering gaze of museum patrons and racial scientists, the albino African American time and again suffers estrangement from humankind.[40]

With the appearance of white aboriginal bodies in narratives of travel and exploration as well as the exhibitions in museum spaces, the pull between the beauty of pure whiteness and the unnaturalness consequently attributed to it unmasks the anxiety produced by a colonial utopian fantasy and the apparent achievement of that fantasy in the body of another. By gazing at the albino's purified whiteness, the not-as-white observers—especially the near-white shipmates and museum patrons—grow disoriented as scrutiny returns to their own insufficient complexion. In the reformed body of Homi Bhabha's mimic of European manners, "the excess or slippage produced by the ambivalence of mimicry (almost the same, *but not quite*) does not merely 'rupture' the discourse, but becomes transformed into an uncertainty which fixes the colonial subject as a 'partial' presence."[41] The figure of the white

Negro produces similar slippage. In the body of the dark-skinned native reformed to apparent whiteness, the color becomes a persistent uncertainty as it disengages from the identity it has grown to signify and floats free. As a result, the excessive whiteness of the albino's accidental mimicry breeds the contradictory impulses to laud and to denigrate. The long-desired purity of color fosters acrimony toward that purity. In order to protect the boundaries of white membership against this incursion, the excessive whiteness sanctions the albino's dehumanization by reducing the white body to the status of freak and demon.

> Whiteness, alone, is mute, meaningless, unfathomable, pointless, frozen, veiled, curtained, dreaded, senseless, implacable. Or so our writers seem to say.
>
> —Toni Morrison, *Playing in the Dark*, 1993

Long before the man in cream colors entered the stage of the *Fidèle* in *The Confidence-Man*, Melville employed the figure of the aboriginal albino in his narratives of travel and exploration. In *Mardi, and a Voyage Thither*, his South Seas follow-up to *Typee* and *Omoo*, Melville documents the slippage between utopian ideal and its unnerving achievement in the body of another. The narrator of his tale confronts the mystifying whiteness of a beautiful native woman named Yillah. "Did I dream?" he first asks, before he follows the question with an inventory of utopian beauty that anticipates the display of the Circassian women in Barnum's American Museum: "A snow-white skin: blue firmament eyes: Golconda locks." The seemingly indigenous whiteness of Yillah and her appearance among the islanders mesmerizes him as he struggles to rationalize the so-called purity of her complexion: "I could not link this mysterious creature with the tawny strangers. She seemed of another race." To explain her white skin, Yillah offers a tale of racial transformation in which the waters of a magical island have "washed white her olive skin." Rejecting her fairy-tale ballyhoo, the narrator settles the mystery by declaring her an "Albino," yet after she disappears among the islands of Mardi, he learns through another islander tale her true European origin. This knowledge deepens his ardor, as if the revelation has relieved him of any trepidation toward an alien white body. "Oh, Yillah!" he cries, "too late, too late have I learned what thou art!"[42] The white body out of context disorients the narrator as he seeks to account for the aberration: virginal whiteness among darker islander bodies. Once the mystery of the pale complexion is solved, the narrator pines for the whiteness now properly returned to the confines of the European body but lost to the islands and the islanders. The narrative of Yillah's white body maneuvers from a tale of colonial desire for a reformed dark body to a threat of miscegenation leveled against white European womanhood.

Melville continues to survey the ambivalence of the aboriginal albino in the epidermis of another white object of colonial and commercial desire, the whale Moby Dick. As with other efforts to codify nature and define racial difference, Ishmael's attempt to circumscribe the "savage" world in the body of the whale meets with a profound, implacable whiteness, which stymies his aspirations. Confronted with whiteness where he expects blackness, he strives like the early racial scientists to find the seat of color, to submit the dark flesh of other whales to the anatomical knife and lay open the bodies for narrative display. In his dissertation on "The Whiteness of the Whale," Ishmael pursues the permutations of the color, its associations and connotations, in an effort to fix its meaning. Instead, he uncovers its ambivalence, its allure and horror, as his gloss on whiteness unveils contradictory allegorical connections to beauty, purity, decay, and death. He contemplates the psychological and spiritual effect the white body has on its audience, a relationship that recalls the exhibition of the white Negro before the apprehensive near-white patrons of Barnum's museum. Far from a docile body, though, the chromatic double in this narrative sheds any vestige of utopian benevolence and physically threatens the piebald parliament that would pursue and commodify it.

When Melville muses upon the body of the whale, he is mining an extensive catalog of popular images that already associates the white whale with white Negro exhibition. In "Mocha Dick," an earlier tale of a final, fatally successful encounter with a white whale, which likely influenced the composition of *Moby-Dick*, Jeremiah N. Reynolds places the whale hunt in the context of commercial enterprise, rendering the whalemen heroes who "swell the fund of national wealth" through "unparalleled industry and daring enterprise." In this world of commodity and conquest, the whale's preternatural white skin surfaces, compelling a quest for the color's origin. For the white body of a black whale, Reynolds finds a counterpart in the exhibition space of the natural history museum. "From the effect of age," he writes, "or more probably from a freak of nature, as exhibited in the case of the Ethiopian Albino, a singular consequence had resulted—*he was white as wool!*"[43]

By invoking the exhibition of the Ethiopian Albino, Reynolds marks the white whale as akin to the racial display, tapping into the uncertainty, the apprehension, and the fear the albino African American instilled in the near-white onlooker. The narrative of the pursuit, the vainglorious lust for perfect whiteness, draws upon the tropes of white Negro exhibition. Like the presence of young Rudolph Lucasie among the African natives, the white whale fills one harpooner with "superstitious dread." To racialize further his display and to establish his whiteness as extraordinary, the whale appears among "the black shapes of the rampant herd, tossing and plunging, like a legion of maddened demons." In the final gesture toward albino exhibition, the Yankee-white Nantucket crew of the whale ship that heedlessly hunts Mocha Dick registers darker against the white skin of the whale. Mocha Dick turns flukes on his pursuers and destroys a whale boat as "the dusky forms of the struggling crew" cling to the wreckage.[44] The exhibited body of the white whale, like that of the white Negro, threatens physically the near-white bodies of those who view and desire him, a parable of white Negro exhibition and its political challenge to an audience consisting of immigrants and the working poor.

In *Moby-Dick*, Melville likewise racializes the common sperm whale by emphasizing its dark color, calling it "black," "jet-black," and, most telling, "Ethiopian."[45] Moby Dick, in manichaean contrast to the jet-blackness of other sperm whales, has a "peculiar snow-white brow" and a "snow-white hump" (201). This contrast, extreme whiteness produced out of extreme blackness, recalls the vocabulary of white Negro exhibition and its origin in colonial contact. Even D. H. Lawrence, in his seminal collection *Studies in Classic American Literature*, intuited the albino display in the white surface of the whale, the mimic, the mocker that reflects Lawrence's own whiteness. Echoing the cant of imperialism, Lawrence anoints Moby Dick as "the deepest blood-being of the white race, . . . our deepest blood-nature. . . . We want to hunt him down. To subject him to our will. And in this maniacal conscious hunt of ourselves we get dark races and pale to help us, red, yellow, and black, east and west, Quaker and fire-worshipper, we get them all to help us in this ghastly maniacal hunt which is our doom and our suicide."[46] To Lawrence, the pursuit of whiteness is a colonial impulse that leads to the subjection of all races and spawns from a need to possess and control whiteness as a commodity, an act necessarily irrational and self-destructive if we consider the results of Ahab's monomania. The presence of whiteness outside of the Anglo-Saxon body stirs a desire to quell the mimic and reaffirm ownership of the color and its implied power.

In the chapter "The Whiteness of the Whale," Melville dissects the colonial allegory of whiteness, revealing its contradictory aesthetics and its hypocritical claims to moral superiority.[47] In the genesis of his thesis, Ishmael first posits the ideology of a normalized whiteness, which gives "the white man ideal mastership over every dusky tribe," only to undermine it with the presence of the white whale and, consequently, the white Negro. The effect of the albino on the audience troubles his speculations. "What is it that in the Albino man so peculiarly repels and often shocks the eye," he asks. "The

Albino is as well made as other men—has no substantive deformity—and yet this mere aspect of all-pervading whiteness makes him more strangely hideous than the ugliest abortion" (191). In spite of his efforts to reduce the albino by rendering its production a still-birth, Ishmael figures the surface of the white whale/white Negro as an inexplicable and irreducible complication in the construction of whiteness. Before the spectacle of the whale's albino skin, Ishmael fashions the nonwhiteness of a crew "chiefly made up of mongrel renegades, and castaways, and cannibals" (162). Ishmael's display of pure-white bodies eventually limits white membership to essentially one member—the "albino whale"—with all others, including the crew of the *Pequod*, all Europeans, and even himself, demoted to the position of savage. Ishmael resists the inclination of travel narrative writers to homogenize the crew into a white fraternity and opts instead to place himself among an "Anarcharsis Clootz deputation from all the isles of the sea, and the ends of the earth," a fraternity that acknowledges the inequality inherent in commercial imperialism, in which, he muses, "the native American liberally provides the brains, the rest of the world as generously supplying the muscles" (270). As a member of this subjugated piebald parliament, Ishmael's declaration can only be interpreted as ironic, a sad admission of guilt for the destructive efforts to expand the empire of whiteness.

Like Jefferson and the racial scientists who followed, Ishmael greets the mystery of racial difference and the subsequent disruption of aboriginal whiteness with the desire to submit dark skin to the anatomical knife. To fix the essence of the whale, Ishmael takes on the task of dissection, figuratively slicing through layers of blubber to uncover some essence of the whale, to define and segregate it from its fellow creatures. In the end, the nature of skin eludes Ishmael the anatomist. He cannot discern its demarcation from the blubber. As he admires the captured corpse of the whale, its body peeled to expose the blubber, bones, and viscera, he uncovers the arbitrary nature of atomizing the body and naming of its parts. The question he asks—"what and where is the skin of the whale?"—articulates the difficulty and sometime absurdity of definition (305). To begin his inventory of parts, Ishmael assesses the blubber as the skin, yet he must still address its covering, "the skin of the skin," as he calls it (306). "True," he admits, "from the unmarred dead body of the whale, you may scrape off with your hand an infinitely thin, transparent substance, somewhat resembling the thinnest shreds of isinglass" (305). This clear epidermis, empty of coloring matter, is too insignificant for his consideration because it does not match the grandeur of his subject matter, a supposition that betrays the capriciousness of scientific classification and the prejudice that informs its scrutiny. His efforts echo the racial scientist's quest for the seat of color as it seems to retreat into the flesh; his dissecting imagination hesitates at the borders of the transparent scarf skin, refusing to grant it significance or even a name. Ishmael's reluctance to distinguish and itemize parts challenges the confidence of the racial scientist to measure and delineate difference. In *Melville's Anatomies*, Samuel Otter testifies to Melville's attempt to disarticulate the efforts of the racial scientists, especially the skull-gathering Samuel George Morton, to fix racial difference in the body and to assess moral inferiority through corporeal allegory. "Part of Melville's project in the whale-anatomy chapters of *Moby-Dick*," he argues, "is to unhinge these catachreses in which characteristics are confounded with character, head with person, and sight with touch."[48] The skin of the albino whale poses a danger to scientific certainty. Ishmael ultimately discards "the skin of skins" because its clarity, its lack of identifying color, prevents him from assigning meaning.

Ahab affirms the danger of whiteness unmoored from the Anglo-Saxon body, signifier and signified separated, the unnatural and fraudulent relationship between the color and moral superiority now open to scrutiny. "All visible objects," he explains to Stubb and Starbuck, "are but as a pasteboard mask." The white whale embodies "the unreasoning mask" that thwarts any effort to master the world through the comprehension and classification of visible phenomena. Even though Ahab suspects that "there is naught beyond," the mask now located in the white surface of the whale, he is vexed by a need to assign its essence. That fraudulence of surfaces detected, the artifice of whiteness unveiled in the body of a racialized albino whale, Ahab can only react with violent frustration: he attempts to "strike through the mask" by striking through the "inscrutable" white skin of the whale to which he can no longer attach meaning (164).

In her reading of Ahab's monomania, Toni Morrison proposes that "the white whale is the ideology of race," a destructive, "savage" force that traumatizes "the racist and the victim" with "severe fragmentation of the self." Ahab's (and consequently Ishmael's) pursuit evidences an effort to attack "the very concept of whiteness as an inhuman idea," a pilgrimage that will leave the pursuer "very alone, very desperate, and very doomed." Although she may be overstating and oversimplifying the symbolism of a whale that always seems to elude reduction, she is correct that "Melville is not exploring white people, but whiteness idealized," and whiteness idealized first in the complicated and transgressive figure of the white Negro.[49] Like the white whale, the figure of the albino African American embodies and confounds the ideology of race. The ambivalence of the white body's mimicry, its excess and slippage, fosters its pursuit by racial scientists, philosophers, and near-white museum patrons who need to fix difference to the skin. This single-minded effort, though, promotes its own demise.

PINKY'S DOUBLE BIND

The white whale haunts American culture, its whiteness sounding from time to time as a metaphor for racial duplicity. Whiteness where blackness should reside. Blackness dissolving into whiteness. And every time the whale sounds, the figure of the white Negro lurks just beneath, a palimpsest of racial transgression. Even recently, critics and scholars have called upon the great white whale to describe the incommensurability of two edifices of contemporary popular culture: the black whiteness of Elvis Presley and the white blackness of Michael Jackson. To counter accusations of Elvis's appropriation of African American music forms, Timothy Parrish declares the singer in the title of his essay "Our White Whale." Only Moby Dick can match Elvis in "his richness, his ambiguity, his mysterious meaning."[50] Comprehension of Elvis, white whale/white Negro, illuminates the miscegenated nature of popular American musical culture. To those who see this miscegenation as a threat to the segregated purity of African American culture, the white whale is the apocalyptic leviathan that portends the death of that culture. Michael Jackson, another performer who courts mystery, draws fire for his popular appeal, his racially indeterminate music, and his pale appearance. Social critic and jazz aficionado Stanley Crouch condemns the gargantuan presence of Jackson in American and world musical culture, clout that he believes is aesthetically undeserved and ultimately dangerous. In a fit of pique, he has sarcastically labeled the self-declared King of Pop "a now bone-colored big, big fish in the media . . . a whale of a success."[51] These employments of the white whale signify the double bind of the albino, neither black enough nor white enough, stuck in a violent cultural crossfire in a world that still demands the security of binary opposition.

As a representation of the power and menace of whiteness, the great white whale of American literature makes a ready target for those who would challenge the seeming omnipotence of its cultural currency. Take on the white whale and you take on the leviathan, you take on the established hierarchy of American literature, you take on the arrogance of people who call themselves white. In Chester Himes's *Blind Man with a Pistol*, the last and arguably most apocalyptic of the Coffin Ed Johnson and Grave Digger Jones detective novels, an African American street-corner preacher attempts to exhort the passing crowd to revolution by invoking the image of the white whale. He shouts to an uncaring crowd, "TONIGHT'S THE NIGHT! We launch our whale boats. Iss the night of the great white whale. You dig me, baby? . . . You want a good house? You got to whale! You want a good car? You got to whale! You want a good job? You got to whale! . . . Whale! Whale! WHALE, WHITEY! WE GOT THE POWER! WE IS BLACK! WE IS

PURE!"[52] Himes appropriates the image of the white whale/white Negro and transforms the great (white) icon of the (white) American literary canon into a target of derision and revolutionary anger; he attacks the aesthetic supremacy of the great white body. He puns on the word *whale*, investing each repetition with greater violence. "You got to whale": you've got to wail, cry out. "You got to whale": you've got to seek out and attack the white body. "You got to whale": you've got to strike out, thrash. "Whale, Whitey": go ahead and cry out. The street preacher's call to arms not only contends with and inverts the white whale as a symbol of white literary authority, it addresses the body of the white Negro, an exhibition of concentrated, purified whiteness authored by white showmen and scientists. Ambiguity and indecipherability of whiteness is not the concern here; it is its very accretion of meanings, its aesthetic dominance, the imposition of its evil.

Himes does not limit his reprobation of whiteness to the albino whale. Throughout his detective novels, he anathematizes and demonizes the color. Robert E. Skinner has located in these works "an underlying belief that whiteness is inextricably bound up with evil."[53] Coffin Ed Johnson and Grave Digger Jones move through a Harlem landscape twisted and corrupted by the effects of de facto segregation, a Dantean hell of politicos, preachers, drug dealers, pimps, whores, and small-time grifters who feed off the misery imposed by a society that enforces racial difference based on the polar opposition of black and white. Unlike the proposals of the racial scientists, the Coffin Ed Johnson and Grave Digger Jones detective novels present the antipathy between black and white as an unnatural formation that results from systematic oppression by the dominant white culture. In his essay "The Dilemma of the Negro Novelist in the U.S.A.," Himes explains, "Of course, Negroes hate white people, far more actively than white people hate Negroes. . . . Can you abuse, enslave, persecute, segregate and generally oppress a people, and have them love you for it?"[54] Although he clearly states the source of black animosity toward whites, Himes leaves unspoken the origins of white antipathy toward those with dark skins. His depiction of Harlem as occupied territory, a community suffering from prolonged economic dispossession, insinuates an inheritance from European colonialism and the slave trade. Robert Crooks argues that Harlem in Himes's fiction serves as a kind of "urban frontier," a borderland between black and white, criminal and law abiding, savage and civilized, the origin of which Crooks properly locates in the manichean allegory of the colonial project. Far from merely acknowledging this borderland, Crooks further contends, Himes "explores its meaning as an ideological concept marking the exercise of white hegemony."[55] The conflict between white and black is most prevalent in this contested no man's land where identities slip and definitions ultimately fail. As part of a purposeful resistance to this structure of colonial power, Himes assails the notion of light skin color as a sign of racial superiority.

Even in the process of upending the aesthetic and moral dominion of whiteness, Himes maintains an opposition of black and white. In his novels, he associates whiteness with the malicious and depraved exploitation of the African American community. Reminiscent of early narratives of albino exhibitions, the color of his white villains is manifested as peculiarly, even unnaturally pale. In *Cotton Comes to Harlem*, the southern colonel who bankrolls a movement to bring the "American nigra" back to the South is "too mother-raping white."[56] The "hophead" henchman who nearly kills Grave Digger in *The Heat's On* has "a dead-white death's face with colorless lips," a cadaverousness that recalls descriptions of albinos by early racial scientists.[57] Himes places white skin under the anatomical spotlight and reduces it to a morbid, freakish display.

African Americans with albinism and vitiligo likewise people his Harlem. In contrast to the overt evil of white-skinned characters, the minor African American characters with white or whitening skin evidence a relatively neutral morality. Spotty, the short-order cook, is "a big black man with white skin" who "looked like an overgrown Dalmatian." Obviously suffering from the stigma of whiteness, he has "made a peace with life" and, with his albino wife, serves affordable food in his own diner.[58] More than a minor misfortune, whiteness can mark an African American character who permits, even through indifference, the corruption to poison further the community. The passive Daddy Haddy allows his tobacco shop to function as a drop for numbers runners and a connection for junkies. His whiteness manifests as "leprous-looking splotches," an inversion of Benjamin Rush's theory that blackness results from a degenerative disease of the skin (85). Under this new fabrication of racial difference, black becomes the foundational color; the white of vitiligo appears as an incursion onto black skin, a symbol of the evil infecting the Harlem body politic.

With his aspirations to invalidate the presumed supremacy of white skin and disrupt the binary opposition of black and white, it is little surprise that Himes draws upon the trope of white Negro exhibition to display the hybrid body of the albino African American before an often confused not-as-white public. In *The Heat's On*, Himes explores a culture's obsession with the body and the secrets the skin seems to hide. Aside from the aforementioned evil white henchmen and piebald shop owners, the author offers other corporeal exhibitions, the body transformed or mutilated. Dark skin is faded white with creams and preparations. Pale skin is blackened with ink. Bodies are violated, shot, blown up. Throats are slit, necks broken. This mistreatment of black bodies, a spectacle of skin color and violence, summons the memory of the anatomical knife that sliced through the flesh to satisfy the curious. Acting on a hunch that a missing heroin shipment may hide somewhere beneath the skin, Sister Heavenly, faith healer and drug dealer, eviscerates a dog in a Harlem hotel room. Ankle-deep in "blood and filth," she parodies the dissections of nineteenth-century anatomists and, like Ishmael's efforts to understand the inner workings of the white whale, comes up empty (135).

Into this world of bodily violation, Himes introduces as his central character Pinky, an albino African American giant scarred from heroin addiction and years of abuse as a boxer. Unlike the demonized paleness of Himes's other white characters, Pinky's white body does not signify congenital moral wickedness. He is cursed with whiteness, an increasingly repugnant color in the novel. His destructive behavior—his drug abuse, his propensity for violence—derives from the double bind of his reduced status: he is segregated from white society as an African American and exiled from the African American community by virtue of the bodily transgression of his whiteness.

For his initial display of Pinky's white body, Himes retains the trope of the white audience challenged by its potential double. Pinky's "milk-white" skin fosters chromatic confusion among this initial group of spectators (5). In the novel's opening scene, the two uniformed police officers investigate a fire alarm Pinky has pulled and encounter the seeming paradox of his body. For a moment, Pinky's white skin allows him to be ignored by the authorities who, by accepting the naturalness of the color, grant him white membership, but his temporarily "normal" body shifts quickly to the spectacular. One of the police officers "saw the white face with the Negroid features and white hair. He had never seen an albino Negro." Confronted with the white Negro body, this representative of white authority is astonished, then settles his disorientation by thinking that "there was something damn funny about him to be a white man" (9). Like the racial scientists of the nineteenth century, the officer contends with the potential revolutionary nature of the white African American body by seeking markers of difference other than skin color.

Pinky is doubly stigmatized, denied membership in both the white and African American communities. The stigma of his whiteness exposes his body to violence at the same time as it registers the effects of the assault. In the opening scene, as firefighters attempt to subdue the giant by "whaling at him with the hickory handles" of their axes, he begins to develop "deep purple welts on [his] sensitive white skin" (12). In a parody of the racial transformations performed in nineteenth-century white Negro exhibitions, Pinky grows dark and bestial from the violence, the bruises effacing his whiteness until he looks like "some unknown monster" (65). In this first scene of exhibition, Himes offers the absurdity of white authority figures pummeling white skin to secure the blackness of an African American, a perverse Just-So story of skin color that suitably assigns its violent origin to the colonial need for racial difference. At the same time as it gives evidence of violence visited upon the black body, the communicative sensitivity of Pinky's white skin underscores the silencing of those with darker skin. Kid Blackie, Pinky's former trainer, explains to Coffin Ed that Pinky's boxing career was cut short by his tendency to show the results of violence. "Bruises too easily," he says. "Touch him with a feather and he'll turn black-and-blue. In the ring it always looks like he's getting beat to death when he ain't even hurt" (120). White skin displays all abuse it suffers. Black skin experiences pain but is silenced, still saddled in part with the insensitivity racial scientists attributed to black skin as a rationalization for slavery. Here the albino African American body emerges as a point of resistance, a chronicle of violence that issues from the blind adherence to definitions of racial difference.

The threat of violence inherent in exhibition demands other manipulations, other transgressions and slippages to escape the blows directed at displayed white skin. Pinky's bodily defiance to the easy binary opposition of black and white hints at other possible racial transformations—in this case, the blurring of boundaries through the marking of skin with cork and paint. Later, to elude detection and the violence directed at his white body, Pinky dyes his skin to minstrel-like exaggeration.[59] By blacking up, Pinky passes as African American before the scrutiny of white authorities, who now can categorize him according to recognizable prosaic and exotic black stereotypes "as either an African politician, a Cuban revolutionary, a Brazilian snake charmer, or just a plain ordinary Harlem shoeshine boy" (81). In spite of Pinky's telling height and demeanor, not even the sharp-eyed Coffin Ed can initially identify him. He only sees a "black giant, so black that he looked dark purple in the bright light, the blackest man [he] had ever seen" (169). As the embodiment of the colonial manichean allegory, Pinky serves as the whitest of the novel's characters as well as the blackest, yet his ability to slip between extremities, to don identities in a world that attributes essence to superficial markers of difference, affords him resistance to the allegory that would otherwise destroy him.

THE AMBASSADOR FROM MARS

> Whether the process of mixture is presented as fatal or redemptive, we must be prepared to give up the illusion that cultural and ethnic purity has ever existed.
>
> —Paul Gilroy, *Against Race*, 2000

As the call of the street preacher to whale whitey in *Blind Man with a Pistol* indicates, white skin is a focus for black anger and frustration. Unable to direct appropriate violence toward white people and their institutions in this landscape of unequal justice, African Americans must satisfy themselves by abusing the exposed white skin of albinos. This abuse of a surrogate white body, though, surfaces as natural and inevitable under the colonial myths of the manichean allegory. In nineteenth-century ballyhoos, the natives in Madagascar chased the young albino Rudolph Lucasie, driven by some sense of a natural antipathy between black and white, while white European explorers saved Unzie the Australian Aboriginal Beauty from native sacrifice. In *The Heat's On*, these tales from albino exhibition provide the motive for the detective story's central mystery: who killed Gus, the man Pinky called his father? As he finally confesses to the murder, Pinky reveals his reasons: Gus refused to take him to Africa because Gus "said I was too white. He said all them black Africans wouldn't like colored people white as I is, and they'd kill me" (173). Disowned, alienated, threatened with death by African hands, Pinky in essence commits patricide, an ultimately self-destructive act that cuts his communal ties to blackness. The ambiguity of Pinky's pale body may allow him to slip between racial oppositions, but the manichean allegory is still in place to determine and enforce the extremes. In the end, it is this severe maintenance of the borders of black and white that dooms Pinky.

The benefits of inverting the racial hierarchy are limited. As emotionally and politically satisfying as it may be to turn the tables on white supremacy, the glorification of blackness that comes at the expense of a violated whiteness does little more than further entrench the racial binary. Still essentialized and antagonistic, white and black merely switch positions of presumed dominance and subordination. In *Against Race*, Paul Gilroy warns of the danger posed by all political communities that base membership upon imagined biological difference, even those solidarities constructed as a response to white supremacy. Raciology inhibits the utopian ideals of "human mutuality and cosmopolitan democracy" for which Gilroy yearns. But asking communities to abandon racial pride and the social ties that have developed over centuries of slavery, racial science, and Jim Crow laws risks accusations of treason. "For many racialized populations," Gilroy admits, "'race' and the hard-won oppositional identities it supports are not to be lightly or prematurely given up." For those who would dare to betray the community and expose themselves to the "ultraconservative forms of political culture and social regulation" that arise in the defense of racial integrity, danger lurks.[60] To disengage from the idea of racial difference, to challenge the so-called natural antipathy between black and white, submits those who transgress boundaries to exile, violence, and even death.

In its apparent rebellion, the albino body registers these dangers. In his novel *Sent for You Yesterday*, John Edgar Wideman presents Brother Tate, an albino African American on daily exhibition in the destitute world of Home-wood. The segregated neighborhood—"a world apart"—suffers under the imposition of racial difference polarized into black and white.[61] Mute as Melville's man in cream colors, Brother serves not as an opposition to black-ness but as an unsettling refutation of the manichean allegory. A child at the time, Doot, the narrator, remembers Brother's "strange color, or lack of color, that made him less nigger and more nigger at the same time," in terms of a double bind that both withholds and overdetermines his racial identity (17). His fluxing presence impugns the presumptions of racial science and causes those who view him—in this case, an audience of other African Americans—to consider in the possible colorlessness of Brother's albino body a world detached from the dual fictions of whiteness and blackness.

Brother's history reads like a nineteenth-century freak show ballyhoo. Abandoned on a doorstep as a baby, he has no parents, no genealogy, no point of origin. His lack of family tree fires the imagination of those who view him. They invent sources for his pale skin, all the while rejecting the idea that his transgressive body can generate from the blackness of the commu-nity. His best friend, Carl French, wonders "where Brother came from. Won-ders if there are two ghosts someplace, white like Brother, who are his mother and father" (28). Like those earlier exhibitions, the spectacle of Brother's albino body also spurs contemplation upon the genesis of color. Carl's father, John French, a frustrated artist reduced by discrimination to wallpapering, considers where color initially came from. "What was the right color of the sky?" he wonders. "The first color? Did it start out one color before it began going through all those changes?" (62). The quest for the first color of the sky is an absurd pursuit and inspires his next absurd inquiry—the nature of skin color. In a violent daydream, John French theorizes on the albino body: "Carl's friend Brother was like somebody had used a chisel on him. A chisel then sandpaper to get down to the whiteness underneath the nigger. Because the little bugger looked chipped clean. Down to the first color or no color at all. Skin like waxed paper you could see through" (62–63). John French encapsulates more than two centuries of conjecture upon the white African American body. According to this inheritance, the original color of humanity is white. The eradication of black skin that philosophers, racial scientists, and museum entrepreneurs have long sought can be achieved through the proper application of violence.

Brother's contingent color challenges the folks of Homewood to contend with his place in their community. They initially target the whiteness they see in his skin and punish him with epithets. To diminish his status, they describe him as "lumpy, colorless piedough," "a cream-of-wheat mother-fucker," and "ugly as a frog's tummy" (36, 94, 190). His complete lack of blackness, the marker that would give him racial membership, compels his audience to exile him, to cast out his whiteness. Snubbed and slurred, Brother becomes a foreign object, an otherworldly manifestation in their eyes. They label him a ghost, "some kind of hoodoo or trickster" (133). Brother's fall from racialized humanity mirrors the fate of white Negro exhibitions in the early twentieth century, where indeterminacy no longer drew crowds. More outlandish narratives were needed to sell the spectacle. In the 1930s, the Ringling Brothers and Barnum and Bailey Circus exhibited Eko and Iko, dreadlocked brothers with albinism, proclaimed the "Ambassadors from Mars" yet also rumored to be Willie and George, African Americans from Louisiana.[62] Reduced to an extraterrestrial cipher, the albino display still poses utopian possibilities, even in this diminished circumstance. A fable of Martian dignitaries crash-landing in the Mojave Desert makes it possible to imagine a place elsewhere beyond color, a planet uncolonized by divisions of black and white.

As a ghost and a fellow ambassador from Mars, Brother also points to an escape from racial difference. All attempts to attribute whiteness fail to settle permanently in Brother's body. Other characters continue to recite John French's dilemma between color and no color. Doot tries to explain the optical effect of Brother's skin: "If you looked closely, Brother had no color. He was lighter than anybody else, so white was a word some people used to picture him, but he wasn't white, not white like snow or paper, not even white like the people who called us black." Brother's body allows the neighborhood an opportunity to scrutinize and dismantle the polarity of black and white by rendering its assumption of chromatic purity absurd and untenable. Unfortunately, they never meet the challenge. The most disturbing aspect of Brother's skin, Doot realizes, is that "there was no color to stop my eyes, no color which said there's a black man or white man in front of you" (15). Brother's transparency, his lack of the most telling identifying marker of race, momentarily removes him from the opposition of black and white, enabling his surface to flicker briefly into that realm beyond the binary. In the confusion of Brother's color is hope for the demolition of the firewall that segregates black and white, but years of living under the authority of the manichean allegory will not allow observers to relinquish Brother's potential whiteness.

Brother's quiet insurrection against the binary of racial difference corporealizes in the body of Junebug, the albino child he has with the equally enigmatic Samantha. Subject as well to the imagined extremities of racial difference, Samantha serves as the antithesis to Brother, his chromatic opposite under the imposed binary of black and white. As Doot makes clear, she is "a coal-black beautiful woman," a "beautiful African queen. . . . Ninety-nine

FIG. 21. "Eko & Iko." From author's collection.

and forty-four one hundred percent black. Ivory Snow black" (17, 123). Immediately repelled by Brother's whiteness, she gradually recognizes the contradiction of this "white Blackman." Even though the incongruity of his body continues to oscillate in her mind, the cultural expectation of the antipathy that blackness should have for white skin gives her pause: "He was white, a color she hated, yet nigger, blackest, purest kind stamped in his features" (131). The disorientation that Brother's body creates presents the opportunity for Samantha to reject the prejudice that infects her life.

Samantha has struggled to remove herself from the institutions that have nursed the aesthetic dominance of whiteness and endorsed the tenets of racial science; nevertheless, her retreat from whiteness into blackness does not disengage her from the binary. Her education, "three years at Fisk," yielded only lessons in chromatic and moral inferiority, a time "when she had believed crossing *t*'s and dotting *i*'s had something to do with becoming a human being and blackness was the chaos you had to whip into shape in order to be a person who counted." Under the institutions of racial science, blackness is a disorder to sanction, a disease to treat. Among the courses "prescribed to cure blackness," she singles out "Biology I," a locus of scientific and racist authority (135). She received her education in the wake of the early-twentieth-century passion for eugenics, the belief that proper attention to heredity could improve the human stock. The cure for blackness promoted by the textbook is not merely metaphorical. State governments used the science of eugenics to support their laws against miscegenation.[63]

Samantha counters this attack on blackness by practicing her own inverted eugenics. She "slept only with the blackest men" in order to produce "pure African children" (134). In her rebellion against the authority of whiteness, she still embraces the manichean allegory that produces and maintains its power. She is intent to protect, to preserve blackness in the imagined "Ark" of her house, which resembles the hold of a middle-passage slave ship, her "perfect black" children sleeping "spoon fashion" on the crowded floor. "When this old Ark docks," she muses, "be whole lotta strong niggers clamber out on the Promised Land" (132). As she hungers for a promised land and an unsullied black race, Samantha expresses a wish to counteract the evils of the black and white binary, the demonizing of dark skin, yet by exalting blackness, she further encourages its antipathy to whiteness.

At first, Samantha imagines Brother's complexion as a threat to her imagined blackness, a possible contaminant to its purity and her efforts to produce a rarefied black skin in her children. In bed with him, she "was afraid his white sweat would stain her body. . . . As soon as he left she inspected every square inch of her glossy black skin." She combats her antipathy to Brother's perceived whiteness by returning to the racism of the biology textbooks. The dry prose of scientific authority teaches her that "melanin is the brown to black pigment that colors the skin, hair, and eyes" (134). However, she transforms this knowledge and its authority by reinventing its narrative through her own mother wit, what "she had known all along" before the anatomical scrutiny of science textbooks "had peeled back her skin" (136). She envisions "the wanderlust of blackness [that] sent melanocytes migrating through the mysterious terrain of the body. Blackness seeking a resting place, a home in the transparent baby" (135). The embryonic original color is no longer white but no color at all.

By reimagining the science textbook and taking control of its narrative of blackness, Samantha tries to appropriate whiteness, not to mimic it, not to absorb its accompanying assumptions of moral superiority, but to disengage it from the destructive binary of black and white. The residual antipathies of the manichean allegory, the hatred of black for white, presents an obstacle to this attempt at disengagement. When the albino Junebug is born, his brothers and sisters recoil. "Learned I could hate my children," Samantha realizes. "Learned I could hate the white one cause the black ones hated him. . . . If I loved Junebug I had to hate the other when they did those terrible things to him" (138). Influenced by the polarization of racial difference, Samantha sets up a false dilemma between love of blackness and love of whiteness. Her choice to oppose whiteness, even in the body of her own child, leads to Junebug's horrific death by fire, presumably at the hands of her other children.

Gilroy warns that until "the color of skin has no more significance than the color of eyes, there will be war. Hostilities are being conducted on both sides of the color line."[64] The road to this utopia, though, holds nothing but hazards. The result of Samantha's attempt to disengage from the manichean allegory is silence, madness, and death. Junebug's immolation eventually drives Samantha to a mental institution. In her cell, Samantha retreats to the authoritarian language of the science textbook until she "could see the words, could say them after all these years—tyrosinase, melanocytes. Remember how they marched across the pages of the medical textbook but she couldn't recall the names of her babies" (137). Samantha finally embraces Junebug and imagines herself in her madness to be "inside June's white skin" (141). Hopelessly distraught over the death of Junebug, Brother goes down to the tracks, lays his head on the rails, and meets his death. Resistance destroys, yet these moments of destruction, inherited and recalled through the imagination of Doot, the witness to the display of Brother's troubling albino body, survive in their retelling, exhibited again in a continuing effort to dismantle the tyranny of racial difference.

Like the piebald body of Barnum's Leopard Child, the figure of the albino
African American confounds the efforts of science to assign definitive and
discrete racial categories. This defiance, though, isolates the albino African
American and creates out of the stunning whiteness a tragic figure. The
white skin exiles the albino African American from the African American
community, and, in turn, the expectation of blackness taints the hueless surface, providing an obstacle to white citizenship. Even more than the predica-
ment of the black body in the midst of transformation, the hybridity of the
albino African American endangers the exotic white body. The tragic double
bind the figure suffers, the trope of a completely and ideally white African
American body, offers an opportunity in its exhibition to question critically
all adherence to racial paradigms. As a product of the spectacle, the violence
directed toward the albino African American condemns blind devotion to
racial difference and the binary of black and white, rendering it at once
untenable and potentially apocalyptic.

"A Better Skin"

S C E N E S   F R O M   T H E
E X H I B I T I O N

et us return to the scene of exhibition.
Enter the public house, the lecture room, the museum hall, where we
shall judge and compare complexions. Consider again Henry Moss,
James the White Negro, the Leopard Boy, the Negro Turning White.

As we have seen from these spectacles, the philosophers who plumb the mysteries of race stage the spectacle, take notes, and rig the comparisons. Vain in its ability to read the signs of racial difference, the audience of near-white rubes and ruffians is nearly always duped by the display, haplessly unaware of its own insufficient whiteness yet still embracing the color as its property.

Revisit once more the scene of exhibition in the late summer of 1791. Charles Willson Peale—museum owner, artist, natural philosopher— displays his *Portrait of James the White Negro* before a tavern crowd and recognizes in the fading darkness of the slave's skin its revolutionary potential. As he carefully describes the quality of James's newly acquired pallor to the American Philosophical Society, he compares it to the complexion of those who view the portrait. "His skin," he writes, "is of a clear wholesome white, fair, and what would be called, *a better skin*, than any number of white people who were present."[1]

A better skin.

For us, as for his audience, the phrase resonates, upsets. A better skin. Whiteness in its exotic purity is exalted. Whiteness in its so-called natural form is diminished. Completely deprived of melanin, the better skin presents an impossible ideal. No Caucasian, no Anglo-Saxon, no white can be that white. Only the white Negro, the racial cross-dresser, the spotted symbol of miscegenation can achieve that purity.

In this first scene staged at a public house in Maryland, Peale presents the three elements of early Republic white Negro exhibition: the impresario, the transforming body, and the audience that the impresario likewise reduces to an exhibit. Positioned before a better skin, those in the audience suffer scrutiny, comparison. Their skin validates the purity of the exhibit's amazing whiteness and places into question their own status as citizens in the white community. This allegedly better skin, its challenge to whiteness and its promise to invert the hierarchy between slave and free, establishes the trope of white Negro exhibition. Now a rhetorical figure, the spectacle of the whitening African American body authors a handy script for other exhibitions of skin color—showman, exhibit, audience, and, of course, better skin arranged into dramas of racial confusion.

This mutating scene of exhibition replays throughout the nineteenth century as the concern over slavery and, after emancipation, the fears of unfettered miscegenation foster narratives about the color line and its transgressors. Fair-skinned slaves deceive hopeful captors; handsome mulattoes pass for white and even marry the unsuspecting Anglo-Saxon. In these literary spectacles, as in the museum exhibitions, a showman displays an African body with white skin to an audience, then subjects the exhibit and the audience to a comparison of color, members of the audience predictably suffering in the comparison. The exhibition briefly allows the body to join the audience, to tease it with membership in the white community, yet the body's status as an exhibit prevents that membership from becoming stable and permanent. This scene of exhibition continues to restage yet changes venues, shifting inevitably from the tavern and museum to literary presentations of the auction block, the scientist's laboratory, and the courtroom where the white Negro will participate in the creation of the legal fictions of race, the whiteness of skin removed from the display and replaced with tainted blood and natal fingerprints. Even with the change of venues, the script of the white Negro exhibition endures. The barker's voice still promotes the whiteness of the skin and stages the comparisons.

"REAL ALBINO"

> Oh! Sally! hearken to my vows!
>   Yield up thy sooty charms—
> My best belov'd! my more than spouse,
>   Oh! take me to thy arms!

—Anonymous, *Richmond Recorder*, 1802

As the scene of exhibition switched from the museum space, the white Negro began to signify the body grown white through generations of racial interrelationships—the mulatto, the quadroon, the octoroon, the blackness reduced to diminishing, yet still ruling, fractions. The suspected source of the whiteness was no longer the climate nor the remission of leprosy; the white Negro was now evidence of interracial couplings, an illicit perquisite of the master, the rape of the African American body inherent in the institution of slavery. Slavery bred exhibitions of whitened skins, master and slave by each generation increasingly indistinguishable. Just as with the exhibition of the anomalous African American body with albinism or vitiligo, the growing whiteness offered hope to those who wished to end slavery by eliminating blackness and bestowed anxiety to those threatened by fluidity between racial categories.

To begin his 1853 novel *Clotel*, William Wells Brown invokes the specter of a miscegenated society, warning his reader that with "the growing population of slaves in the Southern states of America, there is a fearful increase of half whites, most of whose fathers are slave owners, and their mothers slaves." This "amalgamation of the races," Brown argues, derives directly from "the degraded and immoral condition of the relation between master and slave."[2] The employment of "amalgamation" in his argument allows Brown to use the white public's distaste for interracial couplings and their offspring as a catalyst for antislavery sentiments. Just three years prior to the publication of *Clotel* in England, the national census of 1850 was the first to acknowledge biraciality by counting mulattoes.[3] To count the biracial population, census-takers relied solely on their sight and the presumptuous ability to discern evidence of whiteness in the slave body. Any reliance upon birth records or slave interviews would have implicated the master in the production of dangerously white bodies. Brown, though, does not shrink from accusation. To highlight the corruption at the heart of slavery, he names as the author of his initial white Negro display the revered Founding Father Thomas Jefferson, progenitor of slaves.[4] The primary evidence of his transgression is the body of his daughter, Brown's title character.

The rumor and innuendo Brown relies upon to accuse Jefferson first surfaced in 1802 in the poison-pen journalism of James Callender. Imprisoned for six months under the Alien and Sedition Acts of 1798 for a vicious book on John Adams and his administration, Callender turned his attentions to Jefferson, who he thought had abandoned him to the vengeance of the Federalists. In a series of articles for the *Richmond Recorder*, he claimed Jefferson had fathered children through one of his slaves, a young woman Callender named in bold type as "SALLY."[5] The gossip he mined for his attack had circulated among Jefferson's neighbors and confidantes, as well as the slave community, for nearly a decade before Callender made the story public. The tale of Jefferson's liaisons with Sally Hemings continued as a well-known secret among Virginians, black and white, at least until the Civil War.[6] Confirmation of these rumors, though, did not come until recent DNA testing pinpointed kinship between Jefferson and Hemings's descendants.[7]

In spite of early and plentiful evidence of interracial offspring populating plantation households, antebellum racial scientists attempted to mitigate the threat of an ever-whitening slave community by promoting a theory of separate creations. Josiah Nott explained in 1843 that racial amalgamation produced a hybrid of distinct species which, like other hybrids, was less sturdy in constitution and virtually infertile. To allow blacks and whites to marry, he argued, would lead to the mutual extinction of both races.[8] In this emphatic statement, Nott rendered the mulatto inconsequential, a growing whiteness that would literally hit a dead end. This theory of amalgamation gained considerable scientific and popular currency in the years before the Civil War. Even the esteemed natural scientist Louis Agassiz believed mulattoes to be sterile.[9] In the face of this discourse on the degenerate and physically weak bodies of mulattoes, Brown introduces the white beauty of Clotel to refute the premise of black inferiority and bestiality.

Brown's seminar on racial amalgamation performs as a freak show ballyhoo for the coming spectacle of Clotel's white body. The scene of this first exhibition is the auction block, the quadroon daughter of a president displayed before the rabble who endeavor to buy her. In his sales pitch, the auctioneer introduces her as a "real albino."[10] In this playful exaggeration of her whiteness, Brown connects the "fearful increase of half whites" through amalgamation to the physical embodiment of hybridity and racial transformation: the spectacle of the white Negro body. By invoking the trope of white Negro exhibition in this context, Brown figures whiteness as a stigma, the skin of the mulatto and quadroon bearing the testimony of rape and adultery.

A real albino.

When he invokes the exhibition of the white Negro body, Brown also summons its script. The showman-auctioneer displays the white Negro body before an audience. The white and near-white spectators face the whiteness that they have created through their toleration of the institution of slavery. Brown, the showman-author, compares Clotel's pure "albino" color to the mob who gapes. "There she stood," Brown continues, "with a complexion as white as most of those who were waiting with a wish to become her purchasers; her features as finely defined as any of her sex of pure Anglo-Saxon." Exposed to her better skin, Clotel's audience suffers the display as well; the spectacle of her body figures them as lower class and subsequently less white through their crass behavior, their "[l]aughing, joking, swearing, smoking, spitting."[11] Like exhibited white Negroes before her, Clotel is allowed briefly to join this audience of slave merchants and gawkers by virtue of her perceived whiteness, yet her status—as African American, as slave, as exhibit—

denies her membership. Brown's description of the slave auction as a freak show spectacle challenges the status of the audience, establishing a provisional whiteness that includes and excludes the mulatto slave at the same time as it includes and excludes the audience.

By conjuring the figure of the albino in introducing Clotel, the auctioneer also calls upon the erotic appeal of exoticized whiteness, the pale hue of the miscegenated body that issues an invitation for further illicit interracial liaisons. Clotel's mother, Currer, already corrupted by the attentions of Thomas Jefferson and the institution of slavery, grooms her daughters for careers as slave concubines, to "attract attention, especially at balls and parties," where affluent and middle-class white men can shop for mistresses. To underscore the perversity of this harem economy, Brown culminates this dissertation on the production of exotic whiteness with its marketplace presentation. The auctioneer's ballyhoo to the leering near-white crowd highlights Clotel's appealing pale color and, as a clincher to the sales pitch, her virginity. "The chastity of this girl is pure," the auctioneer touts, "she has never been from under her mother's care; she is a virtuous creature."[12] Her price leaps another four hundred dollars at this announcement, which suggests the violence of rape and the spilling of hymeneal blood. The display of so-called tainted white skin on the auction block tenders fantasies of seduction and the seraglio, Circassian women powerless before the bidding pashas, the fiendish and lustful Turk now located in the body of the southern plantation slave master.

This scene of exhibition—the display of Clotel's whiteness and virtue—sets a literary precedent. Barbara Christian has argued that "Brown's description of the mulatta became the model for other black novels" until at least the 1940s.[13] The theater of white skin, its display before and its comparison to the white or near-white audience, perpetuates as the literary figure of the tragic mulatto, the light-skinned African American martyred before the idol of slavery and irrational racial prejudice. As indicated by Brown's presentation of Clotel's "albino" whiteness, the presence of the white Negro in the exhibition spaces of natural history museums and lyceum stages authors this literary trope. The staging of the exhibition accompanies the white Negro's arrival as part of a literary institution: the whiteness of the exhibit's skin, the near-white audience, the impresario who makes clear the inadequacy of the patron's skin before the exhibit.

The display of the whiter-than-white virgin beauty before the lecherous rabble provides a subversive prelude for the sentimental marriage plot of Clotel. "Marriage," Brown proclaims early on, "is, indeed, the first and most important institution of human existence."[14] Ann DuCille explains that "in Brown's antislavery text marriage rites and the right to marry . . . function as the primary signifiers of freedom and humanity."[15] Slaves, though, are prevented from marrying, which perverts the domestic landscape and, for the reader of the sentimental novel, thwarts any expectation of a happy ending, further dramatizing the tragedy of slavery. The reduction of Clotel to the status of an eroticized albino stands as an emblem for this perversity. Like Barnum's Circassians and his albino beauties, she is confined by her exotic whiteness, chained, so to speak, to the exhibition. Her audience of plantation owners lust after the pale skin of the mulattoes and quadroons they buy and breed, neglecting in their profligacy their own wives and families.

After the exhibition on the auction block, Clotel's better skin—achieved through generations of extramarital affairs—suffers additional comparisons of color that expose her to sexual exploitation and further weaken the institution of marriage. The continued exhibitions of white skin mine the fears of the sexual competition engendered by miscegenation.[16] William, the slave who eventually helps Clotel escape her bondage, characterizes the conflict between the light-skinned household slave and her mistress. "You are much fairer," he tells Clotel, "than many of the white women of the South."[17] Reprised in this blunt pronouncement, Clotel's better skin augurs a new exhibition: the now less-white body of southern womanhood.

At the slave auction, Horace Green, Clotel's white lover, buys her, and although they stage a wedding ceremony, Clotel understands that her status as a slave "would give her no legal hold on Horatio's constancy." As expected, Horatio acquires a legal wife, Clotel's connubial twin, who, "though inferior in beauty, was yet a pretty contrast to her rival." Clotel bears Horatio's child, a further production and enhancement of whiteness. The child Mary's "complexion was still lighter than her mother. Indeed she was not darker than other white children." This new and improved semblance to whiteness foretokens a future comparison to Horatio's expected heirs through the new wife, Gertrude, half-brothers and half-sisters, dermal twins of Mary who will contrast with her better skin. The presence of the slave-child galls Gertrude and provokes her to enact a racial transformation by exposing Mary to the sun.[18] Although the sun darkens the skin, Mary still resembles Gertrude's husband, serving as a living reminder of the slave concubine, the better-skinned rival for her husband's affections.[19]

Brown's continuing exhibition of white bodies pricks at the sexual and racial anxieties of his white audience. The depravity of slavery—the spectacle of indistinguishable slave and free children in blended households—begets genealogical confusion. The familial bounds between husband and wife, parent and child, brother and sister, deviate and dissolve. Family trees split and twist in polygamous and adulterous tangles. The distinction between racial categories fades. The simple eyeballing of racial difference fails.

Darwin's Spotted Negro

The sexual competition between indistinguishable white bodies flew in the face of the idea of incompatible, immutable racial essences promoted by the apologists for slavery. Like Barnum's Negro Turning White, the white Negro exhibitions of pale-skinned mulattoes and quadroons undermined the central assumptions of racial science. There were no radical differences between black and white, no natural antipathies. Clotel's favorable comparison to the bloom of white southern womanhood, her ability to attract wayward Southern plantation owners, anticipates a radical change in nineteenth-century racial theory: natural selection.

When he published his 1859 groundbreaking treatise, *The Origin of Species*, Darwin replaced the model of a static living world. Instead of a planet populated with species unchanged since their creation by a divine intelligence, he imagined a world where creatures were modified through the process of the struggle for existence. At first blush, it would seem that this assault on the fixity of species would chagrin the racial scientists, yet those theorists with less of an attachment to Christian doctrine readily embraced the possibility that fundamental differences between the races could develop over long periods of competition. Evolution merely offered a new reason for white superiority. Even Josiah Nott, the champion of polygenesis, saw little conflict with evolutionary theory, which, he declared, "would not controvert the facts and deductions I have laid down."[20] It may have taken millions of years, he reasoned, but the Negro was still inferior by nature.

When he turned his attention to the origins of the human species in his 1871 work *The Descent of Man*, Darwin quickly discarded the theories that buttressed antebellum arguments of white superiority. Evolution, he knew, rendered the claims of both monogenesis and polygenesis obsolete. The whole of any species cannot be traced to a founding single pair of progenitors. More specifically, the environmentalism that formed the influential theories of Samuel Stanhope Smith was "not tenable." Restricting the various racial groups to the status of separate creations was "a hopeless endeavor." As he dismissed the foundational assumptions of racial science, Darwin maintained the dichotomy of savage and civilized, as well as the extreme difference of Africans. And the days of those savages were numbered. "At some future period," he forecasts, "not very distant as measured by centuries, the civilized races of man will almost certainly exterminate, and replace, the savage races throughout the world." As violent as this prediction sounds, the extinction of a people derives mostly from the inability of that group to compete with supposedly better equipped groups for the same resources. Darwin even attributed the success of the Anglo-Saxons on the North American continent to natural selection.[21] Manifest Destiny, it seems, was merely part of the evolutionary process.

Hence, with great glee white supremacists swiftly incorporated Darwin into their claims of superiority. Cultural historian George Fredrickson sees "the full triumph of Darwinism in American thought" by the time of the 1890 census, which seemed to document a decline in the African American population.[22] By the turn of the twentieth century, ethnologists and statisticians were declaring that African Americans "will follow the fate of the Indians, that the great majority will disappear before the whites."[23] Released from the protection of slavery, the argument goes, African Americans will shrink before the unregulated competition with the superior Anglo-Saxon. Charles Chesnutt parodied these self-serving proclamations in his 1901 novel *The Marrow of Tradition*. To overthrow the Reconstruction government in Wellington, North Carolina, a coterie of white supremacists scheme to foment a small populist coup. Major Carteret, the leader of the group, writes editorials for the newspaper he owns to assert "the unfitness of the negro to participate in government." This racist belief in a general unfitness graduates to a Darwinian fantasy of a future in which Africans Americans "are eliminated by the stress of competition." Not isolated to a few disgruntled Southern men, this prediction of a black apocalypse extends even to liberals on a fact-finding mission from the Northern states, who observe "a dying race, unable to withstand the competition of a superior type."[24] In answer to this dire prophecy, Chesnutt demonstrates the capability of African Americans to compete intellectually and physically. The novel's protagonist, Dr. William Miller, has thrived as an African American physician in spite of the obstacles in his path. Both the racist Major Carteret and the good doctor Miller have infant sons. Miller's son is healthy until he is shot by the rioters Carteret originally agitated. The sickly young Carteret, though, needs the healing hand of a black doctor to survive a bout with the croup.

Chesnutt is careful to cast the African American as more than up to the task of racial competition, especially with the mass of Anglo-Saxons that populate the town of Wellington. Most of them are nearly savage poor white people, the violent "baser element . . . from the wharves and the saloons," who burn down hospitals during the riot, and "white women with tallow complexions and snuff-stained lips." Even the scions of old plantation families are dissipated fools, prone to avarice and murder. Chesnutt expresses the fitness of the African American in Darwinian terms. "The negro was here before the Anglo-Saxon was evolved," he writes, "and his thick lips and heavy-lidded eyes looked out from the inscrutable face of the Sphinx across the sands of Egypt while yet the ancestors of those who now oppress him were living in caves, practicing human sacrifice, and painting themselves with woad—and the negro is here yet."[25] The proud Anglo-Saxon is new to this game of natural selection and probably not as well prepared.

Yet beyond the claims of intellectual and physical inferiority lie the racist anxieties over sexual competition. In the aftermath of emancipation, racial scientists still worried about unfettered black and white coupling and mixed-race children, but now these concerns acquired the jargon of heredity and natural selection. Unable through his hybridity to adapt to either the warmth of the South or the cold of the North, the tale unfolds, the mulatto child would not survive, accelerating the expected demise of the African American.[26] Darwin, as well, approached the question of miscegenation and the possibility that mulattoes were the offspring of distinct species, and, like his predecessors, he, too, had to contend with the white Negro. Dismissing the old arguments of sterility, he stated that the "ordinary result of a cross is the production of a blended or intermediate form." He follows this supposition with a report from a doctor in Africa who witnessed that "the offspring of negroes crossed with members of other races [were] either completely black, or completely white, or rarely piebald."[27] Although he does not further dwell on the rare appearance of a white Negro, Darwin is clearly haunted by this relic of racial science, the possibility that miscegenation could mark the skin black and white. Possibly in response to Darwin's incomplete speculations, a man from Alabama sent the evolutionist a photograph of a six-year-old Leopard Boy, which Darwin subsequently presented, without comment, to the Museum of the Royal College of Surgeons.[28] It seems the piebald nightmares of the reconstructed South found their way into the halls of the new evolutionary science.

As embodied by the white Negro body, the anxiety over sexual competition troubles the plot of *The Marrow of Tradition*. The wives of Major Carteret and Dr. Miller are half-sisters by the same father, looking as much alike, the Carteret family nurse explains, "ez ef dey wuz twins." By virtue of her pure-white blood, Olivia Carteret has inherited her father's land, the money, and the old house; as the child of a secret second marriage to an African American housekeeper, Janet Miller received nothing save the indignation of Olivia. To the white half-sister, her black twin is a rival for her father's affections. When she uncovers her father's lost will, Olivia is relieved that he intended to leave Janet much less land and money, since it proves that he "had not preferred her to another."[29] Olivia's consistent tantrums from the sight of the light-skinned Janet are a neurotic manifestation of sexual competition she feels in the presence of her half-sister.

In the climatic moment of the novel, Chesnutt calls upon the trope of white Negro exhibition to illustrate the worthiness of African Americans in the theater of natural selection. With every white doctor indisposed in a town ripped apart by racial violence, Olivia goes to the Miller's house to beg Janet for the services of her husband to save the life of the Carteret infant. Janet, we discover, is mourning the loss of her own child. At this time of partial concil-iation, Chesnutt displays the complexions of the two half-sisters, an exhibi-tion in which Dr. Miller contemplates "the image of his own wife. . . . A little older perhaps, a little fairer of complexion, but with the same form, the same features, marked by the same wild grief."[30] In this case of look-alike siblings, the woman under scrutiny resembles the wife of the spectator, exposing a representative of white Southern womanhood to the African American gaze and, for one brief moment, the vicissitudes of sexual competition. Before the husband, the miscegenated body of the wife is nearly indistinguishable from that of her white half-sister, a similarity of attractiveness that renders the ques-tion of evolutionary hierarchy moot.

THE JIM CROW TWINS

American Darwinists used the principles of natural selection to support the Jim Crow laws that emerged in the wake of emancipation and the even-tual retreat from the policies of Reconstruction. The imposition of social equality in the face of the powerful forces of evolutionary change was folly, they argued.[31] To sanctify the imagined natural hierarchy produced by natu-ral selection, these laws established a society split between black and white — separate accommodations for hotels, restaurants, and transportation all in the name of public health and morality. The policing of these restrictions relied upon visual identification of transgressors. Clerks, maître d's, and train con-ductors rousted the dark-skinned and swarthy from whites-only sections. Like Barnum's patrons before the Albino Family and the Negro Turning White, these agents sought to ensure white citizenship by detecting telltale signs of racial difference. Their efforts, though, produced moments of confusion and suspicion. Among the white bodies in the cars hid the equally white bodies of African Americans. This ever-present doubt inflamed the caretakers of pub-lic spaces to scrutinize whiteness and place all patrons on exhibit.

In 1892, Homer Plessy staged his own exhibition aboard a whites-only car on the East Louisiana Railroad to protest Jim Crow segregation and to pro-vide a legal test case. A light-complected man with an African American great-grandparent, Plessy ceremoniously entered the car and, to ensure his detection, announced to the conductor that he was "colored."[32] When Plessy refused to heed the conductor's requests to leave, a detective for the railroad arrested him for violation of the state law to "promote the comfort of passengers on railway trains" through the provision of "equal but separate accommodations."[33] Plessy's theatrical gesture, the public presentation of his white Negro body, spurred further discussion of his display among other white bodies. In his argument of the case before the United States Supreme Court, Albion Tourgée employed the central conceit of white Negro exhibition: the questionable acumen of authorities to define and decipher racial difference. "Is the officer of a railroad," he asks the court, "competent to decide the question of race? . . . Is not the question of race, scientifically considered, very often impossible of determination?"[34] He disputes the competency of the railroad agents, this white audience, to dictate and enforce white membership.[35] By claiming ultimately the impotence of scientific and legal authorities, he challenges *"the right of the State to label one citizen as white and another as colored,"* an assertion that reduces race to a semantic fiction.[36]

To address the injustice of the Jim Crow laws against all African Americans, Tourgée repeatedly returns his focus to the white body, recognizing in the contradictory surface of the white Negro a breach in the firewall of separate but equal. The appearance of the white Negro suggests its so-called opposite, its more privileged white twin, the two bodies necessarily yoked in exhibition. As with the uneasy distinction between exhibit and patron in Barnum's American Museum, the resulting comparison of light-skinned bodies affords the opportunity for racial transformation or, in this case, a kind of race switch: the disenfranchised "black" body strives for whiteness, the privileged "white" body is consequently threatened with a reciprocal conversion to blackness. For his rhetorical coup de grâce, Tourgée offers the white audience of his white Negro exhibition the nightmare of their own racial transformation. "Suppose a member of this court," he beseeches, "nay, suppose every member of it, by some mysterious dispensation of providence should wake tomorrow with a black skin and curly hair."[37] By exploiting the fantasy of racial transformation that accompanies the figure of the white Negro, Tourgée exposes each justice of the Supreme Court to the possibility of his own blackness and the danger inherent in the legal fiction of race that the Court wishes to impose. The absurd image of the magically transformed justices, a final plea for empathy, burlesques the court and its ultimately futile endeavor to fix and maintain the border between black and white.[38]

> "Bofe of us is imitation white . . . we don't 'mount to noth'n as imitation niggers."
>
> —Roxy to Chambers, Mark Twain, *Pudd'nhead Wilson*, 1894

Born of the same legal bifurcation of American society as the Plessy case, the courtroom scene that culminates Mark Twain's novel *Pudd'nhead Wilson* travesties legal and scientific efforts to define racial difference. During the trial for the murder of Judge Driscoll, Wilson, the lawyer, reveals not only the identity of the murderer as the alleged son Tom Driscoll but also the truth about Tom's secret racial identity. Wilson uncovers the hidden African American parentage through a bloody fingerprint on the murder weapon. Wilson's theatrical demonstration of marks and smudges parodies the efforts of racial scientists to assign racial difference through easily recognizable physical indicators. It also satirizes the efforts of the early eugenicists to acclaim heredity as the sole determining factor of human ability and behavior. Hoping to harness evolutionary science to develop the human gene pool, these scientists designed to give natural selection a little nudge by distinguishing the best and the brightest and encouraging them to propagate. To this aim, they sought signs of difference in the smallest physical attribute. The founder of eugenics, Francis Galton, also developed a system of classifying fingerprints still in use, yet even he failed to find the racial correlation he sought in the whorls, loops, and arches of the fingerprint.[39]

Ironically, Wilson's endeavor to produce a murderer through scientific method results in nothing. In the community's eyes, the crime of patricide is no match for the stigma of Tom's newfound blackness. In a mockery of law, the court commutes his sentence of life imprisonment; instead, the former heir is "sold down the river" as a slave to satisfy the creditors of Judge Driscoll's estate.[40] The presence of Tom Driscoll's white Negro body transforms the court into an exhibition space for Barnum-like speculation and humbuggery. As Eric J. Sundquist explains of the transition, "The rule of law gives way to outright theater, the court becoming an explicit domain of staged opinions and prejudices that burlesque the drift in constitutional law."[41] Overwhelmed by the exhibition of the white Negro, Wilson's hollow victory exposes the irrationality that fueled the Supreme Court's decision in the Plessy case to limit the enfranchisement of African Americans further by establishing the segregation of separate but equal.

The "outright theater" that Sundquist detects results from the influence of white Negro exhibition. As with Tourgée's final act before the Supreme Court, Wilson presents the origin of Tom's masquerade in terms of a magical racial transformation. In a melodramatic gesture, Wilson ballyhoos the infant switch: "A was put into B's cradle in the nursery; B was transferred to the kitchen and became a Negro and a slave . . . but within a quarter of an hour he will stand before you white and free!" (112). Like a sideshow barker, Wilson claims the power to change a man's skin from black to white, an exhibition couched in the authority of racial science yet one that acknowledges the act of semantic invention in the construction of race—Tom's skin has not changed; in the manner of Tourgée's train conductors, Wilson simply declares him white. Although he tries to appropriate the racial transformation as his own invention, twenty-three years stand between the beginning of this white Negro exhibition and the apparent triumph of his scientific scrutiny.

Pudd'nhead Wilson is not the author of this courtroom exhibition. The mantle of showman instead falls to the slave mother of the erstwhile Tom. An unqualified descendent of Clotel, Roxy is "as white as anybody," the product of generations of interracial liaisons between master and slave (8). Although she traces her genealogy through "Ole Cap'n John Smith, de highest blood Ole Virginny ever turned out," she is still owned by Judge Driscoll, who takes equal pride in his "old Virginian ancestry" (70, 4). On the very day that the Driscolls have a son, she gives birth to a boy with "blue eyes and flaxen curls like his white comrade" (9). She realizes early that even Judge Driscoll cannot tell the naked children apart as the two boys share a bath (14). To save her son from a life of slavery, Roxy switches the infants and their races by merely exchanging their clothing, gleefully fooling the community—and the title amateur scientist—with her orchestrated exhibition of the white Negro. Her display of the interchangeable twin white bodies demonstrates the concept of race as, in Twain's words, "a fiction of law and custom" (9).

Otherwise powerless as a slave, Roxy exerts profound influence over the lives of the community by appropriating the exhibition of white bodies. As James M. Cox has observed, "Only Roxanna has the power to create drama and to become the primary force in the world she serves."[42] As exhibitor, Roxy establishes control over her own display, a humbug of white skins, two babies, one slave and one free, virtual twins in complexion. In the first test of this "fiction created by herself," Roxy presents the children before the scientific gaze of Pudd'nhead Wilson, "very anxious that he should admire the great advance in flesh and beauty which the babies had made since he took their fingerprints a month before. He complimented their improvement to her contentment" (19, 16–17). Even with the evidence placed before him "without disguise of jam or other stain," Roxy deceives the careful, authoritative eye of Wilson (17).

Roxy's exhibition of these twin white bodies demonstrates the parallel between spectacle and slavery. Like the exhibition of white Negroes, the display subverts the fictions of racial difference that keep her in bondage, and her appropriation of the exhibition parodies the master's prerogative to cast a body into slavery. She determines the staging of the exhibition, the narration and status of the bodies. She willfully condemns one body to slavery as she exalts its twin. Carolyn Porter has classified the switch of infants as "a specific imitation of the white master's power to enforce . . . inequality."[43] Roxy's act of mimicry, like that of Bhabha's colonial mimic, is "almost the same, but not quite" that of the master.[44] She cannot become white through her performance, but her resemblance to the master, in appearance and now in behavior, disturbs the illusion of white supremacy to the point that the operations of the humbug become visible for a moment, at least to her and, consequently, the reader. She senses her performance as it blurs into learned behavior, and she becomes a victim of her own humbug: her "deceptions intended solely for others gradually grew practically into self-deceptions as well; the mock reverence became real reverence, the mock obsequiousness real obsequiousness, the mock homage real homage; the little counterfeit rift of separation between imitation-slave and imitation-master widened and widened, and became an abyss, and a very real one" (19). Her mimicry reveals the imitations, the fictions of law and custom, that undergird society and its presumption of a natural racial hierarchy. Like the illusions that govern the dominant society, the whiteness she bestows on her son, the "fiction created by herself," takes on its own life. When her son, the master, abuses her, she clings to the only power she has left, that of the showman, the author of the illusion. In her dreams of vengeance, her thoughts turn to "the fancied spectacle of his exposure to the world as an imposter and a slave" (22). To maintain mastery over the master, she can still thrill in the moment of revelation, the ultimate uncovering of the humbug and the crowning of the audience as fools.

In this mental exercise, the slave has power over her master, even if he is a humbug of her own creation. By passing off the slave body as white, she exposes the ever-creaking mechanism of race. Twain's Roxy offers a new twist to the trope of white Negro exhibition: the African American showman who appropriates the white body as a weapon against the presumptions of racial science and white supremacy. Embracing the aesthetic of Barnum, the former exhibit begins to author its own exhibition, wield its own body for a more private audience of its African American peers. Descendants of Clotel and Henry Moss, these bodies at the scene of the exhibition carry a fantasy of transformation, less for the sake of peaceful assimilation and more for the purposes of assaulting the white body and dismantling the tyranny of race.

"FIVE MILLION U. S. WHITE NEGROES"

> passing: i.e. passing for white.
>
> — "Glossary of Negro Words and Phrases," Carl Van Vechten,
> *Nigger Heaven*, 1926

After slavery, the act of passing for white lost its exigency: escape from the whip of the overseer and the dogs of the bounty hunter necessitated the charade, rationalized the temporary defection from blackness. Toward the end of the nineteenth century and into the twentieth, the literary passer began to symbolize a damaged African American solidarity. The characters in Frances E. W. Harper's 1892 novel, *Iola Leroy, or Shadows Uplifted*, express a disdain for passing, that "it would be treason, not only to the race, but to humanity, to have you ignoring your kindred and masquerading as a white man."[45] After an unsuccessful pass in Charles Chesnutt's *The House behind the Cedars*, Rena Walden affirms her blackness and devotes herself to the education of "her people."[46] Editorials and commentaries in African American publications chastised the passer and bemoaned the loss of one more citizen of the race to the white public. Writing for *Opportunity* in 1926, Elmer A. Carter despaired over the "increasing number of these whitewashed Ethiopians who have forever deserted the Lares and Penates of the Negro race."[47] The wish to slip the confinement of racial prejudice may have been understandable, but escape still smelled of treason.

As it acquires the African American gaze, the body of the literary white Negro acquires its critics, its surface an emblem of restricted privilege. Some scholars have accused the passer of betrayal, a reactionary act in which the offender embraces the supremacy of whiteness and, like Roxy, becomes "duped by her own deception" (19). In this line of critical condemnation, the act of crossing over the color line erases identity and demonstrates self-loathing. "'Passing' is an obscene form of salvation," Mary Helen Washington declares, then adds that the "woman who passes over is required to deny everything about her past."[48] Harryette Mullen considers passing less an act of self-denial than "as successful assimilation . . . [and] a process of identifying oneself culturally and genetically with white Americans, while severing associations with African-Americans. Passing is not so much a willful deception or duplicity as it is an attempt to move from the margin to the center of American identity." Her argument targets the literal passer and its literary shadow. All passers, to her mind, endorse whiteness and encourage its hegemony.[49]

The moral hand-wringing over racial transformation, the mourned loss of black men and women to whiteness, is part of the passing narrative tradition. The defection from one's own people most often distills into a painful rejection of family ties, a de rigueur scene of glances, returned glances, and final silences. In Jessie Redmon Fauset's *Plum Bun*, the passer, Angela Murray, waits at a train station for the arrival of her darker-skinned sister, only to forsake her when Angela's white boyfriend shows up unexpectedly.[50] Throughout the rest of the novel, Angela's abandonment haunts her, converting her slowly into a race patriot. Langston Hughes best articulates the bathos of the betrayal in his short story "Passing," a fictional letter from a passing son to his dark-skinned mother. Jack, the letter writer, expresses his dream to "marry white and live white" and not to "get caught in the mire of color again." In the midst of his selfish reverie, he apologizes for passing his mother on the street and "not speaking," an intimate betrayal that he continues to rationalize as necessary in order to escape the bonds of blackness.[51] The passers in these narratives suffer from a self-delusion that eventually exiles them from the security of family and community.

In the project of the passing narrative, the vocabulary of white Negro exhibition survives, even in those morality tales that serve to chastise and punish the transgression of the passer. In his short story "Near-White," Claude McKay presents Angelina Dove, a young African American woman in Harlem, "conscious of her pretty curls, her nice creamy skin, and yet never conscious of how really white she was." Taking the place of the impresario, the narrator echoes Charles Willson Peale in his display of James the White Negro's better skin by proclaiming "that no tangible thing separated her from the respectable white audience . . . , her features being whiter and more regular than many persons' who moved boldly and freely in the privileged circles of the Great Majority." The "blue-eyed" octoroon Eugene Vincent introduces Angie to the theatricality of racial passing. She watches his performance as he helps her temporarily cross the color line and gain entry to the Palace Vaudeville. Reemphasizing the comparison of skin, Vincent instructs her that "we are as white as any of them. Am I not white like any white man you've seen?" Angie happily discovers that her own near-white skin fools her not-as-white audience. But the road to white social acceptance is not an easy one. Her experience with passing meets with frustration and anxiety as she learns from her mother her paradoxical status. Her white skin holds her separate from darker-skinned African Americans at the same time as it encourages greater prejudice from whites. The whites, her mother explains, "hate us even more than they do the blacks. For they're never sure about us, they can't place us."[52] Vilified by virtue of her uncategorizable body, Angie realizes at the end of the story that her light skin will only tease her with entrance into a world she can never attain.

Yet even from under the withering gaze of the passer's critics, the disruptive influence of the white Negro emerges. As I have demonstrated in earlier chapters, the conundrum of the white or whitening African American body unsettles assumptions about the fixity of racial difference and challenges the easy assignment of identity by a mere gaze. Relocated in the figure of the passer, the exhibition of the white African American body retains this play of deceit and detection; it continues to toy with perceptions and assumptions. Like the exhibited Leopard Child and the albino African American, the passing body is both black and white, flickering impossibly between presumed oppositions and essences, and it is in this racial confusion that the figure of the passer achieves its cultural clout. "The specter of passing," Elaine Ginsberg writes, "derives its power . . . as a signification that embodies the anxieties and contradictions of a racially stratified society."[53] Created by the same hypocrisies and absurdities of racism that forged the exhibition of the white Negro, the passer challenges the same audience, frustrates the same pretension to knowledge, irritates the same unease.

The theater of white Negro exhibition and its defiance of racial classification provide a ready-made trope for narratives of passing. At Barnum's scene of exhibition, the white patrons assumed knowledge of racial markers in an attempt to establish their own identity as white. By discerning the African origin of the white Negro, the patrons distinguished themselves from the exhibit. The showman, on the other hand, as the presenter and manufacturer of the humbug, was the only one assured of this knowledge, and, in consequence, he was the only one confirmed as white through the exhibit. At this new scene of exhibition, in the serious game of passing, the white African American body does not so much compete for whiteness as it seeks to confound it.

In the passing narrative, African American authors reemploy the template of white Negro exhibition, inheriting as well Barnum's operational aesthetic. The passing narrative dissolves the showman as the white Negro acquires agency in the exhibition of his or her body. The white or near-white audience remains, certain of its perceptive powers, inquisitive but doomed to ignorance. The easily duped audience provides moments of gleeful and derisive satisfaction for the showman/exhibit. The anonymous narrator of James Weldon Johnson's novel *The Autobiography of an Ex-Colored Man* gloats at the arrogance of his unsuspecting audience and considers the dramatic unveiling of his blackness: "I frequently smiled inwardly at some remark not altogether complimentary to people of color, and more than once I felt like declaiming, 'I am a colored man. Do I not disprove the theory that one drop of Negro blood renders a man unfit?' Many a night when I returned to my room after an enjoyable evening, I laughed heartily over what struck me as the capital joke I was playing."[54] Beneath the Barnumesque joke of the pass lies an act of aggression, an attack on the rubes who watch the passer, the racial scientists who presume the racial inferiority of African Americans.

"You never read Nella Larsen?"
—Langston Hughes, "Who's Passing for Who?," 1952

In 1948, a headline in *Ebony* proclaimed, "5 Million U.S. White Negroes," the dramatic disclosure of a large African American population with light skin, passers all, who had crossed the color line undetected. The accompanying article gave a short history of miscegenation from seventeenth-century Jamestown to twentieth-century one-drop laws and asked the question, "What is it that makes a man a Negro?" The centerpiece of the article was an array of fourteen numbered photographs, each of a handsome, smiling face with pale skin. The photos' caption challenged the reader, "Can you tell who on this page is a Negro and who is white?" The article conceived the pass as a guess-my-race carnival game, enticing its readers—presumably African Americans—to test their mettle in detecting blackness. *Ebony* provided a key. Only three of the fourteen were white.[55] But here the exhibition of white Negroes, forever a bane to easily fooled white and near-white audiences, plagued a group of observers who claimed insider status. Surely, a Negro could spot another Negro, no matter how colorless the complexion. This is hubris, of course. The mere fact of the challenge implies the impossibility of assigning racial origins simply from skin color and other reputed physical markers. In other words, even the in-crowd gets stymied.

The presence of the observer who presumes an intimate understanding of the spectacle is central to the trope of white Negro display. In earlier exhibitions of white Negroes, the showman presented the white African American body before a knowledgeable third party—in these first cases, the white patron who reads the showman's account, witnesses the contrast of color, and understands, with a wink and a nod, the racial nature of the exhibit. What Amy Robinson calls "the triangular theater of the pass" parallels this geometry of white Negro exhibition.[56] In the passing narrative, the figure of the showman fades, and the exhibit achieves agency, seizing command of the white body's display. Robinson's triad registers this combination of showman and exhibit. She identifies two groups of spectators that harken back to Barnum's operational aesthetic: the dupe who cannot discern the "true" nature of the exhibited white body and the member of the in-group who successfully reads the pass and witnesses the deception of the dupe. The exposure of skin for the discerning eye authors a secret theater of detection and concealment for the benefit of one who knows, yet this onlooker is not necessarily innocent nor unaffected by the exhibition. The display that challenges the acumen of the dupe also threatens to disturb the worldly spectator's sense of identity and well-being.

The status of the in-group member is tenuous and conditional. Disorientation happens to African American observers, too. The idea that someone who is black can always detect hidden blackness is just as fallacious as Anglo-Saxon claims to detective prowess. Years after his first didactic tale of passing, Langston Hughes offered a more complex conception of racial cross-dressing and final uncertainty. In his story "Who's Passing for Who?" light-complected characters play a game of racial revelation and counterrevelation. The narrator assumes the stance of a in-crowd member, an African American nightclubber sure of his ability to detect passers. He is mildly annoyed with the white couple who have accompanied his friend Caleb until they tell him, "We've just been *passing* for white for the last fifteen years." Stunned, the narrator and his African American compatriots relax their manners and begin to enjoy themselves. At their departure, though, the couple announces that they weren't "colored" after all. This second disclosure throws the narrator into confusion. "We just stood there on the corner in Harlem dumbfounded—not knowing now *which* way we'd been fooled," he writes. "Were they really white—passing for colored? Or colored—passing for white?"[57] Abandoning the simple act of betrayal he posed in his first story of passing, Hughes uncovers the complex repercussions instigated by the trope of white Negro exhibition: once dependable racial differences now resolved into a final, irreconcilable muddle.

During the early discourse on passing intended to educate the apparently white couple, the African Americans, educated in matters of blackness, ask them, "You never read Nella Larsen?" As the recommended text for study, a central document for the transgression of racial borders, Larsen's short novel *Passing* exploits the trope of white Negro exhibition, staging its challenges and its confusions. The novel's first scene of exhibition hosts two competing displays of essentially twin white Negro bodies and, as a consequence, two competing efforts of spectatorship. Childhood friends, both passing as white, meet by chance in the rooftop restaurant of an exclusive hotel in Chicago. The ocular competition between the two exposes the performances of the pass as potential acts of aggression. Overcome by the summer heat, Irene Redfield has sought refuge in the restaurant. To her, passing is a harmless act of momentary social convenience, a privilege afforded her by her light-complected skin. In her own act of passing, she becomes the unknowing witness to another pass, a dupe to the whiteness of a woman—her friend Clare Kendry—who sits at the next table observing her. Under Clare's unwelcome "steady scrutiny," Irene experiences an extreme self-awareness of the appearance of her skin. She feels "her colour heighten under the continued inspection." The "persistent attention" compels her to check for "a streak of powder somewhere on her face." As she feels a threat to her assumption of whiteness, she tries to "outstare" her rival, yet the insistence of her "rude observer" irritates and begins to instill her with fear.[58] Simultaneously observer and observed, near-white patron and white Negro exhibit, Irene briefly embodies the complex of the white Negro exhibition—the hubris of the spectator, the vulnerability of the exhibit, the smirk of the showman.

Her whiteness challenged, Irene asserts the superiority of her position as an exhibit. Fooled by Clare's performance, Irene glosses upon the arrogance of white spectatorship: "White people were so stupid about such things for all that they usually asserted that they were able to tell; and by the most ridiculous means, fingernails, palms of hands, shapes of ears, teeth, and other equally silly rot. . . . Never, when she was alone, had they even remotely seemed to suspect that she was Negro" (16).[59] Irene's uncomfortable position as both seeing and seen reveals her pitched between performing race as a knowing humbug and falling for own performance as a duped spectator. As she dismisses faith in racial markers, Irene also attempts white spectatorship to detect the still anonymous Clare's particular racial characteristics. Although at first glance Irene notices Clare's "dark, almost black eyes," it is not until much later and she knows at whom she is looking that she identifies the dark eyes as a distinct racial characteristic. "They were Negro eyes," she declares, "mysterious and concealing. And set in that ivory face under that bright hair, there was about them something exotic" (29). As a spectator, she embraces the racial markers she ridicules.

Through this complex dynamic of observation and display, we gain a greater understanding of the effect of the white Negro exhibition on an aspiring near-white body, the disequilibrium it invests, the identity it contests. It is Irene, Jennifer DeVere Brody reminds us, "who harbors a secret desire to be white and not Clare."[60] Irene strives toward an unachievable ideal of whiteness, a middle-class life of security and relative privilege within which she can protect herself from the race self-consciousness the presence of darker (and lower-class) African American bodies instill in her. Larsen biographer Thadious Davis explains that Irene's "attraction to whiteness takes the form of her adoption of white values, standards of beauty, and behavior. In a sense it is an attraction to all that is denied the racialized black person."[61] As a virtual twin, a mirror-self, the white Negro body of Clare embodies everything Irene desires and fears. Clare has successfully passed as white, even married a wealthy white man, yet the blackness of her lower-class origins as a daughter of a drunken janitor and her desire "to see Negroes, to be with them again" makes Irene self-conscious of a racial identity she secretly disdains (71).

In the novel's primary scene of exhibition, Clare's performance further disorients Irene as the passing body serves as a weapon against the presumptions of white spectatorship. In Clare's apartment, Clare, Irene, and Gertrude, another light-skinned African American, all pass as white before John Bellew, Clare's unsuspecting husband and racist dupe. As with Barnum's audiences for white Negro display, John's status as dupe reduces him to an exhibit, one exposed to the derision of a knowing audience. Irene observes, "In Clare's eyes, as she presented her husband, was a queer gleam, a jeer, it might be." Ignorant of both his own performance and the one before him, John narrates a racial transformation in his wife's skin. "When we were first married," he explains, "she was as white as—as—well as white as a lily. But I declare she's gettin' darker and darker. I tell her if she don't look out she'll wake up one of these days and find she's turned into a nigger" (39). His nickname for Clare—"Nig"—underscores his fascination with this transformation and magnifies his ignorance of its meaning.[62] As the duped audience to the exhibition, John loses status and grows less attractively white. The displayed skin of the women proves better than John's "unhealthy-looking dough-coloured face" (38–39).

In this second scene of exhibition, Irene once again suffers as object under observation and knowledgeable observer of the racial display. From her awareness of the exhibition, she can discern the difference between her privileged perspective and that of the dupe: "An onlooker . . . would have thought it a most congenial tea-party, all smiles and jokes and hilarious laughter" (40). The image of the tea party marks Irene's yearnings for a genteel life uncluttered by race, yet her ideal of polite society can only exist by "repressing" the "rage and rebellion" she experiences as a witness to John's racist assault (42). Far from an innocent observer or passive object of exhibition, Irene fully participates in the attack on John's racist presumptions, all the while sneering along with Clare. By asking him about his "dislike" for Negroes, she urges John to continue his diatribe. The fact of the exhibition and John's ignorance of its insidious threat serve as a source of "amusement" to Clare and, in spite of her protests to the contrary, to Irene as well (40). This amusement, though, is for the benefit of the other women, a shared disdain for John's racist rhetoric and his inability to understand.

The production of whiteness that Mullen sees in the act of passing relies upon both "an active denial of black identity only by the individual who passes from black to white" and a "presumption that white identities are racially pure."[63] I would add to that formulation the character's belief in a separate and essential difference between black and white identities. The figure of the white Negro is a quandary to those who embrace those differences as essential. Its shimmering surface that reflects black and white, their mutability and their deception, holds an allure for those who long for transformation and poses a threat to the vigilant guardians of the color line. Unable to integrate these two responses, Irene finds herself "caught between two allegiances, different, yet the same. Herself. Her race" (98). These allegiances, a false dilemma between whiteness and blackness, present a real choice between the liberatory possibilities of transformation and the restrictive maintenance of essentialist categories. Clare cannot see the possibilities, only the betrayal. In Clare's presence, Irene "suffered and rebelled because she was unable to disregard the burden of race."[64] Like the nineteenth-century exhibition of white Negroes before other audiences aspiring toward whiteness, the exhibition of Clare's malleable body debunks race as a performance. Martha Cutter argues that Clare's body, performing racial transformations with ease, "throws into question racial divisions, as well as the idea of firm and irrevocable differences between the races."[65] Consumed by her belief in unalterable categories, Irene is unable to rectify the gap between her "black" nature and her "white" dreams.

The control that Clare has seized over her representation and exhibition directly threatens Irene's sense of emotional well-being. Instead of renouncing blackness, Clare renders the boundaries fluid, imaginary, and she crosses boundaries at will. Irene projects her anxieties over Clare's transgressions upon her own marriage to a darker-skinned man. In Irene's skewed logic, Clare's relationships to men mark her passing: if her marriage to John confirms her whiteness, then a relationship with Irene's dark husband will reclaim her blackness. The malleability of Clare's body, its concurrent whiteness and blackness, manifests as the sexual threat of the miscegenated body. Collapsing into madness before Clare's exhibition, Irene pushes her out a window. The sudden death at least temporarily extinguishes the threat of the white Negro body, leaving Irene still haunted with its memory.

LEOPARD BOYS OF SCIENCE

By exerting control over the white Negro body, the writers of passing narratives learn the lessons of white Negro exhibitions in museums and circus freak shows. The showman manipulates the meaning of the humbug, arranges the comparison of bodies, determines and dismantles racial categories. In his novel *Black No More*, George S. Schuyler directly inserts white Negro exhibition into the tradition of the passing narrative. African American scientist and entrepreneur Dr. Junius Crookman straps Harlem man-about-town Max Disher into a machine of his own invention, "a cross between a dentist's chair and the electric chair," and transforms him from black to white.[66] The application of electrical current induces vitiligo, the skin condition that made Henry Moss the talk of Philadelphia and supplied Barnum with an nearly endless parade of Negroes Turning White. The successful transformation of Max Disher, latter-day Leopard Boy, spawns a migration of the African American community from blackness to whiteness. This wholesale conversion creates chaos in a society that relies upon a stable division between black and white. White supremacists panic over the erasure of racial difference and the object of their feelings of superiority. African American leaders fret over the loss of their constituency and source of their political power. The country becomes one large exhibition of white Negroes, white patrons growing increasingly anxious over the display of white skin, uncertain of their own citizenship.

Like its more modest predecessors, Schuyler's narrative of passing *en masse* has been subject to harsh criticism. Schuyler's reputation in his later years as a conservative crank and member of the John Birch Society has inspired a reassessment of his earlier work as, among other things, "reactionary" and "assimilationist."[67] In this light, the image of the entire African American community crossing the color line by racially transforming itself seems an "urge to whiteness."[68] In the most recent and extreme restatement of this criticism, Susan Gubar claims that Schuyler's novel "views the demise of blackness as the only viable solution for African Americans," a scheme that "effectively functions as a form of genocide, threatening to annihilate all African Americans."[69] Put quite simply, this strain of scholarship accuses Schuyler of endorsing and promoting the supremacy of whiteness. This reading, though, ignores one of the primary goals of Schuyler's satire: an attack on racial essentialism by appropriating whiteness and its means of production. In particular, Schuyler draws upon the long history of Anglo-Saxon scientific mastery over whiteness, the periodic efforts to bestow whiteness as a gift to the poor African American stigmatized by black skin. Through the exhibition of technological prowess over the production of racial difference, scientists maintained the property rights for whiteness and its distribution.[70] Eliminating the maternal middleman, so to speak, the white scientists, all male, cast themselves as the color's sole progenitors. But by building a machine that removes melanin from black skin, Schuyler's African American scientist subversively fathers whiteness, eventually flooding the market with bootleg reproductions of white skin and undermining its value.

The early exhibitions of white Negroes resulted from the interests of a scientific community intrigued by the alchemy of racial difference, its origins, its biological mechanism. Although Samuel Stanhope Smith hoped for a gradual whitening of the African American body under the influence of the mild North American climate, other scientists sought to encourage the erasure of blackness. Along with the anatomical knife, Thomas Jefferson suggested the application of solvents to uncover the essence of blackness. Benjamin Rush recorded experiments with sulfuric acid in the attempt to bleach dark skin drastically and facilitate racial transformation, yet the leprosy he saw in African skin did not abate. P. T. Barnum produced his humbug Negro Turning White as a race change resulting from the application of a folk remedy. Consistent through these fantasies of racial transformation, blackness remains to the scientific eye a contagion, an illness to treat. As new technologies emerged, science and pseudoscience still dreamed of Henry Moss, wishing all the while to be the authors of his patches of white.

With their discovery in the late nineteenth century, radium and X rays offered the hope for the cure to a great variety of human ailments. Newspapers hailed the miracle of radiation and the mysteries of the body it unlocked.[71] The new technology allowed physician and layperson to cast aside clothing and peel back the skin and tissue to unveil the bones beneath. The effect of radiation on the blemishes and melanomas on white skin did not go unnoticed. Apparently, the application of X rays could eliminate unwanted and unhealthy dark patches on white skin, a phenomenon of particular interest to hopeful racial scientists. In late December 1903, the *New York Herald* announced a miracle of racial transformation: "Negroes Made White by X-Rays." In a short article, the paper reported that in the process of treating cancer and lupus, Dr. H. K. Pancoast of the University of Pennsylvania "has discovered that it is possible, by means of the X-ray, to so bleach the skin of a negro that to all intents and purposes the subject becomes a white person."[72] With even greater fanfare, the *New York American* reported, "X-Ray to Turn Black Men White." Accompanying the headline was an illustration of an African American man with a patch of white reaching from his forehead to his nose and his cheekbone. Another Philadelphia physician, Dr. Dieffenback, confirmed "the ability to bleach an Ethiopian's skin to the color of that of a Caucasian." The article emphasized the possible appeal of racial transformation to African Americans. "To have the skin of a white man or woman," the article affirmed, "is a thing infinitely desired" in the South. By implication, the radiation treatment would aid incursions of the color line, thereby reducing racial prejudice by reducing blackness. The description of the treatment, though, implied a deadly violence against blackness, the doctors acknowledging an effort to have the color "killed" and "done away with." Although a complete racial transformation unfortunately "might be attended with fatalities," Dr. Dieffenback recommended that the patient "could have his face and hands changed in their color with perfect safety."[73] Presumably, this limited, violent transformation would allow an African American to "be white" while properly clothed in a shirt with long sleeves and buttoned collar. With the growing patches of white on face and hands, this comically partial transition resulted in a kind of induced piebaldism, the Leopard Child scientifically produced and regulated.[74]

Schuyler's Dr. Crookman is a direct descendent of these hopeful scientists. Like them, he concludes that "if there were no Negroes, there would be no Negro problem."[75] In the preface to the novel, Schuyler acknowledges that the inspiration for Crookman and his race-changing process came from reports in the popular press of additional schemes to turn black to white, pronouncements that maintained the tone of a eugenic pogrom against dark skin. In 1929, Dr. Yusaburo Noguchi, a Japanese biologist on a visit to North America, proposed in a series of interviews the possibility of changing dark skin to white through what he called "electrical nutrition and glandular control," the very words Dr. Crookman later uses to describe his procedure. According to newspaper reports, Noguchi claimed his methods not only would effect change "in skin but in what he calls racial characteristics" as well. As part of his mission, he envisioned his work to apply to "the beautification of children," conflating blackness with ugliness. Noguchi admitted that "one could carry his theories on to some sort of Jules Verne finish with electrical nutrition and glandular control, producing a race of supermen capable by physical and mental powers of overthrowing all other people, but he is not interested in that phase of his work at this time."[76] From this disturbing testimony, the logical outcome of the eradication of black skin is a eugenics project that produces a superior whiteness to colonize the less-white.

In the form of chemical solvents, radium, and electricity, scientific innovation eventually found its way to dark skin, applied in the aid of racial science as if melanin were a blight, a curse, a disease. This obsession with dermatological purity culminated in the dreams of eugenicists, the elimination of peoples determined by scientific study to be weak and defective, the horrible logic of ethnic cleansing in service to the construction of racial purity. The scientific application of statistics and Mendelian genetics traced its origin to the earlier efforts of the racial scientists—in particular, the craniometry of Samuel George Morton.[77] Yet the elemental inspiration of these fantasies of racial transformation and assimilation remained the whitening body of the African American with vitiligo. Explaining the inspiration for his electro-chemical process, Schuyler's Dr. Crookman recalls the public display of "a nervous disease known as vitiligo." In his moment of revelation, Crookman observes "a black girl on the street one day who had several irregular patches on her face and hands."[78] The scientist sees in this exhibition of a Leopard Girl the fantasy of racial transformation promoted by racial scientists and reformers before him. Like Benjamin Rush and Samuel Stanhope Smith, who saw in the body of Henry Moss the gradual and inevitable assimilation of the African American, Schuyler re-exhibits the patchy skin of the white Negro to show the folly of these assimilationist hopes and to skewer the arrogance of eugenic scientists by presenting the disruptive force of whitening African American bodies as an outcome of scientific progress.

In Schuyler's satire, the white Negro retains its revolutionary character. Max Disher, the character with the transformed black body, pursues a picaresque journey into the heart of darkness, as it were—a trip down south where he infiltrates the apparatus of popular white supremacy by joining the Knights of Nordica, an organization based upon the Ku Klux Klan.[79] Exploiting the bigotry of the members, he thrives in the organization. He reaches second in command; he marries the Grand Wizard's daughter. In the tradition of the passing narrative and the white Negro exhibition, Max dupes those who witness his white body. The biggest suckers prove to be what Schuyler identifies as "the lower stratum of white working people: hard-faced, lantern-jawed, dull-eyed adult children." Once again, the working poor suffer before the exhibition of the body of the transformed African American. Max preaches before his audience the gospel of white supremacy, "that a white skin was a sure indication of the possession of superior intellect and moral qualities; that all Negroes were inferior to them."[80] All the while, his body proves an ironic counterpoint, a disruptive contradiction that challenges the whiteness and superiority of the easily bamboozled crowd. As J. Martin Favor argues, Max "uses the racist/racialist power structure already in place to dismantle itself. And such a move is possible only because [he], as a black/white man, understands precisely the intricacies of a racist cultural apparatus."[81] As the embodiment of the color line, the white Negro—the body transformed by vitiligo—presents the opportunity to confound racial difference.

The adventures of Max Disher serve as a microcosm for the greater chaos created by a whole population of African Americans transformed by vitiligo. The mass migration threatens the institutions—white and black—that profit either economically or politically from radical racial difference. Through his satire, Schuyler argues that, ironically, racial essentialism benefits white supremacy and African American organizations sworn to fight it. When the opposition between black and white breaks down, it brings the downfall of race improvement associations, bankrupts businesses that sell and manufacture skin lighteners and hair straighteners, and diminishes the circulation of African American newspapers that advertise the products. It is easy to see this racial transformation as a utopian vision of a society rid of difference, blackness eradicated and whiteness exalted. If Schuyler had stopped his satire at the point of a completed white body politic, this reading might have some weight, but he did not end his racial transformations with blackness simply erased. After the achievement of this white utopia, Crookman publishes a report that "in practically every instance the new Caucasians were from two to three shades lighter than the old Caucasians." True to earlier exhibitions, the white Negro once again displays a better skin. "The old Caucasians," Crookman declares, "had never been really white but rather were a pale pink shading down to a sand color and a red."[82] Undaunted by the disappearance of blackness and the new darkness of their own skins, the population formerly known as white attempts to reassert the hegemony of their complexion, re-creating boundaries between black and white or, in this case, between white and near-white. Prejudice arises against the extremely pale.

Caucasians begin to tan and apply stains to accentuate difference. The transformations continue to multiply until whiteness and blackness become clearly arbitrary fluid fictions, the binary dissolving in the chaos created by white Negro exhibition. Schuyler demonstrates that the display of the African American body grown white from vitiligo unsettles racial construction until race itself is dismantled.

As an outcome of this subversion of race, Schuyler writes, "A white face became startlingly rare. America was definitely, enthusiastically mulatto-minded." With the final image of the novel, a newspaper photograph of a happy American family and their friends on a European vacation, Schuyler has his last caustic joke on white supremacy and racial essentialism. The picture displays the remaining players in the novel: the transformed and untransformed African Americans, the former white supremacists who have uncovered their own biracial ancestors, all made darker by the sun. As the centerpiece, Max Disher, the white Negro, and his wife present their son, the utopian "dusky" miscegenated child.[83] The tableau marks an imagined mulatto future, identities mixed, some manufactured, and all claims to purity dismissed.

BLACK OR WHITE

> By 2000 A.D. a full-blooded American Negro may be rare enough to get a job in a museum, and a century from now our American social leaders may be as tanned naturally as they are now striving to become artificially.
>
> —George S. Schuyler, "A Negro Looks Ahead," 1930

To those who wished for an end to slavery, the first exhibitions of Henry Moss represented a hope for an elimination of racial boundaries. For those frustrated by the failures of Reconstruction and disheartened by the increase of violence delivered upon the African American body, the exhibition of a white African American body proposed a possible miscegenated future in which racial prejudice dissolves with the end of racial difference and purposeful interracial couplings result in a settling of the genetic pool and a brown American face born out of the assimilation. In a series of articles for the *Boston Evening Transcript*, Charles Chesnutt challenges the notion that "the future American will consist of a harmonious fusion of the various European elements," eugenically siphoning out all of "their undesirable traits" and keeping the good. Instead, Chesnutt dreams of the ultimate amalgamation of "white, black, and Indian." As a result of this racial blending and elimination of racial difference, he argues, "[t]here would be no inferior race to domineer over; there would be no superior race to oppress those who differed from them in racial externals." Even with the dissolution of blackness, his vision of an amalgamated future retains the hegemony of whiteness, imagining that this new people will "likely" identify itself as white.[84]

As a foundation for his argument, Chesnutt uses what he considers already mixed American bloodlines, cataloging the "Stream of Dark Blood in the Veins of the Southern Whites."[85] This tangled lineage, both acknowledged and unacknowledged, documented and rumored, gives the lie to the purity of southern whiteness and the presumed segregation of the races. Chesnutt points to the intense production of southern legislation against miscegenation, its intricate calculus of blood and descent, as further proof of the extent of this racial transgression. In *Black No More*, Schuyler targets this southern obsession with lineage and presumption of purity. Arthur Snobbcraft, the aristocratic president of the white supremacist Anglo-Saxon Association, and Dr. Samuel Buggerie, his henchman and eugenic statistician, expect that the family trees will exhibit racial purity, whiteness graphically laid out along immaculate lines of descent. Instead, they uncover their own status as white Negroes. Buggerie's "statistics" reveal the secret history of American slavery.[86] Bondmen and bondwomen ancestors cavorted with slaves, masters imposed upon their offspring, children grew whiter and whiter, then passed for white and blended into the population.

The obsession with genealogy in Schuyler's novel, the tracing of inherited traits through family trees, generates in part from the early-twentieth-century passion for eugenics. Through statistical analysis both laughably subjective and biased, Francis Galton determined by his own hierarchical system "a difference of not less than two grades between the black and white races, and it may be more."[87] Karl Pearson, Galton's protégé and biographer, trained legions of eugenicists to draft and study family trees, to trace the sources of defect and recessive traits. In *A Monograph on Albinism in Man*, Pearson and his students plotted the family trees of white Negroes to discover the origin of the whiteness in African skin and confine it to the status of disease. They charted the lineages of Henry Moss, John "Primrose" Boby, Ashley Benjamin, and all of the members of the related Anderson and Davis families, including the women who toured Europe as "The Three Striped Graces."[88] According to their polling and statistical analysis, Pearson and his crew determined that albinism was less prevalent among Anglo-Saxons than in other races, even among the Celts and the Welsh.[89] The imprecision and chauvinism of their casual counting aside, the genealogical tables were markedly incomplete, some casting back only a generation as information about lineage proved scarce and even unreliable.

The threat of invisible blackness—the one drop that Schuyler presents as

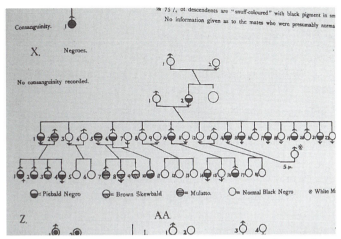

S.p.

◐= Piebald Negro   ◐= Brown Skewbald   ◐= Mulatto.   ○= Normal Black Negro   ✻ White M

Z.   AA

FIG. 22. Anderson and Davis family tree, from Pearson, Nettleship, and Usher's *A Monograph on Albinism in Man*. Loan courtesy of the Iowa State University Library.

FIG. 23. Eliza, James, Bob, and Lillie "Tiger Lily" Davis. From author's collection.

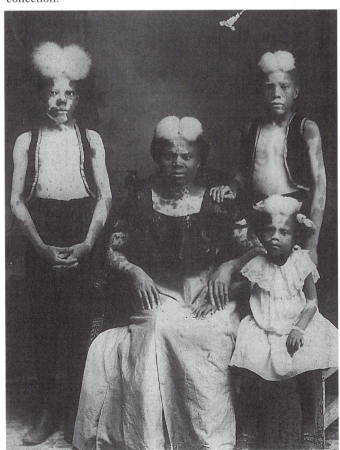

part of most American bloodlines—fosters fears of dark births, babies with African American skin born to couples who presumed themselves white. Werner Sollors has traced the trope of the "Natus Æthiopus" as far back as Aristotle, and such exhibitions were "circumscribed by a small range of options, including the reaction of wonder [and] the suspicion or accusation of adultery."[90] This fascination with sudden unaccountable blackness or whiteness informs the fascination with the white Negro body. Bloodlines accounted for, genealogy traced, the color of the newborn astonished its audience and worried those who feared transgression. This concern surfaces in the passing narratives as the mothers fret over the possible betrayal of their child's darker skin. In Nella Larsen's *Passing*, the women gathered in Clare Kendry's apartment confess the anxiety they feel over the possible birth of "a dark child." "It's only deserters like me," Clare confides, "who have to be afraid of freaks of nature."[91] Darkness must be explained, siblings compared to quell speculation. Different complexions may indicate different fathers and unspeakable transgressions.

At the scene of white Negro exhibition, the image of black and white twins issuing from the same mother hints at interracial sexual transgression, the threat of confused parentage and therewith the blurring of racial categories. Barnum displayed his "Albino Children" alongside their darker siblings and their mother. The spectacle of the black and white siblings together—a piebald family, so to speak—works to establish the binary of black and white, yet the scene insinuates the possibility of a white man lurking in the proverbial woodpile. Although the black and white offspring may prompt a laugh from their white and near-white audience, the humor is tempered by unease. The uncertainty of bloodlines implied by the spectacle fuels the fear of transgression in the white body—the birth of dark-skinned child to presumed white parents. This fear later manifests itself in racist humor, the cuckolded white husband replaced by the cuckolded African American, reduced to coon caricature. In one typical late-nineteenth-century trade card, a midwife in Aunt Jemima attire announces to the man in minstrel-show striped pants and long-tailed blue coat that his wife has just given birth to twins. The midwife also warns him "dat one am kinder white." The final panel of the card features a scene of interracial chaos: two squalling infants—one black, one white—the wife in open-mouthed dismay, the father visibly angry. For the punch line, he tells his wife, "if dat chile dont change color der'l be trouble in dis yer famly." Although this racist joke features the caricature of an African American family, a malignant expression of white superiority, it voices as well an anxiety harbored by its intended white male audience over racial purity and sexual competition from the now ostensibly free African American male body.

"I'M A FARDER"

"AUNTY SAYS DER AM TWO"

"AND DAT ONE AM KINDER WHITE"

"IF DAT CHILE DONT CHANGE COLOR,
DER'L BE TROUBLE IN DIS YER FAM'LY"

F I G . 2 4 . Trade card. From author's collection.

FIG. 25. Sideshow at the Vermont State Fair, photograph by Jack Délano. By permission of the Library of Congress, Prints and Photographs Division, FSA/OWI Collection, [reproduction number, e.g., LC-USF34-9058-C].

The image of the black and white twins resurfaces in the sideshows of state fairs during the 1940s, still bearing the stigma of racial transgression and blurring distinctions. For years, the Strong Twins—African American children, one with dark skin, one apparently with albinism—were displayed in freak shows. "A first in medical history," proclaims the sideshow banner. "One brown eyes, one blue eyes." A large photograph places the children side-by-side for easy comparison of skin color. The spectacle of the children—one white, one black—intimates miscegenation, the physical manifestation of the racist joke, the coon-show father cuckolded, competing sperm ending up in a dead heat. Equally a spectacle, the mother likewise suffers exhibition, a producer of whiteness and, by implication, an adulteress. Confronting their own fears of strange, darker births, the crowd gapes.

The trope of the black and white twins still maintains currency as a modern spectacle, an object lesson for the uncertainties brought about by medical innovation as much as an emblem of racial harmony. In a perverse scene of technological cuckoldry, a white woman from Staten Island recently gave birth to white and black twins. Enough of a spectacle to be reported by the Associated Press and reprinted in major newspapers, including the *New York Times*, the birth and subsequent custody case resulted from a mix-up in embryo implantation at a Manhattan fertility clinic. A lab technician admitted that a catheter used to impregnate the Staten Island woman might have contained some embryos from an African American couple from New Jersey. The newsworthiness of the story turns largely on the spectacle of racial contrast. The lead sentence of the story announces, "A black baby born to a white Staten Island woman." The remainder of the story is largely free of racial anxiety: the couple resolved custody amicably, even though the Staten Island woman had become attached to her African American son; the Staten Island couple would have visitation rights; the couples considered the boys brothers; and they planned to sue the fertility clinic for malpractice and negligence. After the impetus of the article to focus upon racial contrast, the figure of the twins playing together as they grow up offers a utopian image of racial brotherhood, the poster-children of the postmodern blended family, racial divisions trumped by parental love.[92]

By now an apotheosis of harmony and murky lines of descent, the figure of the black and white twins as an image of racial concord surfaces in Michael Jackson's video for his song "Black or White," his anthem for the elimination of racial difference. By themselves, the lyrics of Jackson's song call for an erasure of race at the same time as they summon the binary of racial difference, a world severely divided into distinctions between black and white. "If you're thinking about being my baby," he sings, "it don't matter if you're black or white." In the second half of the song's bridge, Jackson employs a rap punctuated by the declaration, "I'm not going to spend my life being a color." The contradiction voiced by the song—dismissing markers of racial difference and invoking them in the same motion—demonstrates how difficult it is to disengage from race.

Jackson and his director, Jon Landis, mine the catalog of images inherited from white Negro exhibitions, a parade of miscegenated bodies exhibited to challenge racial certainty. Having announced his vitiligo in the form of a public confession, Jackson is himself a conceptual descendant of Barnum's Negro Turning White, a transforming body that defies categorization. Like that of his predecessors, Jackson's ever-whitening surface draws speculation, awe, and anger. Scholars doubt his vitiligo, critics accuse him of racial self-hatred.[93] Regardless, the uncertainty of his white body enthralls, makes good copy. In the initial scene of his exhibition, the dancing African tribesmen who frame his white body intensify his status as a white Negro. They wear bifurcated tribal makeup, split down the middle, half in blackface and half in whiteface. An unconscious reminder of the Leopard Child, the dancers bear the fetish of piebaldism to accompany the exhibition of Jackson's own trans-forming body and his message of cultural and racial hybridity. As a center-piece for the video exhibition, at the bridge of the song, Landis places the two utopian infants—one white, one black—at the North Pole of a globe. As the white child looks on, the black child plays with a snow globe in which Jack-son dances with Cossacks. World peace reduced to child's play, the twins still carry the innuendo of miscegenation and harmony brought about through racial transgression.

This exhibition of racial harmony begins as a colonial travelogue yet, oddly enough, through the influence of Jackson's white Negro body, grows into a guessing game of transforming racial identities.[94] In the prelude to the long version of the video, precocious child-actor Macauley Culkin blasts his musically intolerant father with a guitar power-chord to what appears to be the African veldt to witness from his armchair Jackson trading steps with dancers from various cultures before ever-changing backdrops. Jackson stomps with the Africans, rain dances with Native Americans, cavorts with an Indian dancer, kicks up his heels with Cossacks. In an afterword to the video, a brief denouement of behind-the-scenes materials and outtakes, Landis calls the dancers "ethnic," casting their performance as a *National Geographic* dis-play of cultural difference. Jackson's white body attempts to bridge this differ-ence, adroitly choreographing his way from tradition to tradition, territory to territory, the white Negro mimic as transgressor of boundaries in the guise of a colonial facilitator. Eric Lott emphasizes the artificial nature of the specta-cle, the mimicry of the presentation. The "dancing itself looks patently approximate," he argues, "West Africa by way of Michael Jackson." Race and culture here is "manufactured." Even the Native American child he dances with in the second segment "doesn't look Native American at all."[95]

And here is the danger for the audience of the white Negro exhibition. The transforming and transgressing body calls for definition, challenges all those who witness the spectacle to pinpoint the humbug. To do so, paradoxi-cally, encourages the spectator to reestablish the parameters for essential cat-egories. For a child not to "look Native American," one must affirm the necessary physical characteristics of Native Americans. The white Negro still dupes.

The guessing game of identities reaches its climax in the final set of images for the video of the song. During the coda—a long mantra of "black or white"—a face morphs through a succession of racial and ethnic identi-ties, transforming in turn from Asian to African to European and back. The transformations are neither immediately complete nor abrupt. A change will begin in the eyes or chin; dreadlocks will fall over a white face; a beard will grow over a woman's mouth. In these moments, identities blend, combine, and confuse. These sequential glimpses of technologically miscegenated facial features promote an ideal that circumvents racial distinctiveness and disavows arbitrary physical markers of identity. Presiding over this utopia of constructed and deconstructed identities is the transgressive figure of Michael Jackson, the exhibited white Negro.

The scene of exhibition extends its influence from the early displays before the American Philosophical Society and in Peale's American Museum to Michael Jackson's morphing body before the camera of Jon Landis. The racial transformations that end the video performance of "Black or White" invoke the long history of Negroes Turning White in nineteenth-century museum spaces and the subsequent exhibitions of white skin in twentieth-century narratives of passing, calling upon as well the facility of the white Negro to disrupt the black/white binary and frustrate racial categorization. In the next chapter, I will turn from Jackson's body of work to his body itself to focus upon his apparent purposeful manipulation of skin color and, most importantly, to analyze the near-hysteric public and critical reaction to this transformation—ridicule that further emphasizes the revolutionary effect that the white Negro still has upon its audience.

White Negroes, Leopard Boys, and the King of Pop

Freaks are called freaks and are treated as they are treated—in the main, abominably—because they are human beings who cause to echo, deep within us, our most profound terrors and desires.

—James Baldwin on Michael Jackson, "Freaks and Other Ideals of Manhood," 1985

Two hundred years after the exhibition of Henry Moss at the sign of the Black Horse Inn in Philadelphia, Fox Television aired an installment of *The X-Files* entitled "Teliko." In the 1996 episode, the bodies of murdered black men turn up in the City of Brotherly Love, their skins a sudden and miraculous white from a complete absence of pigment. Theories for the deadly transformation echo the first philosophical speculations upon the white Negro body. The encroaching whiteness on dark skin spurs fears of fever imported from the tropics by immigrants, skin color fancied as a disease spread by black bodies. The spectacle of whiteness reduces Africans and African Americans to specimens for scientific investigation, vulnerable to the anatomical knife as it seeks to uncover the mystery of the skin's transformation. Special FBI agent Mulder eventually speculates, correctly, upon the extraordinary existence of a "lost tribe, a clan of sub-Saharan albinos," pigment vampires who, deprived of pituitary glands, thirst for the melanin that their bodies cannot produce. As the vampire's supply of color depletes and he again grows hungry, telltale patches of white appear and spread like vitiligo across his dark face. We see the West African man feed off the African immigrants. He inserts a thin straw up his victim's nostril until the bone breaks and he reaches the gland. In the final scene, starving for pigment, the killer becomes an albino, now spectral, nearly demonic, in his white depletion.

Blackness is clearly attached to racial and cultural identity in this tale of horror. The murders generate in the immigrant African community tales of the Teliko, an African spirit who feasts on the living. A folkloric reminder of a superstitious past, the white vampire is an albino fright, cannibalistic, yearning for blackness. Limiting himself to the transient community of unattached Nigerian men, the pigment vampire never sucks away the color of nonblack men. Perhaps pale skin lacks the nourishment or the attraction. Or perhaps the vampire seeks in black skin the affirmation of his own identity as he absorbs it into his body. The effect of the attack, unlike those by conventional vampires, is that of a passionless rape, not an erotic seduction. Their noses violated by a tube, their presumed racial essence sucked away, these men are unmanned. Melanin here is life's blood. The removal of color from the African American body, the deprivation of racial identity, brings death.

The body that shifts between white and black—transforming back and again as it feeds and depletes—alters other black bodies, tests the gullible investigators and scientists, and defies their assumptions about racial identity. In the show's initial scene of exhibition, the display of the body to the medical gaze ends in a hoodwinking. Presented with a photograph of the first victim, Special Agent Scully, sometime pathologist, mistakenly identifies him as white. As she is told of other victims, she imagines the possibility of even more undiscovered dead African bodies passing as white in other morgues and mortuaries. She wonders whether the depigmentation may have caused "a problem with identification." Under this insufficient scientific scrutiny, skin color resurrects as the sole indicator of racial difference. Scully first conjectures that the color change results from a pathogen, a plague infecting young African men. As she presides over the cadaver of the first victim, the camera pans slowly over the body, lingering upon the spectacle of his ashy white skin and pale, almost blond hair. The examination of the African man turned white affords her partner, Mulder, the opportunity to compare the skin of the victim to another contemporary white Negro. "I know there's a Michael Jackson joke in there somewhere," he quips, "but I can't seem to find it."

MICHAEL JACKSON, WHITE NEGRO

> They say he used to want to be Diana Ross, now I think he wants to be Olivia Newton-John.
>
> —Don Novello, *Mother Jones*, 1992.

But Mulder's joke is clearly understood, if unspoken. Michael Jackson. King of Pop. Black man with whitening skin. Racial freak. Perennial punch line.

Separate from his recordings and stage performances, Jackson's whitening body generates criticism, disbelief, and an endless stream of jokes. This reaction affords an opportunity to witness the effect a contemporary white Negro has on an audience. The racial transformation in this exhibition pricks at the same adherence to rigid racial boundaries that early Negroes Turning White annoyed, this time offending those who would defend the purity of blackness. Defectors to whiteness, it seems, will not be tolerated.

In one of the exhibitions in George C. Wolfe's play *The Colored Museum*, a character identified only as the Man forsakes his sixties' black revolutionary past in order to assimilate and survive in the corporate present by tossing out emblems of racial solidarity: an Afro comb, a dashiki, a "Free Angela" button, a copy of *Soul on Ice*. The Kid, a manifestation of his younger, rage-filled self, pleads with him not to abandon his seed-time, but the Man confesses, "Being black is too emotionally taxing." At the center of this scene of racial disavowal is the joke of Michael Jackson, white Negro. The Man throws out a series of record albums and 45s until he comes to the Jackson Five's "I Want You Back." The Kid tries to stop him. "Man, you can't throw that away," he says. "It's living proof Michael had a black nose."[1] His nose narrowing, his hair straightening, his dark skin fading with each album cover, Michael Jackson has been reduced to the poster boy of racial self-hatred.

The critical scrutiny of Michael Jackson's body over the final decade and a half of the twentieth century has surpassed all assessment of his music and video performances. We have read the jeering narrative, the ridicule. Critics and cultural observers have presumed his gradually transforming body, his whitening skin, evidence of a treasonous attempt to defect from blackness. From time to time, the derision flares. In these rants, his skin is at turns "decolorized," "blanched," "bone-colored," and "pale as the man in the moon."[2] He has been called "a white zombie," an "artificial human," "the buppy version of Dorian Gray," "America's pre-eminent geek," and a "Toon."[3] Rumors abound of skin bleaches, intensive hydroquinone treatments, chemical peels, and dermabrasions. Further gossip and suspicion circulate about chin implants and numerous nose jobs. The lesser members of his family have chimed in with their taunts and allegations. His brother Jermaine addresses his song "Word to the Badd!" to Michael's transgressions: "Reconstructed/Been abducted/Don't know who you are . . . /Once you were made/You changed your shade/Was your color wrong?" Sister LaToya, who also has a rumored affection for Porcelana bleaching cream, has given contradictory accounts of her brother's acquired whiteness. In 1991, she told a reporter that her brother's skin peculiarities derive from the lupus she claimed at the time he has suffered from since 1979. Later, she denied any skin condition and blamed the white skin on Michael's addiction to skin creams.[4]

At the core of this animosity are allegations that Michael has turned his back on his blackness in order to live his life as a white man. "Jackson conforms to an embarrassing stereotype," Francis Davis claims, "that of the black man altering his features to pass."[5] Greg Tate, in an even more damning fit of vitriolic pique, impeaches Jackson's authenticity, his racial loyalty, charging that he "has crossed so far over the line that there ain't no coming back— assuming through surgical transmutation of his face a singular infamy in the annals of tomming."[6] In the mythology this criticism creates, the transformation of Jackson's body signals a deeper iniquity—the acquiescence to the demands of a white public highlighted, the self-proclaimed King of Pop reduced to the shuffling, agreeable plantation Negro.

At this point, I am careful not to assign any particular motive to Jackson's obviously transforming physiognomy, yet I am willing to entertain all of the possibilities his growing mythology fashions. His alleged surgical procedures, makeup applications, and skin conditions are, at bottom, as much a mystery to me as they are to anyone with limited knowledge of his intentions. The changing surface of the white Negro continues to spark us to speculate, to test our abilities to discern the operation at work, to ferret out the humbug. In the end, the design behind Jackson's manipulations is not nearly as interesting as his audience's fixation on his changing color and, in response, his periodic attempts to seize control of the narrative of his body. Discarding claims to truth about the singer's psychology and behavior, I seek an understanding of that lore as it develops around the figure of Michael Jackson and what it says about our culture's continuing response to the exhibition of the white Negro.

On February 10, 1993, Michael Jackson gave an unprecedented primetime interview to Oprah Winfrey. During the course of the program, Jackson proclaimed his racial pride and explained his ever-whitening body as a product of vitiligo. This pronouncement of an affliction has met with apprehension and downright disbelief. The cover of *Entertainment Weekly* boasted the question, "Can We Really Believe This Guy?"[7] Seemingly to assuage the doubt, an extensive explanation of vitiligo appeared in the *New York Times*, in which Jackson's physician confirmed and documented the condition.[8] Skeptical of the claims of vitiligo, critics pointed to his choice of treatment, the whitening of his divided body as convincing proof that he prefers whiteness over blackness.[9] Although they are correct that some people with vitiligo darken the pigmentless patches, others with extreme cases of the disorder choose to lighten skin if their lack of pigmentation covers a majority of the visible body surface. According to the American Dermatological Association, the decision to lighten or darken is not necessarily a matter of racial preference but of convenience. For some patients with extreme loss of pigment, "the most practical treatment for vitiligo is to remove remaining pigment from normal skin and make the whole body an even white color."[10] Even though the lightening of profoundly depigmented skin appears the most logical and least physically strenuous alternative, the purposeful whitening of skin carries with it the burden of identity politics. With this threat of greater exile and accusations of racial betrayal, most African Americans with vitiligo oppose further whitening of the skin at any cost.[11] As Jackson has learned, the lightening of skin color for any reason results in disbelief and indictment.

As the child of freak shows and racial science, the spectacle of vitiligo still bears the taint of fraud and traitorous racial conversion. The folk wisdom surrounding the disorder associates the appearance of whiteness on dark skin with sexual escapades across the color line. The stigma of whiteness attracts the scrutiny of strangers and charges that the change in color signals a conscious attempt to change identity.[12] In 1981, *Jet* exhibited in its pages Mrs. Eddie Mae Kearney, a woman with vitiligo, whose life "wouldn't be half as bad if she didn't have to face the stares." One photograph renders her body a wonder to the reader, displaying the evidence of spots on her face, hands, and arms. Another shows her with her darker-skinned relatives, a reprise of the contrasts typical of nineteenth-century exhibitions of albino African Americans. The article tells the sad tale of a woman suffering exile from her own community. During the sixties in the still-segregated South, she claims, an African American restaurant refused her service because the waitress believed her to be white.[13] The magazine exhibition of Mrs. Kearney's body presents the tragedy of a woman neither all black nor all white, identity denied and mistrusted in the confusion of changing pigment.

Vitiligo continues to carry connotations of Barnum flimflam and manufactured freakishness. To an audience that still requires essential difference between races, the whiteness of the exhibited Leopard Child must be unnatural, impossible, the product of paint and too much imagination. Whiteness is a choice in this narrative, a willful crime against blackness. In his exhibitions, Henry Moss encouraged the tactile investigation of his skin to assure that the black skin and the white were smoothly joined, natural manifestations and not a deception brought about by his own physical manipulations.[14]

The romance of the freak show as unflinching fraud, though, holds liberatory possibilities. Finessing the body through makeup, fade cream, or surgical procedure, the purposeful construction of a Leopard Child offers the potential to escape the confinement of identification, to become an enigma, both black and white yet neither. In her story "Burning Bush," Michelle Cliff presents the freak show display of a piebald body—a woman labeled "The Girl from Martinique"—as a painted humbug. The printed ballyhoo boasts, "This checkerboard of a woman owes her skin to certain practices of her native land brought with her ancestors from the Dark Continent. She comes directly from Paris . . . appearances before the crowned heads . . . main attraction at the Hippodrome . . . the subject of study by the greatest scientific minds of the century." This hype recalls the history of white Negro exhibition: the exotic, colonized African body displayed as imperial bounty, the exhibition of Maria Sabina, a Barnum display in the New York Hippodrome, the body submitted to the gaze of the racial scientist. The Girl from Martinique admits that she is a "pretend" freak, a fraud concocted to escape a life of prostitution or servitude. Her light-skinned child, produced with the show's Lobster Man, undergoes the same treatment, a "patchwork" cultivated with "a couple bottles of white shoe polish."[15] Once again, the Leopard Child resurfaces as a visual representation of miscegenation. In this case, though, the exhibited body seizes control of the exhibition, manipulating her body, managing her presentation, authorizing her own status as a freak. Suzanne Bost argues that the aggrandized bodies of The Girl from Martinique and her child "simulate, mock, or parody the biological production of half-black, half-white children . . . turning racial mixture to her own economic advantage, and reimagining biracialism as a constructed self-chosen artifice."[16] The application of shoe polish — in this instance, a parodic whitening of the body — manifests as a rebellion against the unalterable binary of black and white racial identities figured in the epidermis. Cliff proposes a dangerous possibility for the employment of the Leopard Child, symbol of the miscegenated body: a constructed biraciality, a performative shell that frustrates categorization. The patchwork fabricated by The Girl from Martinique externalizes what she feels herself to be, neither black nor white yet a creative combination of her own device.

Through the conscious engineering of his body as a spectacle, Michael Jackson, contemporary Leopard Boy, has constructed an identity for himself—biracial, nonracial, even freakish. He has changed his face, his color, possibly even his story, to affect and frustrate an audience presumptuous enough to pin him down. By announcing his vitiligo before a national audience, he begins a riff on Barnum's Leopard Child, the transgressive figure that threatens to dissolve racial boundaries, an act Jackson more than likely has schooled himself in through his obsessive fascination with Victorian freaks.[17] Reproducing the advertisements of nineteenth-century albinos, doctors testify to the skin disorder and provide documentation; the public speculates and scoffs in disbelief. Jackson's reinvention of his body does not so much attack the notion of racial identity as replicate its confusion and exacerbate its reliance upon physical markers of difference.[18] Each transformation, each shade lighter, each snip of the knife tests the enforcement of racial qualifications.

LEOPARD CHILD AS RACE TRAITOR

Five little nigger boys grinning in a row
  Watch "Mummy Flannigan" scrub "Jim Crow;"
Five little nigger boys screaming with delight
  Golly! Massa Cook's Soap turns black white!!

—Cook's "Lightning" Soap advertisement, ca. 1890

Early in his 1789 narrative, African-born Olaudah Equiano gives an account of his experience as a naïf to European manners and culture. As a young slave in England, he tries to bring about his own racial transformation with plain soap and water and a little elbow grease, after he witnesses the bathing of a six-year-old white girl. "I had often observed," he writes, "that when her mother washed her face it looked very rosy; but when she washed mine it did not look so; I therefore tried often times myself if I could not by washing make my face of the same colour as my little playmate . . . , but it was all in vain." Preoccupied with personal hygiene, Equiano peppers the account of his early life with assertions of African cleanliness in an effort to argue against the racist notion of Africans as dirty, uncivilized subhumans.[19] In this disturbing scene of racial envy, though, Equiano's longing for a pale complexion conforms to a colonial fantasy that linked civilization with soap—the washing of the unwashed, so to speak, the conversion of the heathen by scrubbing away the darkness and revealing the true and original whiteness beneath.

As discussed in chapter 2, colonizers dreamed of dark natives translated to a white semblance. In the late nineteenth century, British and American soap manufacturers mined the fantasy of black bodies turned miraculously white to advertise their product and persuade the white buying public that a weekly bath would distinguish them from the sullied races. Anne McClintock places soap advertising "at the vanguard of Britain's . . . civilizing mission" and, as a result, at the core of its national identity.[20] In the United States, the ads employed the script of white Negro exhibition to demonstrate that their products could change the leopard's spots and wash the Ethiop white. Trade cards and magazine inserts staged scene after scene of African American men and African American children scoured of blackness.[21] Irish servants soaked dark-skinned boys in bubbly tubs of Cook's "Lightning" Soap; black mammies proudly displayed children whitened by Pearline Washing Compound; even a young George Washington could not "tell a lie" that he had removed the color from a grinning, barefoot slave with Fairbank's White Star Soap. Like the earlier spectacles of spotted children and Negroes Turning White, these advertisements and their ubiquitous reproduction conveyed to the public a vision of racial transformation, the always incomplete conversion marketing the pipe dream of a body politic cleansed of blackness.

The extensive distribution of these cheaply produced lithographic trade cards, McClintock has argued, brought scientific racism to a wider white and near-white audience.[22] To the African American public, the mass-produced images of whitening skin could only reinforce the aesthetics of white supremacy and induce feelings of their own racial inferiority. In Toni Morrison's first novel, *The Bluest Eye*, commercial representations of idealized whiteness instigate in her African American characters a neurotic self-loathing. The resulting desire for racial transformation leads to madness. The novel tells the story of two parallel childhoods spent in the shadow of whiteness and its hegemony. The tragically abused Pecola Breedlove and the spunky yet nevertheless affected Claudia MacTeer endure the daily barrage of aestheticized whiteness from World War II–era popular culture: the movies of Shirley Temple dancing with Bill "Bojangles" Robinson; the Christmas gifts of "blue-eyed, yellow-haired, pink-skinned" dolls; the elementary school reading books sporting the adventures of rosy-cheeked Dick and Jane, Alice and Jerry.[23] These white images of beauty author the Breedlove family's belief in their own ugliness and unworthiness: "The master had said, 'You are ugly people.' They had looked upon themselves and saw nothing to contradict the statement; saw, in fact, support for it leaning at them from every billboard, every movie, every glance, 'Yes,' they had said. 'You are right'" (39). In her self-hatred, Claudia avenges herself on white dolls, turning the anatomical knife—under which African Americans have suffered for centuries—upon her abuser; unable to express her rage sufficiently, however, the hatred turns inward, and she learns to love the white doll and its blondness. Deprived of the same emotional reserve, Pecola can only dream of racial transformation. She longs for blue eyes, believing that "if those eyes of hers were different, that is to say, beautiful, she herself would be different" (46).

Her transformation comes at the hands of the misanthropic pedophile Soaphead Church, so-named from his efforts at straightening his "tight, curly hair" with a pomade of soap lather (167). Both his hatred of people and love for "the breasts of little girls" spawn from his family's generations-long obsessive, incestuous longing for whiteness and its reproduction (178). From centuries of Western aesthetics, he has inherited its association of blackness with dirt as well as his consequent desire for cleanliness and innocence, which manifests in the children's bodies. Pecola seeks the help of Soaphead as a reputed "Reader, Adviser, and Interpreter of Dreams," a semimagical appellation that suggests to the young, desperate girl the power of a shaman (165). She asks the pedophile for blue eyes, and he grants them. He has her feed poisoned meat to his landlady's dog—an act of abuse upon an animal that disgusts him—and tells her that the dog's convulsions, his odd behavior, will be her sign that her wish has come true. "No one will see her blue eyes," he angrily addresses God. "But she will" (182). Soaphead blames God for putting the child in an impossible situation: to yearn for beauty in a world that will forever deny it to her. By

FIG. 26. Advertisement for Cook's "Lightning" Soap. From author's collection.

F I G . 2 7 . Advertisement for Pearline Washing Compound. From author's collection.

F I G . 2 8 . Advertisement for Fairbank's White Star Soap. From author's collection.

achieving this symbol of whiteness, Pecola falls into madness. Mumbling to herself in public, she has now lost herself to her newfound beauty and the illusion of her racial transformation.

In the figure of the pedophile granting whiteness to a young girl going mad, Morrison presents an oddly prescient image of the mythological Michael Jackson as recently narrated in newspapers and tabloids. Professed lover of the innocence and beauty of children, black man turning white, accused child molester, Jackson fulfills Morrison's calculus of whiteness as progenitor of self-hatred, perversity, and madness. To see Jackson's manipulations of his body as a symptom of racial self-hatred is to review the history of African American beauty products. From the moment of emancipation, African American newspapers and periodicals advertised products to bleach skin and straighten hair: Black and White Ointment, Ozonized Ox Marrow, Curl-I-Cure, Ro-Zol, Kink-No-More, and the ominously titled Black Skin Remover.[24] These products claimed to alter appearance, to transform the "black" body into one as near white as possible. An early-twentieth-century advertisement for Black Skin Remover vows that it "will turn the skin of a black or brown person four or five shades lighter, and a mulatto person perfectly white." Disavowing the freakish figure of the Leopard Child, the advertisement guarantees that the product "does not turn the skin to spots but bleaches out white, the skin remaining beautiful without continual use."[25] Products that promised racial transformation reinforced the racist, pro-slavery mythology that darkness of skin signified servitude and savagery. Noliwe Rooks argues that late-nineteenth-century advertisements "raise the specter of a return to slavery" by promoting concerns among young African Americans that dark skin "was responsible for [the] enslaved condition" of their parents and grandparents. Embracing the earlier efforts of the racial scientists, manufacturers cast blackness as an "imperfection to be fixed, . . . a disease or blemish" to be cured.[26] These products fed—and continue to feed in advertisements for Porcelana and Ultra-Sheen—upon insecurities and help to reinforce the eminence of whiteness and, in the economy of polarized racial difference, the vilification of dark skin.

Not only did African American newspapers profit from this fantasy of racial transformation through the advertisement of these products in their pages, the manufacturers, often African American, acquired fortunes as well. Reputedly the first African American woman to become a self-made millionaire, Madame C. J. Walker, the popularizer of the straightening comb, developed a whole system for hair treatment. She always denied that she intended her merchandise to erase racial characteristics; nevertheless, her preparations and devices addressed the same feelings of racial inferiority as other beauty items.[27] The folly of racial transformation through the application of skin treatments and the profiteers who grew rich from racial insecurity did not escape the notice of African American writers. In Schuyler's *Black No More,* Dr. Crookman's operation to turn blacks white parodies African American obsession with lightening skin and straightening hair. Part of Max Disher's joy over his new complexion is the end to his application of "kink-no-more lotions" and the "expenditures for skin whiteners" (35). The sudden obsolescence of hair straighteners and skin bleaches that follows the mass transformation of the black population destroys a substantial portion of the African American economy. Newspapers fold from lack of advertisers. Modeled after Madame C. J. Walker, Mme. Sisseretta Blandish, "the beauty specialist, who owned the swellest hair-straightening parlor in Harlem," is driven out of business as the population thins and whitens (47). Like the other African American characters in Schuyler's novel, though, she proves adaptable to the new economics of whiteness. In a nation now self-conscious about the stigma of light skin, Blandish, as the newly white Mrs. Sari Blandine, develops "a skin stain that would impart a long-wearing light-brown tinge to the pigment" (221).

The reconstruction of an identity through the manipulation of the body generates criticism of racial dishonesty. To snip some cartilage is to hate one's race. To apply makeup a shade or two lighter, to smooth in a dollop of Porcelana, signals pitiable neurosis. Drawing upon the long history of skin- and hair-care products and the fantasy of transformation they endorse, African American authors have used the image of pale, blotchy patches of skin to satirize racial self-hatred and the failed efforts of some African Americans to eradicate the assumed social stigma of black skin. Those characters who try to achieve white skin become derided traitors to their race, pathetic victims of the fiction of white beauty.

This perception of treason in the whitening body, a denial of racial identity through chemical processes, twists fictional characters into wickedness, the growing whiteness a symbol of Caucasian avarice and deceit. In chapter 3, I addressed the demonization of white skin in the work of Chester Himes. Through his characters with albinism and vitiligo, he positions whiteness as unnatural, an encroaching evil on dark skin. In his novel *The Heat's On,* the manipulative heroin dealer and faith healer Sister Heavenly suffers an aversion for her own black skin so profound as to make of her a racial freak. "As a young woman," Himes writes, "her skin had been black; but daily application of bleach creams for more than half a century had lightened her complexion to the color of pigskin. Her toothpick arms, extending from the pink jacket, were purple hued at the top, graduating to parchment-colored hands so thin and fragile-looking as to appear transparent" (39). Her body registers the progress of her attempt at racial transformation, a Leopard Child grown old, her skin irregularly covered with "pink splotches" (96). Her use of skin bleaches, products that exploit African American self-hatred, marks her willingness to profit from the weakness of her own people and from their drug addictions.

The vilification of racial transformation creates a conundrum for the guardians of racial difference—the potential for black to become white bothers equally the racial sensibilities of African Americans and Anglo-Saxons. The same fantasy that derives from insecurity inflames the anxieties of those who would protect the sanctity of whiteness. Jerry Letlow, the obsequious porter who serves the junta of white supremacists in Charles Chesnutt's *The Marrow of Tradition*, desires a better lot in life and, as a result of the racism he sees daily, prays, "I wush ter Gawd I wuz w'ite."[28] He tries to effect this change through the application of bleach advertised in the local African American newspaper. The announcement is almost a word-for-word transcription of the actual Black Skin Remover advertisement, promising that the product will make the skin "of a mulatto perfectly white." The ad disturbs the Anglo-Saxon powerbrokers nearly as much as the accompanying article, which claims that criminal acts of miscegenation derive not from sexual assaults by African American men but from mutually desired couplings. The bleaching and the interracial relationships both raise the threat of African American assimilation into Anglo-Saxon society. Aspiring to whiteness and social advancement, Jerry applies the bleach to his skin with disastrous results. One of the white supremacists, General Belmont, observes that the servant's "black face is splotched with brown and yellow patches." The transgressive image of the spotted Leopard Child marks Jerry's folly, and his yearning to pass as white earns him the remonstrations from the defenders of white purity. Jerry's employer, the chief Anglo-Saxon Major Carteret, interprets this attempt at racial transformation as a sign that African Americans understand and accept the superiority of the white race. "More pathetic even than Jerry's efforts to escape from the universal doom of his race," the major thinks to himself, "was his ignorance that even if he could, by some strange alchemy, bleach his skin and straighten his hair, there would still remain, underneath it all, only the unbleached darky,—the ass in the lion's skin."[29] Like the racial scientists before him, the major has deflected the gaze away from the skin as the seat of racial difference and toward a less visible and more nebulous claim to an essential blackness that secrets itself somewhere beneath the skin.

Faced with the stigma of splotchy skin and the shame of his transgression given to him by the supremacists, Jerry tries to wash out the straightener and smooth out his color: "An attempt to darken the lighter spots in his cuticle by the application of printer's ink had not proved equally successful,—the retouching left the spots as much too dark as they had formerly been too light."[30] Jerry's failed transformations express a tragic self-hatred as well as the sneaking suspicion that racial difference is a construction, alterable, negotiable, vulnerable to sabotage. In his manipulations, Jerry anticipates the dilemma of Michael Jackson: darken the white patches or lighten his dark skin. He also prefigures the derision of Jackson's audience toward the assessed perversity of his transforming body, the presumptive self-evident mental illness of the man the British tabloid press have dubbed "Wacko Jacko."

"YOU LOOK JUST LIKE A COW!"

In late 1993, public accusations of child molestation reinaugurated Michael Jackson as a site for the discussion of bodily iniquities, his white-and-black skin primary evidence of his madness, his perversity, his crimes. During the course of a nasty child custody case, the father of one of the many adolescent boys with whom Jackson surrounded himself accused the singer of groping his son. In the frenzy that followed, reports of juridical punch and counterpunch, gossip about eyewitnesses and subpoenas, damning testimony and prying searches, the narrative turned time and again to the mysterious body of Michael Jackson and the character of his skin. The case never went to trial, though. With a payout rumored as high as fifty million dollars, Jackson settled with the boy's family with no admission of guilt. The legacy of the accusations lives on in the public spectacle of Jackson's body, a restaging of white Negro exhibitions, gathering further connotations of sin and disobedience. As it enters this legal arena, the display of the transformed white African American body converts the old misdemeanors of self-hatred and the desire to pass as white into a sordid tale of sexual misdeeds. Contemporary taboos supplant interracial couplings as the horror before the public eye. In Jackson's case, his spotted body betrays the iniquities of homosexuality and pedophilia.

In the endless exhibition of the white Negro, the curiosity of a black body turning white still requires exposure to satisfy its audience. The observers want to witness the extent of the change, its mutating geography, to confirm sneaking suspicions. Under legal and popular scrutiny, Michael Jackson struggled again for control over his body and its revelation. News and tabloid reports of the case delighted in the potential disclosure of his transforming body, the truth of his suspect vitiligo unveiled. If something happened between the singer and the boy, the tabloid sensibility seemed to reason, then the child saw the body, was witness to its changes, and these changes, these spots will condemn him. The focus of this scrutiny narrowed further until it spotlighted Michael Jackson's penis, marked by vitiligo, the root and emblem of his sins. John Nguyet Erni explains that at this moment of official investigation and unofficial speculation, "the penis stands for the alleged 'crime scene,'" a problematic jurisdiction, since "the penis is a notoriously wandering object." Isolated, it offers no proof, carries no tangible trace evidence, like blood or fingernail trimmings. The potential identification of the penis by the boy works circumstantially, metaphorically, implying nighttime liaisons, intentional exposures, dirty old men in trench coats. "Hence the attempt to pin it down," Erni adds, "and the urge to mark its perversity."[31]

We witness this exhibition second-hand in tabloid narratives and unauthorized accounts that provoke our imaginations and feed our curiosity. The boy maps the body, assigns the territories of whiteness and blackness, describes the penis in detail, colors in the diagrams.[32] We discover through this child-witness that Jackson is "half black and half white," his color oddly divided at the belt, his legs largely retaining his original color. When Jackson exhibited his naked body, the story goes, the boy exclaimed, "You look like a cow! You look just like a cow!" From the exhibitions by Barnum, the idea of the Leopard Child continues to prompt fantasies of chicanery, of altering the body to change its contours and hide its true, essential markings. Investigators fear Jackson fleeing to Mexico for dermatological treatments to shift his spots and frustrate the inquiry.[33]

In the final grand exhibition, the Santa Barbara County District Attorney subpoenaed the body of Michael Jackson and called for the exposure of his penis before the lens of a video camera. On December 20, sheriff officers submitted Jackson to official documentation and probing eyes to secure its testimony and contain its transgression. Although the videotape record of the exhibition has never been released, the narrative endures, the descriptions lurid and precise, the vocabulary of display still registering the companion responses of salacious wonder and scientific sobriety. The detectives present at the unveiling were "astonished" before his transformed body.[34] The account of the spectacle presented in *Vanity Fair* swears to its authenticity, its access to affidavits and unnamed sources in the investigation. The statements certify "definite markings on Jackson's genital area, . . . a discoloration on his testicles," as well as "a dark spot on the lower left side of [his] penis."[35] According to the magazine, the boy's careful drawing of Jackson's genitals reveals the ominous dark spot, the original darkness Jackson supposedly rejected, now figured as an anomaly, the telling mark of guilt. In the court of popular opinion, his penis finally exposed, the case is closed.

The earliest speculation upon the origin of dark skin color casts its eye toward the penis as a dependable identifier of racial difference. To affix difference to the genitals symbolically restricted blackness and its attendant allegories to African bodies. There, too, could be found the inheritance of savagery, immorality, and sexual profligacy. Eighteenth-century European natural philosophers contended that the pigmentation of the genitals in infants signified the eventual and true color of the child.[36] Comte de Buffon theorized that "the children of Negroes, as soon as they come into the world, have black genitals, and a black spot at the roots of their nails."[37] Through this observation, he concluded that blackness was inherited from the parents and thus restricted to the African body rather than acquired by exposure to the tropical sun. As a consequence of these meditations on the fixity of color, early white Negro exhibition tended to cast a curious gaze to the genitals. John Morgan's 1784 display of the transforming slave-children Adelaide and Jean Pierre lingers upon the whiteness of their private parts. He describes the extent of Adelaide's whiteness to her "loins and buttocks to the junction of the thighs, and the pudendum."[38] With Jean Pierre, Morgan also carefully locates "a white spot in the upper part of the penis."[39] Although he presents no opinion on the genital markings, Morgan shows through his exhibition a concern with the origin of racial transformation and the erasure of a supposedly fixed identifier of difference.[40] The interest in the genitals of white Negroes persists in scientific literature at the beginning of the twentieth century. The monumental study in eugenics *A Monograph on Albinism in Man* pays particular attention to the alteration of color in the penis under the influence of vitiligo. The eugenicists devote photographic plates and meticulous diagrams (showing "dorsal and ventral aspects") to the disembodied whitening tips of African penises. Pages upon pages of genealogical charts tracing the lineage of the aberrant whiteness accompany the almost-prurient fascination with whitening genitals, an attempt to unman the penis, so to speak, to circumscribe and diffuse its latent potency by mapping the descent of whiteness through purely African sources. In the body of Michael Jackson, his worrisome penis legally chronicled and scientifically secured, the troubling white spot of potential transformation evolves into the dark evidence of transgression, immobilized and rendered impotent by the camera.

Jackson's response to the intrusion of cameras is storied as well. He rebels against the imposed exhibition. He grows "enraged . . . , hysterical and completely uncontrollable." Refusing to complete the session, Jackson shouts, "I've said I have vitiligo; so what? Why do you have to examine me?"[41] Reported as examples of childish petulance and the telling disobedience of a guilty man, these acts also demonstrate the efforts of an exhibited white Negro body to refuse to remain passive before gawking onlookers and achieve some kind of agency. On December 22, two days after the videotaping of his body, Michael Jackson moved one last time to take control of his body's exhibition and narration. In a four-minute speech, carried live on CNN and shown taped on broadcast network affiliates, Jackson claimed his

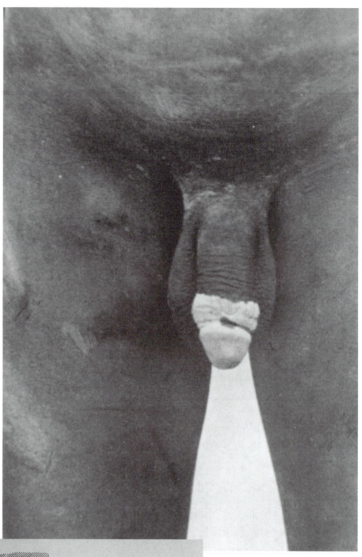

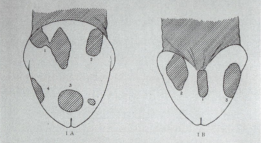

I A AND I B. DORSAL AND VENTRAL ASPECTS, OF THE GLANS PENIS, SHOWING
THE DISTRIBUTION OF THE PIGMENTED (SHADED) AREAS.

FIGS. 29 AND 30. From Pearson, Nettleship, and Usher's *A Monograph on Albinism in Man*. Loan courtesy of the Iowa State University Library.

innocence and described his exhibition before the cameras of the Santa Barbara County Sheriff. Nearly weeping, he recounted the humiliation: "They served a search warrant on me which allowed them to view and photograph my body, including my penis." Experts in voice stress analysis, a new field of anthropometry, found his performance damning, unbelievable.[42] By telling his own story, Jackson makes a bid to reclaim his self-construction as a white Negro and gives voice to the display of his own body; still, the measurers of anatomy and the evidence seekers, heirs of the craniometrists of nineteenth-century racial science, try to impede his agency and define him solely as an exhibit, to be quantified, confined, silenced.

CODA

Jackson's appeal, the narrative display of his penis, returns us to the efforts of Henry Moss to narrate his body to a crowd that would interpret it for him, read his spots like tea leaves, and tell his fortune as a citizen or a servant. Stripping for quarters in a tavern, Moss revealed the story of his penis to European traveler François la Rochefoucault, who translates that Moss's "private parts, he says, are less advanced in this progress, although the change is begun in them."[43] Even with Henry Moss, the audience demanded full exposure—an intimate knowledge of his body and its portentous changing surface. Moss's agency remains for us second-hand, filtered through newspaper accounts, scientific papers, and legal testimony. We witness the ghost of Henry Moss in the talking head of Michael Jackson, pleading his case on television, his pale face partially hidden by sunglasses, forever plagued by those who would presume to know his body.

And now, one last exhibition. In 1808, a relatively minor paternity case in New York grew sensational and brought together the city's most esteemed doctors to debate over the body of the infant the origin of skin color. In the case, the commissioners of the city almshouse sued Alexander Whistelo, "a Black man," to provide for the child of Lucy Williams, "a Yellow woman."[44] For his defense, Whistelo claimed that the child was not his by virtue of the child's complexion, which was lighter than either alleged parent, and "its hair which has every appearance of its being the offspring of a white person." The doctors all thoroughly inspected the child's naked body. The investigation touched upon the genealogy of both parents, the early generation of color in infants, and the effect of the maternal imagination. Lucy Williams claimed that, during her pregnancy, a white man with a gun frightened her and may have affected the color of her developing child.[45] The bulk of the debate, though, centered upon the white bodies of albinos.

Most of the doctors rejected the idea of the child as an albino. Although some had never seen one, those with more experience testified to the lack of resemblance. All but one had apparently never witnessed a case of vitiligo. To argue the possibility that Whistelo may have fathered the light-skinned child, Dr. Samuel L. Mitchell offered into evidence the body of Henry Moss. He read into the record his account of the exhibition, which he had witnessed over ten years previous in Philadelphia. "The skin is of the white carnation hue," he recited, "and the blue veins plainly visible through it."[46] The child, Mitchell implies, could have undergone a similar process, a preternatural whitening of skin that would not preclude the dark-skinned Whistelo as the father.

Sampson, the counselor for the defense, was not impressed by the presentation of Henry Moss. He discounted the transformation, confusing Mitchell's testimony with the other proposed theory of maternal imagination. "The world," he scoffed, "has been in ignorance on another subject, which this trial has promulgated—First, all negroes were supposed to be black. In the process of time it was discovered that some were white;—and now it appears that others are pye-balled. He that doctor Mitchell saw, in the very act of metamorphose, was a full grown man, and could not be influenced, one would think at that time, by any affection of his mama to change his color." In the conclusion to his rebuttal of Moss's transformation, the prosecutor satirically presented a fanciful tableau of racial transformation, a utopian display of never-ending variety in human form and color. "How pretty and pleasant to see little natural Harlequins playing about!" he exclaims. "But for the ignorance of our fathers we might have been burnished like game cocks, and had wives like birds of paradise, and daughters like cockatoos."[47]

Sarcasm aside, this ridiculer of Henry Moss's transforming body reveals the truly disruptive effect of white Negro exhibition: with the fixity of racial difference undermined, a multitude of constructed identities are possible, all endlessly mutable, elusive of definition, defiant of categorization. Escaping the harmful binary of black and white, we are left with contingencies, harlequins, burnished gamecocks, birds of paradise, the anarchy of Melville's piebald parliament.

Requiem for
a Wigger

When the subject of Michael Jackson's body comes up in conversation, questions arise, brows knit. People ask me, "Do you *really* believe that he has vitiligo?" Although the evidence of an affliction may be inconclusive, based largely on innuendo and third-hand reports from anonymous sources, the question itself is telling. It says much about our own reading of the white-black body and a lingering political need to love the blackness and reciprocally shame whiteness for its centuries-long hegemony. To achieve this soul-satisfying censure, we still rely on the binary and maintain its boundaries. The hybrid, the border crosser that slips the bonds of our racial definitions, provokes us. In our history of living along the color line, we still expect traitors in our midst.

Over the past four years of working on this project, I have noticed in my family and friends glimmers of recognition and sometimes wistful memories of racial transgressors and adolescent name-calling. More than one interested party have responded with a knowing nod, "Ah, you mean wiggers." I have to admit that prior to my investigations, I had never heard the epithet. Clarence Major finds the term's source in contemporary African American slang as a reference to "a young white person who affects the manners and speech associated with stock black street culture."[1] A conflation of *white nigger*, the term connotes transgression, racial treason. David Roediger remembers first hearing the term in 1989, and he has traced its usage through the Midwest and the northern East Coast.[2] I suspect broader use and more distant origins touching upon an old tendency to employ the white Negro body—the African American with albinism or vitiligo—for metaphorical purposes.

Companion to the allegorized black and white bodies, the white Negro performs its own little slippery allegory. Over the centuries, it has accumulated meanings in its frequent exhibitions. We have witnessed in these pages the moniker serve to describe the miscegenated body, the tragic mulatto and

quadroon of the nineteenth century, the passer and race traitor of the twentieth. The term *white Negro* labels the wannabes: blacks who aspire to whiteness, whites who long for an imagined liberation in the application of
blackness. It has named a derisive no man's land occupied by racial exiles
ruined beyond redemption.

In 1786, when he gave his "History of the White Negro," Josiah Meigs, the
Connecticut Wit, joined the fate of the albino African American to that of
the debt-burdened white citizen "transformed" from a free person to "this
species of slaves."[3] The white Negro, the white nigger, is a badge of shame, a
fall from independent white manhood. Sinful indebtedness enslaves and
banishes the body from whiteness. Thomas Chandler Haliburton, in the
voice of his Yankee peddler Sam Slick of Slickville, sustains this association
of social dependency with racial transformation. In an 1836 tale, Slick
describes a Nova Scotian slave auction of one town's poorest citizens. The
spectacle stuns the Yankee, who deems slavery appropriate only for the
African American population. This dissolution of racial difference creates a
new creature in the Yankee's eyes. To his dismay, the Nova Scotian town
"approbates no distinction in colours, and when reduced to poverty, is
reduced to slavery, and is sold—*a White Nigger.*"[4]

Cousin to the albino white Negro, the white nigger presents the frightful
prospect of divided loyalties, biracial alliances, the too easy slippage into
blackness. From the end of the American Civil War through Reconstruction
and its white supremacist backlash, defenders of the white race labeled its
traitors white Negroes and white niggers. In 1867, the editors of *Old Guard*
chastised the Honorable W. D. Kelly for supposedly promoting amalgamation as a solution to the race problem by calling him "the white-negro member of Congress from Philadelphia."[5] At the turn of the twentieth century,
followers of "Pitchfork" Ben Tillman reserved the appellation "white nigger"
for southern Republicans who sought the African American vote. The epithet signaled racial duplicity and implied further sexual transgressions—
African American mistresses as the strange bedfellows that politics sometimes
makes.[6]

White supremacists and firebrand populists were not the only ones to use
the white Negro to mark the line between black and white. The border crossing always carries the hint of sedition, double agents, and insidious imper-
sonation. For African American writers, the white Negro has represented the
racial pretenders. In his essay "The World and the Jug," Ralph Ellison chides
critic Irving Howe for presuming to speak for African American writers.
Accusing Howe of "appearing suddenly in blackface," as he puts it, Ellison
proposes that "most Negroes can spot a paper-thin 'white negro' every time
simply because those who masquerade missed what others were forced to

pick up along the way." Ellison employs the term *white Negro* in two ways here: to indicate a body passing for black and, paradoxically, a once-black body passing as white. As a Jewish intellectual, Howe has forgotten his white Negro past, Ellison implies, an immigrant history of exclusion from white membership. "Speaking personally," Ellison adds, "I would like to see the more positive distinctions between whites and Jewish Americans maintained."[7] Even in Ellison's imagination, the white Negro signals the unforgivable transgressions of treason and amnesia.

Rich with metaphoric possibilities, the white Negro is still with us as a body that aspires to straddle the color line and evade its police. The white Negro can be the rebel, the revolutionary creeping at the margins. Even in its most clumsy manifestations, it chides and provokes. Norman Mailer recovers the figure of the Leopard Child to title his essay on racial envy and social rebellion, "The White Negro." In his paean to the white hipster and the orgasm, Mailer finds an answer to American society's lapse into "conformity and depression" in the adoption of the primitive emotions and the free sexual expression he sees among African Americans. To defeat the forces of totalitarianism, he argues, one must become a white Negro. Although he obviously reaches for the destructive stereotypes argued by Jefferson and the racial scientists, Mailer utilizes the figure of the white Negro to signify racial treason, a necessary exile into "all those moral wildernesses of civilized life which the Square automatically condemns as delinquent or evil or immature or morbid or self-destructive or corrupt."[8] In spite of the racist imagining of a primitive, sexually uncontrollable black body, and perhaps even disturbingly flattered by the sexual envy, Eldridge Cleaver defends Mailer's articulation of the white Negro, proposing that the figure expresses a longing to be free of categorization. "People," Cleaver writes, "are feverishly, and at great psychic and social expense, seeking *fundamental and irrevocable liberation*—and, what is more important, *are succeeding in escaping*—from the big white lies that compose the monolithic myth of White Supremacy/Black Inferiority, in a desperate attempt on the part of a new generation of white Americans to enter into the cosmopolitan egalitarian spirit of the twentieth century."[9] In Cleaver's idea of liberation, though, blackness—and the pronounced image of masculinity it represents for him—maintains its opposition to whiteness. The metaphoric white Negro, as Mailer imagines the figure and its historical accretion of meanings, represents a destruction of the binary of black and white.

In the prologue of his novel *Invisible Man*, Ralph Ellison initially rejects the physical conversion implied by the exhibition of the white Negro. His narrator claims that the invisibility from which he suffers is not "exactly a matter of a biochemical accident to my epidermis." No utopian metamorphosis into whiteness here, no manipulation of melanin through radiation therapy, fade creams, or the distillation of a mysterious weed. Though he turns away from the fantasy of racial transformation, Ellison explores in his epilogue the metaphorical possibilities of vitiligo to explain his gradual understanding of his condition, his journey through the novel. "I carry my sickness," the narrator explains. "It came upon me slowly, like that strange disease that affects those black men whom you see turning slowly from black to albino, their pigment disappearing as under the radiation of some cruel, invisible ray. You go along for years knowing something is wrong, then suddenly you discover that you're as transparent as air." This metaphoric transformation from black to albino results in the odd contradiction of racial exhibition, the exposed body "naked and shivering before the millions of eyes who look through you unseeingly."[10] He is a latter-day Henry Moss, a sideshow attraction, stripped to the waist before eyes distracted by a need for polar oppositions and extremes of racial difference.

To express his sickness, this coming to knowledge, Ellison interestingly employs vitiligo, the image of growing whiteness, not blackness. This strategy does not embrace the idea of assimilation. To cave in to cultural demand and become white in appearance or behavior are anathema to the narrator. He asks, "Whence all this passion toward conformity anyway?—diversity is the word. . . . Why, if they follow this conformity business they'll end up by forcing me, an invisible man to become white, which is not a color but the lack of one." False choices between black and white, color or no color result from reckless adherence to the binary. Under these constrictions, transformations may oscillate between the two oppositions, but racial difference still remains, blackness and whiteness continuing its incestuous dance. "Thus," the narrator explains, "one of the greatest jokes in the world is the spectacle of the whites busy escaping blackness and becoming blacker every day, and the blacks striving toward whiteness, becoming quite dull and gray." By invoking the figure of the white Negro, Ellison rediscovers a way out from the binary, the destructiveness of the manichean allegory. The Leopard Boy, the piebald child, the transforming body of Henry Moss pose a separate metaphoric prospect, one that points beyond the limitations of black and white or the restrictive nonchoice between exile and assimilation. Defiant, dissident, the white Negro affords new imaginings, new territories for the construction and maintenance of identities. The narrator knows that his sickness is not the end of his journey and the white Negro is not the paragon but a step. When he decides that he "must shake off the old skin," he has moved toward that greater possibility anticipated by the white Negro.[11]

We may hate to admit it, but we still marvel at the white African American body. The photos startle, the lithographs fascinate, Michael Jackson puzzles.

We may want to consign the figure to insignificance, to declare it dead and bury it deep. Yet even when we try to put away the phantasm of race, the spectacle of the white Negro continues to resurrect to remind us of the boundaries we still maintain, the prejudices of color we still harbor. At this moment at the beginning of the twenty-first century, the Albino Family and the Leopard Child still haunt our discussions of racial difference, indeterminate, slippery, resistant to definition, the embodiment of our fantasies of elusive, self-determined transformation.

NOTES

INTRODUCTION

1. From its first coinage, the term *white Negro* exclusively applied to the exhibition of African Americans with albinism or vitiligo. Over the years, the term has gathered other meanings and mutations, some entirely derogatory. While acknowledging its anachronism and its potential to offend, I will continue to use the appellation as indicative of these first exhibitions and offer the term to signify the displays of light-complected African American bodies that have followed in order to demonstrate the persistent social and political importance of the figure.

2. Leslie Fiedler, *Freaks: Myths and Images of the Secret Self* (New York: Simon and Schuster, 1978), 171.

3. Ibid., 27, 24. Since roughly 1847, according to the *Oxford English Dictionary*, the often derogatory term *freak* has labeled and defined bodies of certain individuals as radically different. I recognize the inflammatory nature of the word, yet I will continue to employ it because it best names the restrictive status of those designated as abnormal for the purpose of exhibition. In other words, for my purposes, *freak* always denotes a social construction of difference, never a naturalized condition.

4. Susan Stewart, *On Longing: Narratives of the Miniature, the Gigantic, the Souvenir, the Collection* (Durham, N.C.: Duke University Press, 1993), 132, 133, 109.

5. Current critical discussions of the extraordinary body identify vitiligo and albinism as a disability in the same context as one with blindness, obesity, or paralysis. These skin conditions cause little or no physical debilitation, yet the stigma assessed to them is the same as those that more greatly hinder negotiation with the world. Our language acknowledges this. We call albinism a disease, a disorder; we consider a person to "suffer" from vitiligo. Although the term *disability* traditionally applies to a body treated by society as essentially different through an excess or lack that inhibits movement or hinders the senses, I use it here in the manner of Rosemary Garland Thomson and other scholars of disability studies—as a limiting cultural construction not unlike race or gender that results from the diligent policing of "normalcy" by rendering bodily difference deviant. Rosemarie Garland Thomson explains that "disability is not bodily insufficiency, but instead arises from the interaction of physical differences with an environment. . . . Disability is the unorthodox made flesh." Under these conditions and critical rubric, the skin "disease" vitiligo qualifies as a disability. Rosemarie Garland Thomson, *Extraordinary Bodies: Figuring Disability in American Culture and Literature* (New York: Columbia University Press, 1996), 23, 24.

6. Robert Bogdan, *Freak Show: Presenting Human Oddities for Amusement and Profit* (Chicago: University of Chicago Press, 1988), 95.

7. Thomson, *Extraordinary*, 8, 31, 42, 43.

8. Mikhail Bakhtin, *Rabelais and His World*, trans. Hélène Iswolsky (Blooming-ton: Indiana University Press, 1984), 230.

9. Thomson, *Extraordinary*, 56, 57.

10. Ibid., 57.

11. Peter Stallybrass and Allon White, *The Politics and Poetics of Transgression* (London: Methuen, 1986), 28.

12. Bakhtin acknowledges in this cosmology the figure of the rogue, the clown, and the fool to upend and recenter, to which Thomson appends the extraordinary body. I should note that Bakhtin is discussing literature here, not the fair, but he tends to collapse these two discourses in his arguments. Mikhail Bakhtin, *The Dialogic Imagination*, trans. Caryl Emerson and Michael Holquist (Austin: University of Texas Press, 1981), 159; Thomson, *Extraordinary*, 150n.

13. Stallybrass and White, *Politics*, 38, 40, 27, 44.

14. Jean-Paul Ortonne, David Mosher, and Thomas B. Fitzgerald, *Vitiligo and Other Hypomelanoses of Hair and Skin* (New York: Plenum, 1983), 61.

15. Abdul JanMohamed, "The Economy of Manichean Allegory: The Function of Racial Difference in Colonialist Literature," in *"Race," Writing, and Difference*, ed. Henry Louis Gates Jr. (Chicago: University of Chicago Press, 1994), 80, 82.

16. Theodore W. Allen, *The Invention of the White Race*, vol. 1, *Racial Oppression and Social Control* (New York: Verso, 1994), 22.

17. Homi K. Bhabha, *The Location of Culture* (New York: Routledge, 1994), 87, 90.

18. Bhabha offers another disruption of colonialism in the figure of the English book. Colonizers distributed the translated book, often the King James Bible, in an effort to "civilize" the natives, but the translation into a new language and cultural context inspires more ambiguity than authority, as the transformed book provides a critique of those behaviors as the new readers speculate upon the meaning of the hybrid text and openly debate its contradictions and insufficiencies. Bhabha, *Location*, 107.

19. Steven Mullaney, "Strange Things, Gross Terms, Curious Customs: The Rehearsal of Cultures in the Late Renaissance," *Representations* 3 (1983): 45–48; Stephen Greenblatt, *Marvelous Possessions* (Chicago: University of Chicago Press, 1991), 109–112.

20. Mullaney, "Strange," 48, 44.

21. Maja-Lisa von Sneidern, "Joined At the Hip: A Monster, Colonialism, and the Scriblerian Project," *Eighteenth-Century Studies* 30 (1997): 223.

22. Leonard Cassuto, *The Inhuman Race: The Racial Grotesque in American Literature and Culture* (New York: Columbia University Press, 1997), 1, 16.

23. Ibid., 6.

24. Karl Pearson, E. Nettleship, and C. H. Usher, *A Monograph on Albinism in Man, Text, Part One* (Cambridge: Cambridge University Press, 1911), 230.

25. James Parsons, "An Account of the White Negro Shown before the Royal Society," *Transactions of the Royal Philosophical Society* 55 (1765): 50. One of these copies currently resides in the collection of the Colonial Williamsburg Foundation. Another copy can be found in London at the Royal College of Surgeons.

26. Greenblatt, *Marvelous*, 120. Concurrent with the proliferation of Maria Sabina's image in the 1740s, the exhibition of a young albino girl created a sensation

in the salons of Paris and inspired Maupertuis to wax upon the power of the maternal imagination to create monstrous births in his treatise *Dissertation Physique a l'Occasion du Nègre Blanc*. Other contemporary paintings of white Negroes reside in European collections: the Musée d'Histoire de la Médecine in Paris owns Joaquim Miguel da Rocha's *Pied Negress*; the Musée de l'Homme, another Paris museum, counts Le Masurier's *Ad vivum accuratissime pingebat in Martinica* among its holdings.

27. "Obituary," *Bell Weekly Messenger*, February 7, 1813, 3.

28. Robert Chambers, *The Book of Days* (London: Chambers, 1862), 267.

29. William Byrd II, "An Account of a Negro-Boy That Is Dappel'd in Several Places of His Body with White Spots," *Transactions of the Royal Philosophical Society* 19 (1695–1697): 781.

30. James Bate, "An Account of the Remarkable Alteration of Colour in a Negro Woman," *Transactions of the Royal Philosophical Society* 51 (1759): 176.

31. Dana D. Nelson, *National Manhood: Capitalist Citizenship and the Imagined Fraternity of White Men* (Durham, N.C.: Duke University Press, 1998), 52.

32. David Roediger implements John Bukowczykj's term "not-yet-white" to describe ethnic groups temporarily excluded from the privileges of whiteness. Roediger acquired the term from an unpublished paper delivered by Barry Goldberg. I have altered the term to emphasize further the tenuousness of white membership, which is never guaranteed and not always achievable. David Roediger, *Toward the Abolition of Whiteness* (New York: Verso, 1994), 184, 195n.

33. David Roediger, *The Wages of Whiteness*, rev. ed. (New York: Verso, 1999), 22.

34. Alexander Saxton, *The Rise and Fall of the White Republic: Class Politics and Mass Culture in Nineteenth-Century America* (New York: Verso, 1990), 385.

35. Stallybrass and White are careful to establish the instability of the audience/exhibit binary, positioning the "observer at the fair" as "a potential participant and so the relation between observer and observed is never fixed. Indeed . . . the plebeian fair-goers were themselves part of the spectacle for the bourgeois observer." Stallybrass and White, *Politics*, 42.

36. Winthrop Jordan, *White Over Black* (Chapel Hill: University of North Carolina Press, 1968), 521–525.

37. Eva Cherniavsky, *That Pale Mother Rising: Sentimental Discourses and the Imitation of Motherhood in Nineteenth-Century America* (Bloomington: Indiana University Press, 1995), 18, 3.

38. Nelson, *National*, ix, 58.

39. Toni Morrison, *Playing in the Dark: Whiteness and the Literary Imagination* (New York: Random House, 1992), 5.

40. Herman Melville, *The Confidence-Man*, (1857; reprint, Evanston, Ill.: Northwestern University Press, 1984), 9.

CHAPTER 1: THE WHITE NEGRO IN THE EARLY REPUBLIC

1. *Papers of Thomas Jefferson*, ed. Julian Boyd, vol. 6 (Princeton: Princeton University Press, 1950–), 423.

2. Georges Buffon, *Natural History, General and Particular*, vol. 5 (Creech, 1780), 404–405.

3. Although a fully developed idea of a racialized Anglo-Saxonism would not arrive until later in the nineteenth century, British colonists and, consequently,

citizens of the newly founded United States in the late eighteenth century were seeking political and linguistic heritage in the fiction of an Anglo-Saxon England. In his *Notes*, Jefferson recommended as an addition to college studies "the ancient languages and literature of the North, on account of their connection with our own language, laws, customs, and history." The myth of the Anglo-Saxon helped Reformation England to develop a political identity separate from continental Europe while still feeling a kinship to the Protestant northern countries. Likewise, the idea of a shared Anglo-Saxon past aided the new United States to find some sense of solidarity and limit white citizenship. I use the term in the spirit of this developing, and limiting, American racial identity. Thomas Jefferson, *Notes on the State of Virginia* (1787; reprint, Chapel Hill: University of North Carolina Press, 1955), 151. For more on the early history of Anglo-Saxonism as an idea, see Reginald Horsman, *Race and Manifest Destiny: Origins of American Racial Anglo-Saxonism* (Cambridge, Mass.: Harvard University Press, 1981), 1–24.

4. Skipwith to Jefferson, January 20, 1784, *Papers*, vol. 6, 473–474.

5. Carter to Jefferson, February 9, 1784, *Papers*, vol. 6, 534.

6. Jefferson calls his white Negroes "Albinos." Although it is generally considered derogatory, I will maintain the term as it defines a culturally constructed category that reduces a person to one physical characteristic and allows for the dehumanization of that person.

7. Jefferson, *Notes*, 70.

8. Robert A. Ferguson, "'Mysterious Obligation': Jefferson's *Notes on the State of Virginia*," *American Literature* 52 (1980): 383.

9. Robert A. Ferguson, "'We Hold These Truths': Strategies of Control in the Literature of the Founders," in *Reconstructing American Literary History*, ed. Sacvan Bercovitch (Cambridge, Mass.: Harvard University Press, 1986), 14.

10. Christopher Looby, "The Constitution of Nature: Taxonomy as Politics in Jefferson, Peale, and Bartram," *Early American Literature* 22 (1987): 253.

11. Jefferson, *Notes*, 70.

12. In his work on Jefferson's complicated theories of racial difference, John Chester Miller never mentions the white Negroes. John Chester Miller, *The Wolf by the Ears: Thomas Jefferson and Slavery* (Charlottesville: University of Virginia Press, 1991). For similar omissions, see also John P. Diggins, "Slavery, Race, and Equality: Jefferson and the Pathos of the Enlightenment," *American Quarterly* 28 (1976): 206–228; Jean Yarbrough, "Race and the Moral Foundation of the American Republic: Another Look at the *Declaration* and the *Notes on Virginia*," *Journal of Politics* 53 (1991): 91–105; Frank Shuffelton, "Thomas Jefferson: Race, Culture, and the Failure of the Anthropological Method," in *A Mixed Race: Ethnicity in Early America*, ed. Frank Shuffelton (New York: Oxford University Press, 1993), 257–277; and Alexander O. Boulton, "The American Paradox: Jeffersonian Equality and Racial Science," *American Quarterly* 47 (1995): 467–492.

13. Jefferson, *Notes*, 70.

14. Oddly enough, Jordan never notices the similarities between the white Negroes in the Skipwith and Carter letters and those in Jefferson's *Notes*. He interprets the white Negroes in the letters as a continued interest in the phenomenon after the 1781 date of composition Jefferson gives for *Notes*. Although Jefferson may have had a continued interest in the whitening skin of slaves, these letters are obviously not evidence of it. Jordan, *White*, 523n.

15. Mitchell Breitweiser, "Jefferson's Prospect," *Prospects* 10 (1985): 333.

16. Jefferson, *Notes*, 71.

17. Scholars also tend not to distinguish between the body with albinism and the body with vitiligo, combining both bodies under the designation "albino." See David R. Brigham, *Public Culture in the Early Republic: Peale's Museum and Its Audience* (Washington: Smithsonian Institution Press, 1995), 130–134; Cherniavsky, *Pale Mother*, 22; Breitwieser, "Jefferson's," 333; and Nelson, *National*, 56.

18. Jefferson, *Notes*, 70.

19. Although the *Transactions of the American Philosophical Society* gives the year as 1784, the minutes of the society set the date of Morgan's presentation as May 5, 1786. "Early Proceedings of the American Philosophical Society, 1744–1838," *Proceedings of the American Philosophical Society* 22.1 (1984): 143.

20. John Morgan, "Some Account of a Motley Coloured, or Pye Negro Girl and Mulatto Boy, Exhibited before the Society in the Month of May, 1784," *Transactions of the American Philosophical Society* 2 (1786): 393, 394.

21. Ibid., 393, 394, 395.

22. A theory that holds the mother responsible for any congenital deformities, Barbara Maria Stafford argues, "freed God of any guilt of having created chaotic traits, and placed the burden instead on unrestrained passions and innate human concupiscence." Barbara Maria Stafford, *Body Criticism: Imaging the Unseen in Enlightenment Art and Medicine* (Cambridge, Mass.: MIT Press, 1991), 306. For a further history of the maternal imagination theory, see Marie-Hèléne Huet, *Monstrous Imagination* (Cambridge, Mass.: Harvard University Press, 1993).

23. Morgan, "Some Account," 395.

24. For the reprint of Morgan's account of Adelaide and Jean-Pierre, see *American Museum* 4 (1789): 501–502. For additional reprinted articles on white Negroes, see James Bate, "An Account of the Remarkable Alteration of Colour in a Negro Woman," *American Museum* 5 (1790): 234; and James Parsons, "An Account of the White Negro Shown before the Royal Society," *American Museum* 6 (1791): 243. For original articles critical of slavery, see (among many others) "Constitution of the Pennsylvania Society for Promoting the Abolition of Slavery," "On Slavery," "Petition of an African Slave," and "Address to the Heart, on the Subject of American Slavery," *American Museum* 1 (1786): 460–462, 472, 538–540, 540–544.

25. Madison to Jefferson, December 28, 1786, *Papers*, vol. 9, 643.

26. Ibid.

27. Ramsay to Jefferson, ibid., 441. Ramsay was not alone in declaring the savagery of people in the frontier settlements. Crèvecœur describes the frontier population as "no better than carnivorous animals of a superior rank" and their children as "a mongrel breed, half civilized, half savage." This regressive behavior, he stipulates, generates from "the wildness of the neighborhood." J. Hector St. John Crèvecœur, *Letters from an American Farmer*, ed. Albert E. Stone (1782; reprint, New York: Penguin, 1986), 72, 77, 76.

28. Josiah Meigs, "The History of White Negroes," *New-Haven Gazette, and the Connecticut Magazine* 1 (1786), 65

29. Ibid., 65, 66.

30. Ibid., 66.

31. Jared Gardner, *Master Plots: Race and the Founding of an American Literature* (Baltimore: Johns Hopkins University Press, 1998), 15.

32. *The Selected Papers of Charles Willson Peale and His Family*, ed. Lillian B. Smith, vol. 1 (New Haven, Conn.: Yale University Press, 1983–), 620n.

33. Peale to John Callahan, October 30, 1791, *Selected Papers*, vol. 1, 625.

34. According to all sources, the *Portrait of James the White Negro* has still not been located, possibly the victim of one of the early fires in Barnum's American Museum.

35. David S. Shields demonstrates how British American belles lettres helped reform tavern discourse from a potential battlefield for class and political conflict and an arena for crass commercial negotiations into a stage for polite cohabitation where "[m]astering the discursive manners . . . secured one's happiness." David S. Shields, *Civil Tongues and Polite Letters in British America* (Chapel Hill: University of North Carolina Press, 1997), xxvii.

36. Peter Thompson, *Rum Punch and Revolution: Taverngoing and Public Life in Eighteenth-Century Philadelphia* (Philadelphia: University of Pennsylvania Press, 1999), 145.

37. Stallybrass and White, *Politics*, 83.

38. John Adams, *Works*, ed. Charles Francis Adams, vol. 2 (Boston: Little and Brown, 1850), 85.

39. He also published the account in the *Universal Asylum and Columbian Magazine* and the *Maryland Gazette, or the Baltimore General Advertiser*.

40. Peale, "Account of a Black Man Turned White," in *Selected Papers*, vol. 1, 621.

41. "Concerning a Negro Who Turned White," Peale Family Papers, American Philosophical Society.

42. Peale, "Account," 621.

43. Ibid.

44. Charles Willson Peale, "Address to the Public," *Aurora*, January 27, 1800.

45. Philip Fisher defines the democratic social space as "a homogenous, cellular medium of life," a field of reproducible, uniform units of experience that aims to create "a common identity" out of diverse immigrant pasts. Most important to my purposes, the democratic space is "transparent and intelligible." In other words, all relationships are immediately understood by a citizen within the space. I disagree, however, with Fisher's contention that the space "provides for no observers, for no oppositional positions." Although those within the space observe each other without a privileged position, the architect of the space always occupies the place of an observer separate from the multitudes. In Peale's museum, Peale watches and manipulates his patrons. As an artifice, the democratic social space in its practical form is inherently divided and, in Fisher's words, "damaged." Philip Fisher, *Still the New World: American Literature in a Culture of Creative Destruction* (Cambridge, Mass.: Harvard University Press, 1999), 37, 38, 49, 50, 51.

46. Peale, "First Advertisement for the Museum," in *Selected Papers*, vol. 1, 448.

47. Peale, "Introduction to a Course of Lectures on Natural History Delivered in the University of Pennsylvania, November 16, 1799," in *Selected Papers*, vol. 2, 265.

48. Peale, "Advertisement for Subscription to A Scientific and Descriptive Catalogue of Peale's Museum," in *Selected Papers*, vol. 2, 128.

49. Charles Willson Peale, *Discourse Introductory to a Course of Lectures on the Science of Nature* (Philadelphia: Poulson, 1800), 39.

50. Peale to William Findley, February 18, 1800, *Selected Papers*, vol. 2, 278.

51. Peale, "Broadside: Peale's Museum," *Selected Papers*, vol. 1, 580.

52. Peale, quoted in Roger B. Stein, "Charles Willson Peale's Expressive Design: *The Artist in the Museum*," in *New Perspectives on Charles Willson Peale: A 250th Anniversary Celebration*, ed. Lillian Miller and David C. Ward (Pittsburgh: University of Pittsburgh Press, 1991), 184.

53. Peale, *Discourse*, 11.

54. Michel Foucault, *The Order of Things: An Archaeology of the Human Sciences* (New York: Random House, 1970), 134.

55. Brigham, *Public*, 130.

56. Charles Willson Peale, *An Historical Catalogue of Peale's Collection of Paintings* (Philadelphia: Fowell, 1795), 33. In an 1822 watercolor, *The Long Room* by Charles Willson Peale and Titian Ramsay Peale II, Peale's *Portrait of Miss Harvey, the Albiness* appears at the end of the long main exhibition room, separated from the portraits of "great men" and presidents that line the long wall to the left above the bird displays. As a depiction of another anomalous creature, the *Portrait of James the White Negro* would have occupied a similar place, shunted to the side yet still prominently displayed. For detail from the watercolor, see Brigham, *Public*, 46–47.

57. Charles Caldwell, *Autobiography* (Philadelphia: 1855), 268. Ira Berlin locates Moss in Baltimore during the same summer. The city commissioners gave permission to an exhibition of "a Negro turned White as a Show." The time is right for Moss, but the evidence is still inconclusive. Ira Berlin, *Slaves without Masters* (New York: Oxford University Press, 1974), 62.

58. "Account of a Singular Change of Colour in a Negro," *Weekly Magazine* 1 (1798), 110.

59. Caldwell, *Autobiography*, 307.

60. "Account," 110; "Henry Moss," *Americanischer und Land Calendar, Auf das 1797 Jahr Christi* (Philadelphia: Cist, 1796), 39.

61. "Account," 110; "Henry Moss," 40; François la Rochefoucault Liancourt, *Travels through the United States of North America, the Country of the Iroquois, and Upper Canada*, vol. 2 (London: Phillips, 1799), 134.

62. Samuel Stanhope Smith, *An Essay on the Causes of the Variety of Complexion and Figure in the Human Species, Second Edition* (1810; reprint, Cambridge: Harvard University Press, 1965), 59n; "Account," 111; "Henry Moss," 40; "A Great Curiosity," *Aurora*, July 13, 1796, 3.

63. "Henry Moss," 40; Rochefoucault, *Travels*, 134.

64. "Great Curiosity," 3.

65. "Henry Moss," 39.

66. "Great Curiosity," 3. A broadside advertising Moss's July 23 exhibition at the Black Horse Tavern credits the certificate to Joseph Holt. Benjamin Rush, "Commonplace Book," American Philosophical Society.

67. "Account," 110–111.

68. Rochefoucault, *Travels*, 134.

69. "To the Lovers of Natural Philosophy," *Aurora*, August 24, 1796, 3.

70. J. V. Wiesenthal, "Case of a Negro Whose Skin Has Become White," *New England Journal of Medicine and Surgery* 8 (1819): 35.

71. Samuel Stanhope Smith, *An Essay on the Causes of the Variety of Complexion in the Human Species* (Philadelphia: Aitken, 1787), 10n, 104, 13, 104.

72. Smith, *Essay, Second Edition*, 58–59, 59n, 58.

73. Ibid., 58.

74. Samuel Latham Mitchell, "Another Instance of a Negro Turning White," *Medical Repository* 4 (1801): 199–200. For histories of the claims of atheism against Jefferson, see Edwin T. Martin, *Thomas Jefferson: Scientist* (New York: Schuman, 1952), 238–240; and Jordan, *White*, 502–505.

75. Jordan, *White*, 516.

76. Smith, *Essay, Second Edition*, 59n, 100–101, 89, 95–96.

77. Ibid., 43, 45.

78. Ibid., 46.

79. J. H. Powell, *Bring Out Your Dead* (Philadelphia: University of Pennsylvania Press, 1949), 282.

80. Benjamin Rush, *An Account of the Bilious Remitting Yellow Fever, as It Appeared in the City of Philadelphia in the Year 1793* (Philadelphia: Dobson, 1794), 6.

81. Benjamin Rush, *Letters*, ed. L. H. Butterfield, vol. 2 (Princeton, N.J.: Princeton University Press, 1951), 785.

82. Ibid., 786.

83. Benjamin Rush, "Observations Intended to Favour a Supposition that the Black Color (as It Is Called) of the Negroes Is Derived from the Leprosy," *Transactions of the American Philosophical Society* 4 (1799): 289.

84. Ibid., 296–297, 294.

85. Ibid., 297, 295.

86. Jan Nederveen Pieterse, *White on Black: Images of Africa and Blacks in Western Popular Culture* (New Haven, Conn.: Yale University Press, 1992), 195.

87. For extensive examples of this proverb in sixteenth-century literature, see Robert Ralston Cawley, *The Voyagers and Elizabethan Drama* (New York: Modern Language Association, 1938), 87–88.

88. Washington to William McHenry, September 30, 1798, George Washington, *Writings*, ed. John C. Fitzpatrick, vol. 36 (Washington, D.C.: Government Printing Office, 1931–1944), 474.

89. Hugh Henry Brackenridge, *Modern Chivalry* (1792–1815; reprint, New York: American Book Company, 1937), 23.

90. Ibid., 75.

91. Ibid., 25.

92. Ibid., 26, 27.

93. Ibid., 116.

94. Brackenridge, *Modern Chivalry*, 117. Intentionally or not, Brackenridge's Adam looks remarkably like Thomas Jefferson, which can only be a serendipitous anticipation of the Sally Hemings scandal.

95. Emory Elliott, *Revolutionary Writers: Literature and Authority in the New Republic, 1725–1810* (New York: Oxford University Press, 1982), 183.

96. Grantland S. Rice, *The Transformation of Authorship in America* (Chicago: University of Chicago Press, 1997), 133.

97. The origin of color was a favorite subject for minstrel-show stump speeches. In 1873, Dan Emmett gave a "Negro Sermon" in which, among other things, he proposed Adam and Eve "was boaf brack men." Quoted in Hans Nathan, *Dan Emmett and the Rise of Early Negro Minstrelsy* (Norman: University of Oklahoma Press, 1962), 411.

CHAPTER 2: BARNUM'S LEOPARD BOY

1. Jefferson, *Notes*, 138.

2. Ibid., 138.

3. Ibid., 139, 138.

4. Ibid., 143.

5. As discussed in chapter 1, taxonomy served as an organizing principle and foundational philosophy for the early Republic. Foucault identifies in the various taxonomical exhibitions of natural history—the museums, the gardens—"unencumbered spaces in which things are juxtaposed . . . a non-temporal rectangle in which, stripped of all commentary, of all enveloping language, creatures present themselves one beside another, their surfaces visible, grouped according to their common features, and thus already virtually analysed, and bearers of nothing but their own individual names." By reducing all of nature to a system of easily recognizable qualities, taxonomy renders the natural sciences democratically accessible to all. The satisfaction of the democratic impulse, though, also reduces people to their most visibly identifiable feature: in this case, skin color. Michel Foucault, *The Order of Things* (New York: Random House, 1975), 131.

6. Rush, "Observations," 296.

7. Ibid., 297.

8. For an extended discussion of the controversy over Jefferson's racial theories during his presidential campaigns, see Martin, *Thomas Jefferson*, 212–240.

9. For a more extensive account of polygenetic theories, see William Stanton, *The Leopard's Spots: Scientific Attitudes toward Race in America, 1815–59* (Chicago: University of Chicago Press, 1960); and George Fredrickson, *The Black Image in the White Mind: The Debate on Afro-American Character and Destiny, 1817–1914* (New York: Harper and Row, 1971), 71–96.

10. Charles Caldwell, *Autobiography* (Philadelphia: Lippincott, Grambo, 1855), 269, 164.

11. Ibid., 164.

12. Ibid., 268.

13. In January 1831, the Massachusetts state legislature passed "An act more effectively to Protect the Sepulchres of the Dead and to Legalize the Study of Anatomy in Certain Cases" in order to allow medical schools to perform the dissections necessary for their students' education and to remove the impetus for body snatching by these same students and professors. Prior to this act and ones that followed in other states, medical schools could only legally obtain the bodies of condemned criminals whose ultimate punishment was the defilement of their bodies through dissection. Frederick C. Waite, "The Development of Anatomical Laws in the States of New England," *New England Journal of Medicine* 233 (1945): 721.

14. Samuel George Morton, *Crania Americana* (Philadelphia: Dobson, 1839), 290.

15. Samuel George Morton, *Crania Aegyptiaca* (Philadelphia: Pennington, 1844), 66.

16. Samuel A. Cartwright, "Report on the Diseases and Physical Peculiarities of the Negro Race," *New Orleans Medical and Surgical Journal* 7 (1851): 692. Cartwright's observations received a wider readership when they were shortly thereafter republished as "Diseases and Peculiarities of the Negro Race" in *Debow's Commercial Review*.

17. Waite, "Development," 719. Foucault has argued that "the opposition of religion, morality, and stubborn prejudice to the opening of corpses," a common narrative in the histories of comparative anatomy and medical education, was a convenient myth of a struggle between "a young corpus of knowledge and old beliefs" created to rationalize the necessity for dissection. Michel Foucault, *The Birth of the Clinic: An Archaeology of Medical Perception* (New York: Random House, 1975), 124, 126. This myth, though, has a basis in fact. In the young United States, where only convicted murderers could suffer the indignities of the knife, the unauthorized robbing of graves by medical students—a real and documented phenomenon—resulted in protest and riots, the most famous of which was "The Doctors' Mob" of 1788 in New York City. Armed by improvised weapons and the rumor of a child's dissection at the hands of a medical professor, a crowd of workers, including a number of free African Americans, rioted for three days. At one point, a group of city officials, including DeWitt Clinton, John Jay, Alexander Hamilton, and Baron von Steuben, unsuccessfully faced down the mob. Jules Calvin Ladenheim, "'The Doctors' Mob' of 1788," *Journal of the History of Medicine and Applied Science* 5 (1950): 33. The riot helped spur legislation to provide officially cadavers for medical schools in New York State. Although Foucault may be correct to assume that the opposition between knowledge and superstition is a fiction created to authorize the professionalism of the anatomist, the opposition to dissection by members of the working poor and African American populations in the United States was real.

18. Michael Sappol, "The Cultural Politics of Anatomy in 19th-Century America: Death, Dissection, and Embodied Social Identity" (Ph.D. diss., Columbia University, 1997), 41.

19. The southwestern humorists counted among themselves middle-class merchants, doctors, and lawyers, all politically conservative supporters of patrician interests and critics of the newly enfranchised Jacksonian rabble. Kenneth Lynn observes, "To call the roll of the best-known Southwestern humorists in the twenty-year period from 1833 to 1853 . . . is to call in vain for a supporter of Andrew Jackson." The politics of George Washington Harris, though, are a bit more complicated: a vilifier of the North and its politics, he criticized those authority figures of largely antisecessionist Knoxville whom he believed had betrayed the cause of southern autonomy. Though his figure Sut Lovingood follows in the tradition of the quaint, lower-class object of middle-class derision, he largely uses this figure to demonstrate the hypocrisy and moral degradation of the town's authority figures. Kenneth Lynn, *Mark Twain and Southwestern Humor* (Boston: Little, Brown, 1959), 52, 131.

20. Henry Clay Lewis, *Odd Leaves from the Life of a Louisiana Swamp Doctor* (1843; reprint, Baton Rouge: Louisiana State University Press, 1997), 133.

21. Ibid., 134.

22. David Rattlehead [Marcus Byrn], *The Life and Adventures of an Arkansaw Doctor* (1851; reprint, Fayetteville: University of Arkansas Press, 1989), 123, 124.

23. Lewis, *Odd Leaves*, 79.

24. Ibid., 76–77.

25. From 1844 to 1845, Lewis attended the Louisville Medical Institute, the academy Charles Caldwell founded. Caldwell served as one of Lewis's instructors. In this story, Lewis may be parodying his teacher's obsession with white Negroes, as well as the fascination of other racial scientists with the subject. Nonetheless, this connection to Caldwell presents a provocative lineage from Caldwell's mentor, Benjamin

Rush, who hailed the whitening skin of Henry Moss, to Lewis, who literally reduces the white Negro to a horrifying flap of skin.

26. In an early article, Alan H. Rose argues that Lewis's depiction of the southern African American "completely enacts the fear that haunted the entire society, the murder of the Southern white by a black demon." Alan H. Rose, "The Image of the Negro in the Writings of Henry Clay Lewis," *American Literature* 41 (1969): 256. As Rose later develops his argument in book form, the African American becomes more a symbol of "disorder" that psychologically threatens the author and the narrator. Alan H. Rose, *Demonic Vision: Racial Fantasy and Southern Fiction* (New York: Archon, 1976), 29.

27. Lewis, *Odd Leaves*, 77.

28. Ibid., 75, 76.

29. The display of people with disabilities, even those with aesthetic anomalies that do not affect the ability physically to negotiate the world, serves to define boundaries between groups and classes. Rosemarie Garland Thomson argues that the freak show helps "consolidate a version of American selfhood that was capable, rational, and normative, but that strove toward an ontological sameness upon which the notion of democratic equality is predicated." Thomson, *Extraordinary*, 64.

30. George Washington Harris, "Sut Lovingood Escapes Assassination," in *High Times and Hard Times*, ed. M. Thomas Inge (Nashville, Tenn.: Vanderbilt University Press, 1967), 130.

31. Ibid.

32. Neil Harris, *Humbug: The Art of P. T. Barnum* (Chicago: University of Chicago Press, 1973), 57, 79.

33. A. H. Saxon, *P. T. Barnum: The Legend and the Man* (New York: Columbia University Press, 1989), 107.

34. The 1850 guidebook to the museum assures that the "most fastidious may take their families there, without the least apprehension of their being offended by word or deed." *Barnum's American Museum Illustrated* (New York: Van Norden and Leslie, 1850), 2.

35. Bluford Adams, *E Pluribus Barnum: The Great Showman and U.S. Popular Culture* (Minneapolis: University of Minnesota Press, 1997), 90.

36. "A Word about Museums," *Nation*, July 27, 1865, 113.

37. P. T. Barnum, "Mr. Barnum on Museums," *Nation*, August 10, 1865, 171.

38. Adams, *E Pluribus*, 95.

39. P. T. Barnum, *Struggles and Triumphs* (Hartford, Conn.: Burr, 1869), 89.

40. Noel Ignatiev, *How the Irish Became White* (New York: Routledge, 1995), 109–112.

41. Roediger, *Towards*, 184.

42. Benjamin Reiss claims that Barnum displayed African Americans with vitiligo as "missing links," yet I have found no evidence of that, although the term does hint at such an exhibition. Benjamin Reiss, "P. T. Barnum, Joice Heth, and the Antebellum Spectacles of Race," *American Quarterly* 51 (1999): 85. Long after the American Museum, during Reconstruction when the fantasy of racial transformation begins to lose some currency among the museum-going public, exhibitors tried other narratives. A slip of an advertisement glued on the back of an 1884 photograph in the Harvard Theatre Collection of "John W. Nash, Age 12 years, Born in Philadelphia, Pa.," reads, "Leopard Boy. The spotted link between the human and feline kingdom."

43. Josef Warkany, "Congenital Malformations in the Past," *Journal of Chronic Diseases* 10 (1959): 90–92.

44. Werner Sollors has identified an extensive international literature that yokes miscegenation with another taboo sexual practice—incest. Werner Sollors, *Neither Black nor White yet Both: Thematic Explorations of Interracial Literature* (New York: Oxford University Press, 1997), 285–335.

45. Josiah C. Nott, "The Mulatto a Hybrid—Probable Extermination of the Two Races If the Whites and Blacks Are Allowed to Intermarry," *American Journal of the Medical Sciences* 6 (1843): 256. This theory quickly took hold in popular thinking, leading one Ohio senator to declare in 1864 that "the mulatto does not live; he does not recreate his kind; he is a monster. Such hybrid races by a law of Providence scarcely survive beyond one generation." Quoted in Sidney Kaplan, "The Miscegenation Issue in the Election of 1864," in *American Studies in Black and White: Selected Essays 1949–89* (Amherst: University of Massachusetts Press, 1991), 60.

46. Michael Mitchell, *Monsters of the Gilded Age: The Photographs of Charles Eisenmann* (Toronto: Gage, 1979), 21.

47. Bogdan, *Freak*, 106.

48. Horsman, *Race and Manifest Destiny*, 9.

49. The term *Leucoaethiope* first surfaces in the writings Greek historians and scientists, including those of Pliny, Ptolemy, and Mela. It derives from the Greek *leukos* (white) and *Aethiopes* (Ethiopian or African). It is not known whether these writers ever applied the term to Africans with albinism or vitiligo. Pearson, Nettleship, and Usher, *Monograph*, 11. Employed in the nineteenth-century exhibition of white Negroes, the term *Leucoaethiope* maintains currency in a variety of spellings; I have settled on the one used by Barnum's advertisements.

50. "Living Curiosities at Barnum's Museum," *Harper's Weekly*, December 15, 1860, 799.

51. Bogdan, *Freak*, 110. For accounts of the demise of the dime museum and the freak show, see Bogdan, *Freak*, 62–68; and Thomson, *Extraordinary*, 78–80.

52. *The History of Rudolph Lucasie, a Native of Lenabon, Madagascar, and an Albino of the First Class; also a Brief History of His Wife and child; with an Account of the Extraordinary Physical Phenomena Termed "Albinism"* (New York: 1860), 6.

53. *Mr. Clem Foster, the White Negro from Martineque* (Haford, England: May, n.d.), 2.

54. "Living Curiosities," 799.

55. Thomson, *Extraordinary*, 69.

56. James Kinney, *Amalgamation! Race, Sex, and Rhetoric in the Nineteenth-Century Novel* (Westport, Conn.: Greenwood, 1985), 38.

57. Oliver Bolokitten [Jerome B. Holgate], *A Sojourn in the City of Amalgamation in the Year of our Lord 19—* (New York: Bolokitten, 1835), 69, 73, 74.

58. David Croly and George Wakeman, *Miscegenation: The Theory of the Blending of the Races, Applied to the White Man and the Negro* (New York: Dexter, Hamilton, 1864), 65.

59. Theodore Tilton, "The Union of the Races," *New York Independent*, February 25, 1864, 4.

60. Frank J. Webb, *The Garies and Their Friends* (1857; reprint, Baltimore: Johns Hopkins University Press, 1997), 157.

61. Ibid., 322, 329.

62. The significance of the "Sisters at Heart" episode was also not lost on the television industry. The episode received the Governor's Award at the 1971 Emmy Awards. Elizabeth Montgomery, the star of *Bewitched*, expressed her own pleasure with the episode, identifying it as a model for the show's mission. Herbie J. Pilato, *Bewitched Forever* (Arlington, Tex.: Summit, 1996), 10.

63. Eric Lott, *Love and Theft: Blackface Minstrelsy and the American Working Class* (New York: Oxford University Press, 1995), 40.

64. Susan Gubar, *Racechanges: White Skin, Blackface in American Culture* (New York: Oxford University Press, 1997), 55, 78.

65. Lott, *Love*, 6.

66. W. T. Lhamon Jr., *Raising Cain: Blackface Performance from Jim Crow to Hip Hop* (Cambridge, Mass.: Harvard University Press, 1998), 42.

67. Dale Cockrell asserts, "Although the whole notion of blackface masquerade among the common peoples of northern Europe might have first followed from direct contact with dark-skinned Moors (but probably did not), the facts seem to be that the rituals using chimney soot soon lost much if not all of the racial association, and blackface masking became a means of expressing removal from time and place through disguise." Dale Cockrell, *Demons of Disorder: Early Blackface Minstrels and Their World* (Cambridge, U. K.: Cambridge University Press, 1997), 52.

68. Lhamon, *Raising*, 43.

69. Although it is difficult to pinpoint the cause and effect of any folk expression, scholars now appear to agree that the wearing of blackface mask by this youth population expressed some hopeful empathy with the condition of free African Americans. Even Lott has posed that "the blackness of the oppressed could itself become an idiom of class dissent—a fact that implied some sense of cross-racial identification." Lott, *Love*, 84. Less reluctant, though still cognizant that "it sounds naive and openly controversial," Cockrell argues that these youths "saw an ally in the black laborer against their common superiors, not simply an inevitable enemy." Cockrell, *Demons*, 161. Lhamon presents the identification between these two groups as inevitable, since "[y]ouths in blackface were almost as estranged from the bourgeois inflections of the slavery quarrel as were the blacks whom they therefore chose to figure their dilemma and emphasize their distance." Lhamon, *Raising*, 43.

70. In Byron Christy's late 1840s' version of the play, the father, now a merchant, owns a museum, a reference to Barnum's new American Museum. Thomas Dartmouth Rice, *The Virginny Mummy, a Negro Farce in One Act and Two Scenes, Property of Byron Christy*, Pennsylvania Historical Society, Philadelphia.

71. Thomas Dartmouth Rice, *The Virginny Mummy*, in *Jump Jim Crow: Plays, Lyrics and Street Prose of the First Atlantic Popular Culture*, ed. W. T. Lhamon, Jr. (1835; reprint, Cambridge, Mass.: Harvard University Press, forthcoming). Unless otherwise noted, all further references to the play are to this version and edition.

72. Morton, *Crania Aegyptiaca*, 65.

73. Josiah C. Nott, *Two Lectures on the Natural History of the Caucasians and Negro Races* (Mobile, Ala.: Dade and Thompson, 1844), 16.

74. All quotes from Rice, *The Virginny Mummy, a Negro Farce*.

75. William Bobo, *Glimpses of New-York City, by a South Carolinian, Who Had Nothing Else to Do* (Charleston, S.C.: McCarter, 1852), 96, 97.

76. Lhamon, *Raising*, 159.

77. Tilden G. Edelstein, "Othello in America: The Drama of Racial Intermarriage," in *Region, Race and Reconstruction*, ed. J. Morgan Kousser (New York: Oxford University Press, 1982), 179–197.

78. John Quincy Adams, "Misconceptions of Shakespeare upon the Stage," *New England Magazine* 9 (1835): 252.

79. Thomas Dartmouth Rice, *Otello*, in Lhamon, *Jump Jim Crow*. In the 1874 publication of the long-performed play *Old Zip Coon*, the title character speaks, "Well—de massa's goned away and I got his property and marries Sal, and we got a darter—black one side de face an' white todder—an' she won't touch nuffin' short ob a piannum, and dat brings all de high-toned darkies round her, and de white trash dey come roun her thick as flies in a 'lasses hogshead." As with Rice's play, the piebald child results from an interracial marriage. The anonymous author connects the piebald child to class aspiration by African Americans and the white laboring poor, or the near-whites. *Old Zip Coon*, in *This Grotesque Essence: Plays from the American Minstrel Stage*, ed. Gary D. Engle (1874; reprint, Baton Rouge: Louisiana State University Press, 1978), 53.

80. John Howard Griffin, *Black Like Me* (Boston: Houghton Mifflin, 1960), 149.

81. Charles Caldwell, *Thoughts on the Original Unity of the Human Race, Second Edition* (Cincinnati, Ohio: James, 1852), 65, 66, 100. According to the standard textbook on vitiligo, "It is rare for a significant degree of repigmentation to occur and extraordinary for total repigmentation to be seen. Patients need always be aware that there is little hope for spontaneous repigmentation." Jean-Paul Ortonne, David Mosher, and Thomas B. Fitzgerald, *Vitiligo and Other Hypomelanoses of Hair and Skin* (New York: Plenum, 1983), 176.

82. M. R. Werner devotes a paragraph to this Barnum exhibit and claims that "newspapers reported daily the progress of the negro's change in color." I have yet to confirm the press's intensity of coverage, but Werner's interest in a figure that posed "the solution to the slavery problem" confirms the white Negro's continued attraction and cultural currency. M. R. Werner, *Barnum* (New York: Harcourt Brace, 1923), 204.

83. William M. Ramsey, "Melville's and Barnum's Man with a Weed," *American Literature* 61 (1979): 102.

84. Barnum, *Struggles*, 202. This poem survives through all the subsequent yearly updates of his autobiography, including the one published after his death in 1891.

85. William Northall, *Before and Behind the Curtain, or Fifteen Years' Observations among the Theatres of New York* (New York: Burgess, 1851), 163.

86. Melville, *Confidence-Man*, 9. Further quotations from this novel are from this edition and are cited parenthetically in the text.

87. I am grateful for the work of William Ramsey, who first discovered the connection between *The Confidence-Man* and white Negro exhibition.

88. Lott, *Love*, 61.

89. Carolyn L. Karcher, *Shadow over the Promised Land: Slavery, Race, and Violence in Melville's America* (Baton Rouge: Louisiana State University Press, 1980), 206.

CHAPTER 3: THE DOUBLE BIND OF THE ALBINO

1. Lott identifies Black Guinea as a purely blackface performance, a simple masquerade that fools a gullible audience. Lott, *Love*, 61. Such a reading denies the

influence of white Negro exhibition and blunts the importance of its ambivalence. On the other hand, Lhamon testifies to the oscillation that Black Guinea's perform-ance effects, a "vertigo" experienced by members of the piebald parliament that mir-rors the confusion of those who viewed Barnum's "Negro Turning White." Lhamon, *Raising*, 137.

2. In a recent photographic spread of albinos in *Life*, an anonymous young woman with albinism expresses her frustration with the persistent cultural myths about the skin disorder. "I am a woman," she proclaims. "I have feelings. I hear what people say and read what they write. I am not deaf. I do not have red eyes. And I can-not tell the future." Rick Guidotti, "Redefining Beauty," *Life*, June 1998, 66.

3. Edward Leroy Rice, *Monarchs of Minstrelsy, from "Daddy" Rice to Date* (New York: Kenny, 1911), 28.

4. Dale Cockrell, *Excelsior: Journals of the Hutchinson Family Singers, 1842–46* (Stuyvesant, N.Y.: Pendragon, 1989), 297.

5. The "Four Albino Boys" performed in New York from time to time through 1845. Vera Brodsky Lawrence, *Strong on Music*, vol. 1 (New York: Oxford University Press, 1988), 286, 344, 413. An 1837 article in *Burton's Gentleman's Magazine* may record the birth and infancy of two of the boys in this act, two "remarkable speci-mens" of "White Negroes" from Cape May County, New Jersey, "one about four, the other a year older, although born of negro parents, are whiter than the generality of 'the pale faces of the north.'" If this article does refer to boys from the later act, it par-adoxically claims that the mother of the boys "positively objects to the proposals made to her by various interested individuals, and refuses to make her children the object of a show." "White Negroes," *Burton's Gentleman's Magazine* 1 (1837), 220.

6. Pearson, Nettleship, and Usher, *Monograph*, 13.

7. JanMohamed, "Economy," 80. Most scholars have traced the origins of a cod-ified racial difference to the European explorations of Africa and the Americas. Winthrop Jordan begins his study with English exploration in Africa, and although he does not establish a causal relationship between the economic motives of colo-nization and the description of peoples in English texts, he still recognizes that from the beginning "Englishmen actually described Negroes as *black*—an exaggerated term which in itself suggests that the Negro's complexion had powerful impact upon their perceptions." Jordan, *White*, 5. Thomas Gossett vaguely attributes theories of racial difference to the "Age of Exploration," which "led many to speculate on race differences at a period when neither Europeans nor Englishmen were prepared to make allowances for vast cultural diversities." Thomas Gossett, *Race: The History of an Idea in America*, rev. ed. (New York: Oxford University Press, 1997), 16. Not wish-ing to relegate the origins of racial difference to European whim and generosity, Audrey Smedley specifically articulates racism as a "cosmological ordering system structured out of the political, economic, and social realities of peoples who had emerged as expansionist, conquering, dominating nations on a worldwide quest for wealth and power." Audrey Smedley, *Race in North America* (Boulder, Colo.: West-view, 1993), 25. John Hodge identifies the "dualism" that JanMohamed labels "manichean" as an essential and ultimately malevolent component of European cul-ture rather than as a convenient outgrowth of economic necessity. John Hodge, *Cul-tural Bases of Racism and Group Oppression* (Berkeley, Calif.: Two Riders, 1975).

8. Bhabha, *Location*, 86.

9. Edgar Allan Poe, *The Narrative of Arthur Gordon Pym of Nantucket* (1838;

reprint, New York: Penguin, 1975), 162. Further quotations from this novel are from this edition and are cited parenthetically in the text.

10. Henry Clay, *African Repository* 6 (1830): 11.

11. Teresa Goddu, *Gothic America: Narrative, History, and Nation* (New York: Columbia University Press, 1997), 86.

12. Dana D. Nelson, *The Word in Black and White: Reading "Race" in American Literature 1638–1867* (New York: Oxford University Press, 1993), 102.

13. Leonard Cassuto coins the term *racial freak* in his discussion of the racial grotesque in the work of Herman Melville. He observes a conflation between racial science and freak show narratives. The "goal of nineteenth-century science," he writes, "was the same as that of the freak show: to construct and scrutinize the edges of humanity." In the shadow of increased racial tensions from the debates over slavery, the freak show hosted "the deflection of racial anxiety onto a class whose difference was (to the viewer) apparently undeniable and literally spectacular." Cassuto, *Inhuman*, 191, 194.

14. Leslie Fiedler, *Love and Death and the American Novel* (New York: Simon and Schuster, 1978), 394; Carol Peirce and Alexander G. Rose III, "Poe's Reading of Myth: The White Vision of Arthur Gordon Pym," in *Poe's Pym: Critical Explorations*, ed. Richard Kopley (Durham, N.C.: Duke University Press, 1992), 74; John Carlos Rowe, "Poe, Antebellum Slavery, and Modern Criticism," in Kopley, *Poe's Pym*, 126–127.

15. Bhabha, *Location*, 86.

16. For early explanations of the Symmes's influence on Poe, see Robert F. Almy, "J. N. Reynolds: A Brief Biography with Particular Reference to Poe and Symmes," *Colophon*, new series 2.2 (1937), 227–245; and J. O. Bailey, "Sources for Poe's Arthur Gordon Pym, 'Hans Pfaal,' and Other Pieces," *PMLA* 57 (1942), 513–535. For an explanation of Symmes's theories, see John Weld Peck, "Symmes' Theory," *Ohio Archaelogical and Historical Society Publications* 18 (1909): 28–42.

17. Although Symmes's authorship of *Symzonia* is now generally accepted, the evidence is scant and circumstantial at best. For further discussion of the attribution of authorship, see J. O. Bailey, introduction to *Symzonia, a Voyage of Discovery*, by *Captain Adam Seaborn*, by John Cleves Symmes (1820; reprint, Gainesville, Fla.: Scholar's Facsimiles and Reprints, 1965).

18. John Cleves Symmes, *Light Gives Light to Light Discoverer ad Infinitum* (St. Louis: n.p., 1818).

19. Symmes, *Symzonia*, 13. Further quotations from this novel are from this edition and are cited parenthetically in the text.

20. Stephen Greenblatt, *Marvelous Possessions* (Chicago: University of Chicago Press, 1991), 56.

21. *History of Rudolph Lucasie*, 3, 4–5.

22. *History of Rudolph Lucasie, a Native of Lenabon, Madagascar, and an Albino of the First Class; also a Brief History of His Wife and Child: with an account of the Extraordinary Physical Phenomena termed "Albinism"* (Nashville, Tenn.: Ligon, 1869), 3.

23. Ibid., 7

24. Gossett, *Race*, 37.

25. Herman Melville, *Moby-Dick* (1851; reprint, Evanston, Ill.: Northwestern University Press, 1988), 278.

26. Linda Frost argues that the narrative of the Circassian Beauty "seems in part to represent a Northern anxiety about racial mixing, particularly in regard to the anticipated effects of emancipation." Linda Frost, "The Circassian Beauty and the Circassian Slave: Gender, Imperialism, and American Popular Entertainment," in *Freakery: Cultural Spectacles of the Extraordinary*, ed. Rosemarie Garland Thomson (New York: New York University Press, 1995), 250. The superlative eastern European white bodies replace the superlative African white bodies in a fantasy of transformation other than racial: a conversion into citizenship through the assimilation of appropriate "white" behaviors. According to one of the exhibition narratives, the colonized and therefore redeemed "Circassian Girl" becomes "a refined, intelligent and Christian woman . . . enrolled upon the scroll of humanity, in company with the great mass of her countrywomen." *Zoe Meleke: Biographical Sketch of the Circassian Girl* (New York: Barnum's Greatest Show on Earth, 1880), 11–12.

27. Barnum to Hitchcock, February 2, 1856, *Selected Letters of P. T. Barnum*, ed. A. H. Saxon (New York: Columbia University Press, 1983), 92.

28. Barnum, *Struggles*, 581.

29. A. H. Saxon readily accepts Zalumma as the genuine article: her "pedigree," he writes, "was obviously beyond reproach." Saxon, *Barnum*, 102. Robert Bogdan, though, is more dubious. He refers to an unpublished manuscript of John Dingess, which alleges that when a suitable Circassian Beauty could not be found, Barnum created Zalumma. Bogdan, *Freak*, 238.

30. In their history of the circus, John Durant and Alice Durant record the storied use of "stale beer" as a hair rinse to achieve the extraordinary hairstyle of the Circassian Beauty. John Durant and Alice Durant, *Pictorial History of the American Circus* (New York: Barnes, 1957), 121.

31. *The History of Miss Ettie Reynolds, the Madagascar Lady* (New York: New York Popular, n.d.), 6, 1–2.

32. *The History of Unzie, the Australian Aboriginal Beauty* (New York: Dicks, 1893).

33. Durant and Durant, *Pictorial*, 121.

34. Guidotti, "Redefining," 65.

35. Rick Guidotti, "Positive Exposure: Illuminating the Richness of Difference," October 1998, http://www.rickguidotti.com/about.htm.

36. Jefferson, *Notes*, 70.

37. Morgan, "Some Account," 393; Mitchell, "Another Instance," 200.

38. Rush, "Observations," 291.

39. Ludwig Gall, "Pennsylvania through a German's Eyes: The Travels of Ludwig Gall, 1819–1820," trans. Frederic Trautman, *Pennsylvania Magazine of History and Biography* 105 (1981): 43. Another exhibit imported from the Bartholomew Fair, the "Beautiful Albiness," apparently a European woman, was never exhibited as a "white Negro."

40. In the recent end-of-the-millennium film of a satanic apocalypse, *End of Days*, an African American with albinism, spectacularly coifed in large rolls of white hair, serves as a minion of the devil, stalking the man of pure heart, Arnold Schwarzenegger.

41. Bhabha, *Location*, 86.

42. Herman Melville, *Mardi, and a Voyage Thither* (1849; reprint, Evansville, Ill.: Northwestern University Press, 1970), 136–137, 153, 308.

43. Jeremiah N. Reynolds, "Mocha Dick, or the White Whale of the Pacific," *Nickerbocker* 13 (1839): 392, 379. Although he cannot confirm it, Hershel Parker considers the possibility that Melville had read "Mocha Dick." The May 1839 issue of the *Nickerbocker* came out just before Melville sailed for Liverpool, and the account of the white whale was read enough to be discussed for years thereafter. In the earliest drafts of the novel, Melville had his captain call to other ships, "Any news from Mocha Dick?," which he subsequently changes to "Hast seen the white whale?" Hershel Parker, *Herman Melville: A Biography*, vol. 1 (Baltimore: Johns Hopkins University Press, 1996), 181, 695, 697.

44. Reynolds, "Mocha Dick," 384, 387, 388.

45. Melville, *Moby-Dick*, 222, 419, 283. Further quotations from this novel are from this edition and are cited parenthetically in the text. Harry Levin also recognizes the racialization of the whale, as well as Moby Dick's further exile from his "race" through the stigma of his white skin. "All other whales are of Ethiopian hue," he writes, "and Moby Dick is set apart from them by his albinism, as they are set apart by their magnitude from all other created things." Confronted by the exhibition of the whale's white skin, Levin is yet an unbeliever, declaring unequivocally that "there is no such animal as an albino whale." Harry Levin, *The Power of Blackness* (New York: Knopf, 1964), 222, 223.

46. D. H. Lawrence, *Studies in Classic American Literature* (1923; reprint, New York: Penguin, 1977), 169.

47. Valerie Babb sees a connection between Ishmael's "contemplation of the whale" and a "contemplation of racial whiteness." Under this rubric, Ishmael purposely pursues "the daunting task of de-universalizing whiteness." Valerie Babb, *Whiteness Visible: The Meaning of Whiteness* (New York: New York University Press, 1998), 97, 98. Babb's ideas follow a direct line of descent through the recent work of Marsha Vick and Toni Morrison. Following Morrison's figuration of the whale as "the ideology of whiteness," Vick contends that Ishmael "defamiliarizes the trope of whiteness as an essence." Morrison, *Playing*, 15; Marsha C. Vick, "'Defamiliarization' and the Ideology of Race in Moby-Dick," *CLA Journal* 35 (1992): 337.

48. Samuel Otter, *Melville's Anatomies* (Berkeley: University of California Press, 1999), 122.

49. Toni Morrison, "Unspeakable Things Unspoken: The Afro-American Presence in American Literature," *Michigan Quarterly Review* 28 (1989): 15, 16, 17.

50. Timothy Parrish, "Our White Whale, Elvis; or, Democracy Sighted," *Prospects* 20 (1995): 329.

51. Stanley Crouch, "Hooked," *New Republic*, August 21, 1995, 18.

52. Chester Himes, *Blind Man with a Pistol*, (1969; reprint, New York: Random House, 1989), 46.

53. Robert E. Skinner, *Two Guns from Harlem: The Detective Fiction of Chester Himes* (Bowling Green, Ohio: Bowling Green University Press, 1989), 21–22.

54. Chester Himes, "The Dilemma of the Negro Novelist in the U.S.A.," in *Beyond the Angry Black*, ed. John A. Williams (New York: Cooper Square, 1966), 57.

55. Robert Crooks, "From the Far Side of the Urban Frontier: The Detective Fiction of Chester Himes and Walter Mosley," *College Literature* 22.3 (1995): 68, 87n, 74.

56. Chester Himes, *Cotton Comes to Harlem* (1965; reprint, New York: Vintage, 1988), 60.

57. Chester Himes, *The Heat's On* (1966; reprint, New York: Vintage, 1988), 79. Further quotations from this novel are from this edition and are cited parenthetically in the text.

58. Himes, *Cotton*, 132.

59. In *Cotton Comes to Harlem*, Himes employs the blackening of a light-skinned character as minstrel-show degradation. To disguise Iris, the ruthless "high-yellow woman," Grave Digger and Coffin Ed blacken her up, an act that makes Ed fantasize about a racial transformation of his own, "make up to disguise us as white." The successful result, the humiliation of extreme blackness, provokes one of her confidantes to call her "the last of the Topsys." Himes, *Cotton*, 128, 130.

60. Paul Gilroy, *Against Race* (Cambridge, Mass.: Harvard University Press, 2000), 7, 12, 14.

61. John Edgar Wideman, *Sent for You Yesterday* (New York: Avon, 1983), 21. Further quotations from this novel are from this edition and are cited parenthetically in the text.

62. Daniel P. Mannix, *We Who Are Not as Others* (New York: Pocket, 1976), 136.

63. For a more thorough history of the eugenics movement in England and the United States, see Daniel J. Kevles, *In the Name of Eugenics: Genetics and the Uses of Human Heredity* (Cambridge, Mass.: Harvard University Press, 1985).

64. Gilroy, *Against*, 254.

CHAPTER 4: "A BETTER SKIN"

1. Peale, "Account," 620–621.

2. William Wells Brown, *Clotel, or the President's Daughter* (1853; reprint, New York: Carol, 1995), 59.

3. Joel Williamson, *New People: Miscegenation and Mulattoes in the United States* (Baton Rouge: Louisiana State University Press, 1995), 24.

4. Brown, *Clotel*, 63.

5. James Callender, "The President Again," *Richmond Recorder*, September 1, 1802.

6. Joshua D. Rothman, "James Callender and the Social Knowledge of Interracial Sex in Antebellum Virginia," in *Sally Hemings and Thomas Jefferson: History, Memory, and Civic Culture*, ed. Jan Ellen Lewis and Peter S. Onuf (Charlottesville: University of Virginia Press, 1999), 104, 107.

7. Eugene A. Foster, M. A. Jobling, P. G. Taylor, P. Donnelly, P. de Kniff, Rene Miermet, T. Zerjal, and C. Tyler-Smith, "Jefferson Fathered Slave's Last Child," *Nature*, November 5, 1998, 27–28.

8. Nott, "Mulatto," 253.

9. Elizabeth Cary Agassiz, *Louis Agassiz: His Life and Correspondence* (Boston: Houghton Mifflin, 1890), 595.

10. Brown, *Clotel*, 66.

11. Ibid., 66, 67.

12. Ibid., 64, 67.

13. Barbara Christian, *Black Women Novelists: The Development of a Tradition* (Westport, Conn.: Greenwood, 1985), 22–23.

14. Brown, *Clotel*, 61.

15. Ann DuCille, *The Coupling Convention: Sex, Text, and Tradition in Black Women's Fiction* (New York: Oxford University Press, 1993), 19.

16. The presence of light-skinned household slaves served as a daily reminder to plantation wives of infidelities by their husbands. In her diary, Mary Boykin Chesnut describes the genealogical confusion and sexual rivalry that arises through the institution of slavery. "Like the patriarchs of old," she writes, "our men live all in one house with their wives and their concubines, and the mulattoes one sees in every family exactly resemble the white children—and every lady is ready to tell you who is the father of all the mulatto children in everybody's household, but those in her own she seems to think drop from the clouds, or pretends so to think." Mary Boykin Chesnut, *Mary Chesnut's Civil War* (New Haven, Conn.: Yale University Press, 1980), 29.

17. Brown, *Clotel*, 171.

18. Ibid., 84, 85, 158–159.

19. The use of tanning to darken slave skin surfaces as well in Harriet Wilson's *Our Nig*. Sensing sexual rivalry in the light-complected slave, Mrs. Bellmont refuses to let Jane shield her skin from the sun. The mistress "was determined the sun should have full power to darken the shade which nature had first bestowed upon her as best befitting." Harriet Wilson, *Our Nig*, in *Three Classic African American Novels*, ed. William L. Andrews (1859; reprint, New York: Penguin, 1990), 307.

20. Josiah C. Nott, *The Negro Race: Its Ethnology and History* (Mobile, Ala.: n.p., 1866), 13.

21. Charles Darwin, *The Descent of Man* (1871; reprint, New York: Prometheus Books, 1998), 188, 201, 183, 163, 147.

22. Fredrickson, *Black*, 246.

23. Walter F. Willcox, quoted in Frederickson, *Black*, 252.

24. Charles Chesnutt, *The Marrow of Tradition* (1901; reprint, Ann Arbor: University of Michigan Press, 1969), 31, 86, 115.

25. Ibid., 304, 141, 62.

26. Fredrickson, *Black*, 234–235.

27. Charles Darwin, *The Origin of Species* (1858; reprint, New York: Penguin, 1985), 179.

28. Pearson, Nettleship, and Usher, *Monograph*, 241–242. The child was shipped to Liverpool for an exhibition but died from a stomach ailment shortly after arrival.

29. Chesnutt, *Marrow*, 8, 257.

30. Ibid., 323.

31. Lee D. Baker, *From Savage to Negro: Anthropology and the Construction of Race, 1896–1954* (Berkeley: University of California Press, 1998), 26–38.

32. Otto H. Olsen, *The Thin Disguise* (New York: Humanities, 1967), 14. Documentation is vague on the details of Plessy's arrest. Charles A. Lofgren speculates that at least the confrontation "was surely arranged," since, according to the affidavit of the arresting officer, "the mixture of colored blood [was] not discernible." Charles A. Lofgren, *The Plessy Case: A Legal-Historical Interpretation* (New York: Oxford University Press, 1987), 41.

33. "Preamble of *Act No. 111*," quoted in Olsen, *Thin*, 54.

34. Albion W. Tourgée, "Brief for Homer A. Plessy," quoted in Olsen, *Thin*, 81.

35. In *Up from Slavery*, Booker T. Washington describes the buffoonery of railroad conductors in their attempts to police the Jim Crow cars. In one incident, a conductor is stymied by a light-skinned African American "so white that even an expert would have hard work to classify him as a black man." The conductor pursues all pos-

sible reputed signs of racial difference: "hair, eyes, nose, and hands." This agent of the railroad finally finds his presumed evidence after "examining" the man's feet and leaves him be among the other African American passengers. Although Washington does not directly comment on this episode, it is obvious that the true spectacle of this tale is not the white Negro exhibit but the foolish, and self-deceived, official. Booker T. Washington, *Up from Slavery* (1901; reprint, New York: Penguin, 1986), 100–101.

36. Tourgée, "Brief," 98.

37. Ibid., 102.

38. This fantasy of racial transformation, the reverse of the white Negro figure I have discussed, also has its minor cultural history. Each time, a bigoted character is magically transformed from white to black to teach that character a lesson in racial understanding. See also Charles Chesnutt, "Mars Jeems's Nightmare," in *The Conjure Woman* (1899; reprint, Ann Arbor: University of Michigan Press, 1969), 64–102, as well as the films *Finian's Rainbow* and *Watermelon Man* for other examples of this trope. Considering these works, Susan Gubar cautions that "blackness can remain an anathema in this tradition, especially when it is inflicted as a punishment fitting the crimes of inhumane whites. Only when the boundaries separating black and white are perceived as demonstrably permeable does racial mutability lead to the undermining of race itself as a category." Gubar, *Racechanges*, 25.

39. Francis Galton, *Fingerprints* (1892; reprint, New York: Da Capo, 1965), 17–18. Michael Rogin and Eric Sundquist are ambivalent about Twain's employment of Galton's fingerprint technique as a detector of racial difference. Although they agree that Galton was frustrated in his attempts to uncover a racial marker in the fingerprint, the eventual discovery of Tom Driscoll's race derives solely from his fingerprints. To Rogin, this revelation suggests a defeat for "the true and unique individual 'character'" that the fingerprint represents. Michael Rogin, "Francis Galton and Mark Twain: The Natal Autograph in *Pudd'nhead Wilson*," in *Mark Twain's Pudd'nhead Wilson: Race, Conflict, and Culture*, ed. Susan Gillman and Forrest G. Robinson (Durham, N.C.: Duke University Press, 1990), 79, 80. Sundquist presumes that Twain's intention is "to mock the theory that segregation was rooted in organic laws susceptible to proof by the new scientific and sociological study of heredity" that Galton founded. Eric Sundquist, *To Wake the Nations* (Cambridge: Harvard University Press, 1993), 251, 252.

40. Mark Twain, *Pudd'nhead Wilson* (1894; reprint, New York: Norton, 1980), 115. Further quotations from this novel are from this edition and are cited parenthetically in the text.

41. Sundquist, *Wake*, 253.

42. James M. Cox, *Mark Twain: The Fate of Humor* (Princeton, N.J.: Princeton University Press, 1966), 231.

43. Carolyn Porter, "Roxana's Plot," in Gillman and Robinson, *Twain's "Pudd'nhead Wilson,"* 127.

44. Bhabha, *Location*, 84.

45. Frances E. W. Harper, *Iola Leroy, or Shadows Uplifted* (1892; reprint, New York: Oxford University Press, 1988), 203.

46. Charles Chesnutt, *The House Behind the Cedars* (1900; reprint, New York: Penguin, 1993), 143.

47. Elmer A. Carter, "Crossing Over," *Opportunity* 4 (1925): 377.

48. Mary Helen Washington, *Invented Lives: Narratives of Black Women 1860–1960* (New York: Doubleday, 1988), 164.

49. Harryette Mullen, "Optic White: Blackness and the Production of Whiteness," *diacritics* 24.2–3 (1994): 77. Some passing narratives invite this reading. In James Weldon Johnson's *The Autobiography of an Ex-Colored Man*, the anonymous narrator identifies himself as "a coward, a deserter" for choosing to pass as white. James Weldon Johnson, *The Autobiography of an Ex-Colored Man* (1912; reprint, New York: Random House, 1989), 208.

50. Jessie Redmon Fauset, *Plum Bun* (1929; reprint, Boston: Beacon, 1990), 158–159.

51. Langston Hughes, "Passing," in *The Ways of White Folks* (1934; reprint, New York: Random House, 1990), 53, 54.

52. Claude McKay, "Near-White," in *Gingertown* (New York: Harper, 1932), 76, 78, 96.

53. Elaine K. Ginsberg, "Introduction: The Politics of Passing," in *Passing and the Fictions of Identity*, ed. Elaine K. Ginsberg (Durham, N.C.: Duke University Press, 1996), 8.

54. Johnson, *Autobiography*, 197.

55. Roi Ottley, "Five Million U.S. White Negroes," *Ebony*, March 1948, 22–23.

56. Amy Robinson, "It Takes One to Know One: Passing and Communities of Common Interest," *Critical Inquiry* 20 (1994): 731.

57. Langston Hughes, "Who's Passing For Who?" in *Laughing to Keep from Crying* (New York: Henry Holt, 1952), 6, 7.

58. Nella Larsen, *Passing* (1929; reprint, New York: Penguin, 1997), 15–16. Further quotations from this novel are from this edition and are cited parenthetically in the text.

59. For an extensive history on the trope of the fingernail as a marker of racial difference, see Sollors, *Neither*, 142–161.

60. Jennifer DeVere Brody, "Clare Kendry's 'True' Colors: Race and Class Conflict in Nella Larsen's *Passing*," *Callaloo* 15 (1992): 1055.

61. Thadious Davis, introduction to Larsen, *Passing*, xx.

62. Judith Butler suggests that at some level, John Bellew knows or suspects Clare's biracial parentage. His apparent fixation upon her possible blackness results from a fetishization of her racial ambiguity. "In fact," Butler concludes, "it appears that the uncertain border between black and white is precisely what he eroticizes, what he needs in order to make Clare into the exotic object to be dominated." Judith Butler, "Passing, Queering: Nella Larsen's Psychoanalytical Challenge," in *Female Subjects in Black and White*, ed. Elizabeth Abel, Barbara Christian, and Helene Moglen (Berkeley: University of California Press, 1997), 270. This reading of John's fascination with Clare's body harkens back to the exhibition of the exotic Circassian and albino bodies in the nineteenth century. See chapter 3 for my discussion of Circassian Beauties.

63. Mullen, "Optic," 72.

64. Ibid., 98.

65. Martha J. Cutter, "Sliding Significations: Passing as Narrative and Textual Strategy in Nella Larsen's Fiction," in Ginsberg, *Passing*, 93.

66. George S. Schuyler, *Black No More* (1931; reprint, Boston: Northeastern University Press, 1989), 34.

67. Mullen, "Optic," 75; Robert S. Bone, *The Negro Novel in America*, rev. ed. (New Haven, Conn.: Yale University Press, 1965), 89. For further criticism of

Schuyler's "assimilationism," see Charles R. Larson, introduction to *Black No More*, by George S. Schuyler (New York: Collier, 1971); and Ann Rayson, "George Schuyler: Paradox among 'Assimilationist' Writers," *Black American Literature Forum* 12 (1978): 102–106.

68. Bone, *Negro*, 89.

69. Gubar, *Racechanges*, 18,19.

70. In his argument on behalf of Homer Plessy before the United States Supreme Court, Tourgée argued that "the reputation of belonging to the dominant race, in this instance the white race, is *property*, in the same sense that a tight of action or inheritance is *property*." Tourgée, "Brief," 83. Schuyler makes this abstract conception of whiteness more literal and concrete. For an extensive historical overview of the development of whiteness as a kind of property, see Cheryl I. Harris, "Whiteness as Property," *Harvard Law Review* 106 (1993): 1709–1791.

71. The discovery of X rays founded a popular fascination with radiation and its seemingly magical properties. For a brief history of this hysteria at the turn of the twentieth century, see Bettyann Holtzmann Kevles, *Naked to the Bone: Medical Imaging in the Twentieth Century* (New Brunswick, N.J.: Rutgers University Press, 1997), 24–30.

72. "Negroes Made White by X-Rays," *New York Herald*, December 28, 1903, 5, 10.

73. "X-Ray to Turn Black Men White," *New York American*, December 28, 1903, 9.

74. The *Boston Globe* reprinted a short portion of the *New York Herald* article under the headline "X-Ray Bleached a Negro." *Boston Globe*, December 28, 1903, 10. Clippings from other reports of these experiments are reprinted in an article by David J. DiSantis and Denise M. DiSantis. One of these reports claims that a senior at the University of California will use X rays and radium "to turn the skin of a negro white." David J. DiSantis and Denise M. DiSantis, "Wrong Turns on Radiology's Road to Progress," *Radiographics* 11 (1991): 1137.

75. Schuyler, *Black*, 54.

76. "To Whiten Black and Yellow Races," *Literary Digest*, November 23, 1929, 31–32.

77. Daniel J. Kevles provides a history of the eugenics movement and its entrance into popular culture. Kevles, *Eugenics*, 57–112.

78. Schuyler, *Black*, 26.

79. Michael W. Peplow describes Max as a picaro and links the European tradition of the picaresque to the African American folk tradition of trickster figures such as High John de Conqueror and Brer Rabbit. Michael W. Peplow, *George S. Schuyler* (Boston: Twayne, 1980), 67–68.

80. Schuyler, *Black*, 76, 78.

81. J. Martin Favor, *Authentic Blackness: The Folk in the New Negro Renaissance* (Durham, N.C.: Duke University Press, 1999), 120.

82. Schuyler, *Black*, 218, 219.

83. Ibid., 222.

84. Charles Chesnutt, "The Future American," in *Essays and Speeches*, ed. Joseph R. McElrath Jr., Robert C. Leitz III, and Jesse S. Crisler (Stanford, Calif.: Stanford University Press, 1999), 121, 122, 123, 125.

85. Ibid., 126.

86. Schuyler, *Black*, 178.

87. Francis Galton, *Hereditary Genius: An Inquiry into Its Laws and Conse-quences* (1869; reprint, London: Macmillan, 1914), 327. Galton qualifies racial genius as the ability of a race to produce "judges, statesmen, commanders, men of literature and science, poets, artists, and divines." One of the criteria for the low rank of the African is the feeling of superiority the Anglo-Saxon explorer feels in the pres-ence of "native chief." He writes, "It is seldom that we hear of a white traveler meet-ing with a black chief whom he feels to be the better man." He further theorizes that the discrepancy between the traveler and the chief "may be due to the relative demerits of native education, and . . . to a difference in natural gifts." Galton, *Genius*, 326, 327–328.

88. The family trees of the Anderson and Davis families were the most genealog-ically scrutinized of all performing piebald families. Pearson traces vitiligo as a genetic trait to a Louisiana ex-slave, Lettice Anderson. Those of her children who apparently inherited this trait exhibited themselves as, among other things, South Sea islanders, "The Leopard Family," and "The Three Striped Graces." Known in France as "Les trios Braces tigrées," the "Graces" consisted of varying combinations of Davis and Anderson sisters, cousins, and aunts who sang and danced in American and European variety shows from the turn of the twentieth century to their appar-ently final exhibition at the 1933 Century of Progress Exhibition in Chicago. Dur-ing the first decades of the twentieth century, Lillie Davis performed as the internationally known acrobatic dancer "Tiger Lily." Pearson, Nettleship, and Usher, *Monograph*, 128–130. See also Q. I. Simpson and W. E. Castle, "A Family of Spotted Negroes," *American Naturalist* 47 (1913): 50–56; and Clyde E. Keeler, "The Heredity of a Congenital White Spotting in Negroes," *JAMA* 103 (1934): 179–180.

89. Pearson, Nettleship, and Usher, *Monograph*, 36.

90. Sollors, *Neither*, 49.

91. Larsen, *Passing*, 36, 37.

92. "After Embryo Mix-Up, Genetic Parents Get Baby," *New York Times*, May 27, 1999. In a March 7, 2000, segment on the television newsmagazine 20/20, Barbara Walters reported that the visitation agreement between the two families has col-lapsed, ending, for now, the earlier vision of utopian racial sodality. The persistence of this story further indicates the continuing fascination with white Negro exhibition.

93. David D. Yuan qualifies Jackson's skin disorder as "alleged." David D. Yuan, "The Celebrity Freak: Michael Jackson's 'Grotesque Glory," in Thomson, *Freakery*, 376. Greg Tate has gone the furthest to condemn Jackson for his racial transforma-tion, referring to his "skin job" as "the carpetbagging side of black advancement in the affirmative action era." Greg Tate, "I'm White: What's Wrong with Michael Jack-son," *Village Voice*, September 22, 1997, 16.

94. Drawing upon Bhabha's theories of colonial ambivalence, Cynthia J. Fuchs argues that "Michael Jackson is painfully and erratically 'colonial,'" a body that appears to accept dominance yet challenges categorization by race, gender, or sexu-ality. Cynthia J. Fuchs, "Michael Jackson's Penis," in *Cruising the Performative*, ed. Sue Ellen Case, Philip Brett, and Susan Leigh Foster (Bloomington: Indiana Univer-sity Press, 1995), 16.

95. Eric Lott, "The Aesthetic Ante: Pleasure, Pop Culture, and the Middle Pas-sage," *Callaloo* 17 (1994): 551.

CHAPTER 5: WHITE NEGROES, LEOPARD BOYS, AND THE KING OF POP

1. George C. Wolfe, *The Colored Museum* (New York: Grove, 1985), 33–34, 36.

2. Tate, "I'm White," 15; Crouch, "Hooked," 19; Francis Davis, "Toons," *Atlantic Monthly*, April 1992, 102.

3. Margo Jefferson, "The Image Culture," *Vogue*, March 1988, 127; Tate, "I'm White," 16; Guy Trebay, "The Boy Can't Help It," *Village Voice*, September 22, 1987, 17; Davis, "Toons," 100.

4. Tanarive Due, "Skin Deep," *Miami Herald*, October 2, 1991; Christopher Andersen, *Michael Jackson Unauthorized* (New York: Simon and Schuster, 1994), 210. A 1991 article points an accusing finger at Jermaine and LaToya as well as at Michael, claiming the siblings have also resorted to surgery and bleaching creams. Due, "Skin."

5. Davis, "Toons," 102.

6. Tate, "I'm White," 16.

7. Ken Tucker, "Beyond the Pale," *Entertainment Weekly*, February 26, 1993, 16–21.

8. "Doctor Says Michael Jackson Has a Skin Disease," *New York Times*, February 13, 1993.

9. Among this consensus are Susan Gubar, David Yuan, and Michael Awkward, who agree with the assessment of *Newsweek* writers Mary Talbot and Charles Fleming that "most vitiligo sufferers darken their light patches with makeup to even the tone. Jackson's makeup solution takes the other tack: less ebony, more ivory." Gubar, *Racechanges*, 20; Yuan, "Celebrity," 379; Michael Awkward, *Negotiating Difference: Race, Gender, and the Politics of Positionality* (Chicago: University of Chicago Press, 1995), 178; Mary Talbot with Charles Fleming, "The Two Faces of Michael Jackson," *Newsweek*, February 23, 1993, 57.

10. *Vitiligo* (Schaumburg, Ill.: American Academy of Dermatology, 1994), 6.

11. According to a 1991 study published in the *Journal of Health and Social Behavior*, 54 percent of African Americans with vitiligo "disapprove of total depigmentation as a treatment under any circumstances; 27 percent approve only in very severe cases." The authors of the study account for this reluctance toward additional whitening of the skin by suggesting the importance of skin color as a marker of racial identity. Unfortunately, they do not offer for comparison statistics on approval of depigmentation by white patients. Judith Porter and Ann Hill Beuf, "Racial Variation in Reaction to Physical Stigma: A Study of Degree of Disturbance by Vitiligo among Black and White Patients," *Journal of Health and Social Behavior* 32 (1991): 200.

12. Porter and Beuf, "Racial," 201. One study gave as the typical comment to a person with vitiligo, "You must have got it from fooling around with those honky broads." Ibid., 200.

13. "Woman Suffers Disease Turning Her Skin from Black-to-White-to Black," *Jet*, July 9, 1981, 14, 15.

14. "Account of a Singular Change of Colour in a Negro," *Weekly Magazine* 1 (1798), 110–111. The same account attested that "he was not sensible of the least obstruction, on the passage of a razor from the black to the white, or from the white to the black parts of the face." Ibid., 110.

15. Michelle Cliff, "Burning Bush," in *Bodies of Water* (New York: Dutton, 1990), 76, 77, 78.

16. Suzanne Bost, "Fluidity without Postmodernism: Michelle Cliff and the 'Tragic Mulatta' Tradition," *African American Review* 32 (1998): 684.

17. As a crucial episode of Jackson mythology, his storied attempt to buy the remains of John Merrick, "The Elephant Man," betokens an interest in tragic bodies further twisted by intense public scrutiny. Andersen, *Michael*, 81. David Yuan has also suggested Jackson's knowledge of Leopard Children, adding, "If the Leopard Child represents the static [silent] enfreakment of a human curiosity, Jackson's goal is obviously to defy this fate." Yuan, "Celebrity," 378.

18. Michael Awkward has voiced these same possibilities in the spectacle that Jackson's skin has become. "Jackson's public appearances and discursive perform-ances," Awkward argues, "manifest conceptual slippage between notions of the natu-ral and the socially constructed, between biological determinism and cultural conditioning. His recourse to notions of an essential(ist) black subjectivity evinces not his inconsistencies so much as the ultimately insoluble nature of this debate as it is presently framed." Awkward, *Negotiating*, 175–176.

19. Olaudah Equiano, *The Interesting Narrative* (1789; reprint, New York: Pen-guin, 1995), 69. Paradoxically, Equiano offers a white Negro exhibition in the first chapter of his narrative in an apparent effort to denaturalize the superiority of white skin. "I remember while in Africa," he writes, "to have seen three negro children, who were tawny, and another quite white, who were universally regarded by myself and the natives in general, as deformed." Equiano insists on the extreme hygiene of the African. "Before we taste food," he affirms, "we always wash our hands: indeed our cleanliness on all occasions is extreme; but on this it is an indispensable cere-mony." As a contrast, European habits initially appall him, especially the tendency to eat "with unwashed hands." Ibid., 38, 35, 68.

20. Anne McClintock, *Imperial Leather: Race, Gender and Sexuality in the Colo-nial Contest* (New York: Routledge, 1995), 208

21. I have yet to see an advertisement in which an adult African American woman is washed of her blackness. Much in the spirit of the various nineteenth-century state laws that determined that the racial fate of the child would follow the mother, women in these advertisements were considered more bestowers of racial characteristics than receivers of racial transformation. In one trade card for Dixon's Stove Polish that seems to reverse the process of the soap advertisements, a mammy figure applies the product to the naked body of a young, playful white girl, darkening her legs and torso.

22. McClintock, *Imperial Leather*, 209.

23. Toni Morrison, *The Bluest Eye* (1970; reprint, New York: Penguin, 1993), 19, 20, 46. Further quotations from this novel are from this edition and are cited paren-thetically in the text.

24. A 1925 editorial in the pages of *Opportunity* decries the prevalence of these advertisements in "the most race conscious papers, . . . giving greatest emphasis to the mechanism for obliterating racial characteristics." Charles S. Johnson, "Race Pride and Cosmetics," *Opportunity* 3 (1925): 293.

25. "Black Skin Remover," *St. Louis Palladium* (1901), quoted in Noliwe M. Rooks, *Hair Raising: Beauty, Culture, and African American Women* (New Brunswick, N.J.: Rutgers University Press, 1996), 29.

26. Rooks, *Hair*, 29–30.

27. Kathy Russell, Midge Wilson, and Ronald Hall, *The Color Complex: The Pol-*

itics of Skin Color among African Americans (New York: Harcourt Brace Jovanovich, 1992), 45.

28. Chesnutt, *Marrow*, 36.

29. Ibid., 84, 243, 245.

30. Ibid., 245.

31. John Nguyet Erni, "Queer Figurations in the Media: Critical Reflections on the Michael Jackson Sex Scandal," *Critical Studies in Mass Communication* 15 (1998): 169.

32. Andersen, *Michael*, 381; Maureen Orth, "Nightmare in Neverland," *Vanity Fair*, March 1994, 137.

33. Andersen, *Michael*, 381, 359.

34. Ibid., 381.

35. Maureen Orth, "The Jackson Jive," *Vanity Fair*, September 1995, 116.

36. Sollors, *Neither*, 155.

37. Georges Buffon, *Natural History General and Particular*, new ed., vol. 3, trans. William Smellie (London: Cadell and Davies, 1812), 200–201.

38. Morgan, "Some Account," 392. The scrutiny of Adelaide's genitals foreshadows the intense European interest in the spectacle of Saartjie Bartmann, the "Hottentot Venus," who suffered from steatopygia, or protruding buttocks. From 1810 until her death in 1815, the native South African Baartman was exhibited in the capitals of Europe, her endowments displayed by the wearing of form-hugging, flesh-colored clothes. The medical community also obsessively inspected her genitals. After death, esteemed naturalist Georges Cuvier dissected her body, removing her labia for preservation and further study. According to Sander Gilman, "Bartmann's sexual parts, her genitalia and her buttocks, served as the central image for the black female throughout the nineteenth century." Sander Gilman, "Black Bodies, White Bodies: Toward an Iconography of Female Sexuality in Late Nineteenth-Century Art, Medicine, and Literature," in Gates, "*Race*," 235.

39. Morgan, "Some Account," 394.

40. The use of the genitals as a telltale seat of color and racial difference still retains some currency in contemporary folklore. Russell, Wilson, and Hall record an instance of a young mother inspecting her child's genitals for confirmation of its light complexion. Russell, Wilson, and Hall, *Color*, 95.

41. Orth, "Jackson," 116.

42. Andersen, *Michael*, 383.

43. Rochefoucault, *Travels*, 134.

44. *The Commissioners of the of the Alms-House, vs. Alexander Whistelo, a Black Man; being a remarkable case of bastardy, tried and adjudged by the mayor, recorder, and several aldermen, of the city of New York* (New York: Longworth, 1808), 4.

45. Ibid., 7, 10.

46. Ibid., 20.

47. Ibid., 48–49.

AFTERWORD: REQUIEM FOR A WIGGER

1. Clarence Major, *Juba to Jive: The Dictionary of African-American Slang* (New York: Viking, 1994), 511.

2. David Roediger, "*Guineas, Wiggers,* and the Dramas of Racialized Culture," *American Literary History* 7 (1995): 659–660.

3. Meigs, "History," 65.

4. Thomas Chandler Haliburton, *The Clockmaker, or The Sayings and Doings of Sam Slick, of Slickville* (1836; reprint, Toronto: McClelland and Stewart, 1993), 172.

5. "Editor's Table," *Old Guard* 5 (1867): 954.

6. See Joel Williamson, *The Crucible of Race: Black-White Relations in the American South since Emancipation* (New York: Oxford University Press, 1984), 465–466; and Stephen Kantrowitz, *Ben Tillman and the Reconstruction of White Supremacy* (Chapel Hill, N.C.: University of North Carolina Press, 2000), 5.

7. Ralph Ellison, "The World and the Jug," in *The Collected Essays*, ed. John F. Callahan (New York: Random House, 1995), 153, 171, 173.

8. Norman Mailer, "The White Negro," in *Advertisements for Myself* (New York: Putnam, 1959), 338, 348.

9. Eldridge Cleaver, *Soul on Ice* (1968; reprint, New York: Random House, 1999), 123–124.

10. Ralph Ellison, *Invisible Man* (1952; reprint, New York: Random House, 1989), 3, 575, 577.

11. Ibid., 577, 580.

INDEX

sioners of the Alms-House v. Alexander
Whistelo
White, Allon, 4–5, 29, 189n35
whiteface performance: and blackface
theater, 89–91; in *The Confidence Man*,
88
"White Negro, The" (Mailer), 183
white Negroes: aggrandizement of, 63,
66–67; audience of, 2, 13–14, 21, 92, 111;
blackface theater, 89–91; and class formation, 13, 14, 16, 27, 44–46, 48, 51, 58, 59;
and climate, 38, 40–41, 46; and colonialism, 6, 8, 10, 101, 109; and dissection,
50–55; exhibition conditions, 36–37, 91,
166; and genealogy, 67, 69, 70, 155–156,
179; and immigrants, 13, 14, 16, 48, 51,
58, 59, 92; and manifest destiny, 67; and
maternal impression, 13, 25, 191n22; and
miscegenation, 11, 15, 30, 43, 67, 69,
70–74, 128–129, 167; as missing link,
196–197n27; and national definition, 11,
13, 42–43; and natural history, 14, 22–23,

24, 28; and racial science, 15, 30, 68–69,
101, 102, 114, 117, 118, 120, 124–126;
and racial transformation, 1, 16, 52,
82–83, 86, 87, 149–152, 180, 185; and
racial violence, 50, 119, 120; and slavery,
11, 13, 20, 27, 28, 30, 33, 38–40, 72,
129–130; and social harmony, 15, 41, 43,
44, 81; term, 1, 22, 182, 183, 187n1; *see
also* albinism; albino; Leopard Child;
vitiligo
"Who's Passing for Who" (Hughes), 144
Wideman, John Edgar: *Sent for You Yesterday*, 16–17, 120–122, 124–126
Wiesenthal, J. V., 37
wigger: term, 181; *see also* white Negro
Wilson, Harriet, *Our Nig*, 206n19
Winfrey, Oprah, 165
Wolfe, George C.: *The Colored Museum*, 164
"World and the Jug, The" (Ellison), 182–183

X-Files, The (television show), 162–163
X rays, 150, 209n71

ABOUT THE AUTHOR

Charles D. Martin teaches American Literature at the Florida State University. He continues to investigate the influence of circus and world's fair sideshows on American racial theory.